Couples Therapy:
An Adlerian Perspective

Editors and Authors

Roy M. Kern
Georgia State University

E. Clair Hawes
Counseling Psychologist
British Columbia

and

Oscar C. Christensen
University of Arizona

Copyright 1989
Educational Media Corporation®

Library of Congress Catalog Card No. 89-80325

ISBN 0-932796-26-5

Printing (Last Digit)

9 8 7 6 5 4 3 2 1

Publisher—

EDUCATIONAL MEDIA CORPORATION®
P.O. Box 21311
Minneapolis, MN 55421

Production editor—

Don L. Sorenson

Graphic design—

Earl Sorenson

Acknowledgments

Special thanks to all those involved in the publication of this book. Thanks to Robert Yeakle and David Hornbuckle for editorial and logistics assistance. For typing and editorial comments, special thanks to Mary Brooks and Anita Williams. And finally, special appreciation is extended to Richard Smith, Chair of the Department of Counseling and Psychological Services, Georgia State University, for providing student assistant support when needed.

Acknowledgments

Special thanks are due ...

Introduction

Marital and couples therapy has developed into an exciting as well as difficult task, due to the massive changes in values and society in general. Twenty-five years ago, for example, the therapist would probably count on a couple who were contemplating marriage for the first time, struggling with their relationship as it related to the marital experience or discussions focused on children and adolescents.

Oh what a difference the years make! Now the therapist is faced with couples seeking assistance and who live together but are not married, who have been married not once but possibly three times in a span of ten years, or a couple who have been married for twenty-five years and are deciding on divorce.

If this is not enough, one only needs to recognize or become aware of the social context further complicating the task of the therapist, such as dual career couples, AIDS, equality issues, substance abuses, sexual dysfunctions, economic pressures, career uncertainty and the diversifications related to the ethical and legal issues of surrogate parenting, artificial insemination and the innovative but questionable adoption options.

The question then becomes one of can a theory and therapeutic process which was created some seventy-five years ago be relevant for the couples of the present? Can the Adlerian perspective be implemented within the context of today's concerns? More specifically, have the individuals who adhere to the Adlerian perspective refined and expanded the theoretical constructs into usable techniques for the therapists working with couples today?

To address these foregoing questions, the purpose of this book is to acquaint the reader and practitioner with some of the most relevant knowledge available related to how Adlerian therapists working with couples are employing the approach.

The author(s) of each section, beginning with theory and ending with working with remarried couples, are practicing clinicians with a mean average of actual therapy time with couples of seventeen years.

Couples Therapy: An Adlerian Perspective, however, is more than theory and techniques. The contributors see it more as a social responsibility to put in print their ideas so that their years of learning, experience and application of Adler's ideas may enrich the therapeutic experience for other couples and their families.

Contributors

Editors and Authors

Roy M. Kern is a professor in the Department of Counseling and Psychological Services and is the Coordinator of the Family Education Center at Georgia State University. He is a licensed marriage and family therapist, AAMFT Approved Supervisor and has lectured and taught throughout North America and Europe. Roy has served as a consultant for numerous organizations and has authored several articles and a book, *Case for Adlerian Counseling*. He has led the research and development of instruments that measure the Adlerian concept of Lifestyle (the Wheeler, Kern, Curlette Lifestyle Personality Inventory and the Kern Lifestyle Scale).

E. Clair Hawes is a Counseling Psychologist and has been in private practice specializing in marriage therapy for 16 years. She has authored several articles and books on marriage counseling, marriage enrichment and the family and has lectured and taught throughout North American and Europe on marriage therapy and related issues. Clair is a Sessional Clinical Instructor for the Department of Counseling Psychology at the University of British Columbia.

Oscar C. Christensen is a professor in the Department of Counseling and Guidance at the University of Arizona and considered by many as one of the most highly regarded Adlerian practitioners in North America and Europe. This fact is not only documented by his text, *Adlerian Family Counseling*, but also by the several contributors in the text who have completed degrees under his supervision. Oscar is best known for his ability not only to write about Adlerian principles, but his ability to present these principles through live demonstrations.

G. Hugh Allred, Professor of marriage and family therapy at Brigham Young University and a Fellow and Approved Supervisor of therapists with the American Association for Marriage and Family Therapy, received his doctorate in counseling psychology from the University of Oregon. His major research interests include studying the interaction of husbands and wives, parents and children, and therapists and clients. Hugh's most recent (1986) book was *Teenager: A Survival Guide for Mom and Dad*. Dr. Allred has a private practice in individual, marriage and family therapy.

Carol Davis Evans has a fulltime private practice in sex therapy, individual, marriage and family therapy and is a Clinical Supervisor with the American Association for Marriage and Family Therapy. She received her doctorate in counseling and guidance from the University of Arizona, is the past president of the Arizona division of the American Association for Marriage and Family Therapy, and has had clinical training with Masters and Johnson. Carol is an Adjunct Assistant Professor at the University of Arizona and is CoDirector of the Family Therapy Training Institute of Tucson.

Robert R. Evans is an Assistant Professor of Sociology at the University of Arizona and has a private practice in sex therapy, individual, marriage and family therapy. He is a clinical member of the American Association for Marriage and Family Therapy and is CoDirector of the Family Therapy Training Institute of Tucson. He received his doctorate is social psychology from the University of Wisconsin. Bob and his wife Carol together and separately have had clinical training with Masters and Johnson and other therapists respected in the fields of sex, individual, marriage and family therapies.

Brenda B. Even is in private practice in individual, marriage, family and career counseling at Counseling, Therapy and Mediation Associates. She is also a trained mediator who deals with divorce, school and business mediations. She is affiliated with the American Association for Counseling and Development; the Arizona Counselors Association; the North American Society of Adlerian Psychology; and the American Association for Marriage and Family Therapy. She is a National Certified Counselor and a Certified Clinical Mental Health Counselor. Brenda received her doctorate from the University of Arizona.

Maxine N. Ijams, Co-Founder of Counseling, Therapy and Mediation Associates in Tucson, Arizona, has been an Adjunct Professor in the Counseling Department at the University of Arizona, and a visiting Professor at the University of Vermont and the University of Ottawa, Canada. She is on the governing board of the Center for Counseling and Education, Ottawa, and has presented numerous workshops in the United States and Canada. She has published *Clues and Techniques for Improving Classroom Interaction*, as well as contributing several chapters in several books.

William G. Nicoll is an Assistant Professor of Counseling at the University of Cincinnati in Cincinnati, Ohio. He maintains a private practice in marriage and family counseling and is a frequent consultant and in-service speaker on marriage and family counseling. He has published several articles in professional journals and has a chapter in Christensen and Schramski's (Eds.) *Adlerian Family Counseling*. Bill has been involved with Adlerian Psychology since 1976 and has served on the Delegate Assembly of the North American Society for Adlerian Psychology.

Lynn K. O'Hern is the Director of the Developing Effective Strategies for Counselors Project for the Division of Counseling and Guidance at the University of Arizona. She has written articles and taught numerous workshops/classes on Divorce Transition, Stepparenting and Remarriage and Equity Issues. Lynn is the coauthor (with Frank Williams) of "Stepfamilies" in Christensen and Schramski's (Eds.) *Adlerian Family Counseling*.

Bernard E. Poduska is an Assistant Professor and Director of the Family Financial Counseling Clinic at Brigham Young University. He has a Ph.D. in Marriage and Family Therapy. He has published a college text in the area of personality and adjustment; a trade book on self analysis; and numerous articles in the financial counseling and planning areas that deal primarily with the effects of personality on financial behavior.

Frank R. Williams is the Program Coordinator of the Extension Home Economics and Family Life Specialist for the University of Arizona Cooperative Extension. He has a small private practice specializing in stepfamilies and men and is active in community organizations including Divorce Recovery, Planned Parenthood, Council for Children, and Youth and Families. Frank has authored numerous Cooperative Extension publications and is coauthor (with Lynn O'Hern) Of "Stepfamilies" in Christensen and Schramski's (Eds.) *Adlerian Family Counseling*.

Forward

The text has been organized from a marriage life cycle perspective which begins with "Adlerian Marital Therapy: History, Theory and Process" and concludes with "Working with Remarried Couples."

The first chapter, by Nicoll, provides a summary of Adlerian theory on couples therapy and how the approach in many ways parallels the ideas of the systemic theorist of today. The chapter is designed to create a vocabulary and theory base that will assist the reader who may or may not be acquainted with the Adlerian perspective with a knowledge for the chapters which follow.

Chapter two, by Hawes and Kern, acquaints the reader with how the theory may be operationalized into practical procedures for conducting the first session with the couple. The authors in this chapter have attempted to lead the therapist step-by-step through a typical first interview with a couple. It also is designed to help the therapist set the stage for future sessions related to Lifestyle interviewing and potential intervention strategies.

Chapter three, by Maxine Ijams, provides the therapist with a succinct process analysis and knowledge base of how to conduct the sessions to follow as it relates to Lifestyle analysis and toxic relationship issues created by differences attributed to individual Lifestyle dynamics.

Chapter four, "Therapeutic Interventions in the Marital Relationship," by Hawes, and Chapter five, "Relationship Enhancement Programs," by Allred and Poduska, have been written to assist the therapist to create strategies to help couples deal with toxic issues that evolve during the Lifestyle analysis and future therapy sessions. These two chapters bring together the techniques and interventions employed by some of the most highly recognized Adlerian therapists in North America and Europe.

The remaining three chapters are devoted to special issues in couples work that complete the life cycle of the coupling process. Chapter six, "Sex Therapy: An Adlerian Approach," addresses an issue that will eventually surface when dealing with the marital dyad for any length of time. Carol Davis Evans and Robert Evans provide an extraordinary overview of Adlerian theory, present day theory, and how the problems of couples in the arena of sex mirror the problems within the relationship.

Chapter seven, "Divorce Mediation," by Brenda Even, attempts to confirm and validate that even when the therapy experience ends in divorce, the Adlerian principles of respect, cooperation, encouragement and education are the keys to growth in the time of crisis for the couple.

Chapter eight, "Working with Remarried Couples," by O"Hern and Williams, has been included to assist the therapist, not only to employ Adlerian principles with remarried couples, but to also educate the therapist as to the additional socio-psychological principles one needs to address when dealing with these couples.

In conclusion, the brief overview of each chapter attempts to provide the reader with a logical format of placement of chapters in the text. However, be prepared as a reader: For just as individual therapists have their own style of helping clients and couples grow, each author has a unique style of creating, on paper, an approach to marital and couples therapy.

Table of Contents

Part I:
Adlerian Theory and Process

Chapter 1
Adlerian Marital Therapy: History, Theory and Process
by
William G. Nicoll

Historical Development of Adlerian Marital Therapy

The Viennese psychiatrist, Alfred Adler, recognized marriage (love/intimacy) as one of the basic social tasks or challenges confronting individuals in their socialpsychological development (Ansbacher & Ansbacher, 1956). Adler suggested that each of us has a need to develop in our lives a close, intimate relationship with at least one individual. He described this need in terms of a task or challenge which each of us must solve for our own benefit as well as ultimately for the benefit of community, society and humankind (Adler, 1978). Marriage, he stated, is a task for two people living and working together as a part of humanity and society and thereby connecting the past and the future.

Adler noted, however, that not all individuals are adequately prepared in their psychological development for successfully meeting this life task. Many people have mistaken attitudes and styles for approaching life and relationships and thus experience difficulty in developing a satisfactory intimate relationship with another. Most commonly, this mistake lies in a too self-centered, expecting, getting approach to relationships rather than a "...task-centered, self-transcending, contributing, mature cooperative outlook" (Adler, 1978, p. 336).

Further, Adler noted that many commonly held societal myths often contribute to the development of such mistaken ideas and approaches to marriage. The "they lived happily everafter" myth of many popular books and movies, for example, suggests marriage as a cure for the problems one must face. Instead, Adler suggested marriage must be viewed as the beginning of a new task requiring attitudes of equality, cooperation, mutual responsibility and interest in one another as well as skills in communication, problem-solving and cooperative efforts.

The approach to marriage developed by Adler is therefore primarily educational in nature. Rather than involving diagnosis, treatment and cure of marital pathology, Adlerian Psychology stresses assessment of mistaken approaches and attitudes toward intimate relationships and the teaching or training of some satisfactory, less erroneous approaches to the task of marriage and intimacy. This approach to marital therapy, i.e., identifying mistaken ideas, misconceptions, erroneous/destructive styles of relating and a lack of necessary relationship skills— lends itself not only to remedial efforts in cases of marital conflict, but to preventive approaches in pre-marital counseling, marital enrichment and family life education.

As early as 1926, Alfred Adler was an advocate of marital and premarital counseling (Adler, 1978). Although there does not appear to be any record of him conducting therapy with couples, he did recognize the need for preventive work in this area by stating, "It would be a real blessing for marriage, humanity and the future generation if before every marriage there were some marriage therapy by experienced Individual Psychologists to supplement inadequate preparation and improve erroneous attitudes" (p. 335). It was largely left to the students of Adler and his theory to pursue the development of this area further; that is, the application of Individual Psychology to marital relationships.

Sophie Lazarsfeld, an associate of Adler in Vienna, was probably the first Adlerian marriage therapist. She started her Marriage and Sex Counseling Center in Vienna in 1926 (Adler, 1978). Later the application of Adler's Individual Psychology to marriage was advanced by individuals such as Olga Knopf (1932), who wrote on sex and marriage in her book, *The Art of Being a Woman*; Rudolph Dreikurs, who wrote extensively on marriage and marriage counseling (Dreikurs, 1946, 1968); and Danica

Deutsch, who in the 1950s and 60s conducted marriage counseling and group therapy with couples in New York (Deutsch, 1956, 1967b).

The application of Individual Psychology to the problems of marital relationships was further advanced by Helen Papenek, who in 1965 wrote of her work in group therapy with couples (Papenek, 1965), and William and Miriam Pew, who have described their work with four-track marital therapy (Pew & Pew, 1972). Still more recently, the evolution of applying Adler's Individual Psychology to improving marital relationships has extended to the area of marriage enrichment with such programs as *Couples Growing Together* (Hawes & Hawes, 1986) and *TIME* (Dinkmeyer & Carlson, 1984).

The process and techniques of Adlerian marriage counseling and therapy, as it has been developed by these and other clinicians, are derived from the same set of basic principles and assumptions originally developed by Adler for understanding individual behavior. Adler's theories on human behavior might well be viewed as the first systems-based approach in the field of psychology. In the first quarter of the century, Adler recognized the inadequacy of mechanistic-reductionistic epistemologies for understanding such complex phenomena as human behavior and his psychology was developed instead from a systemic-holistic perspective (Ansbacher & Ansbacher, 1956).

Alfred Adler chose to call his theory Individual Psychology. The term, individual, was taken from the Latin, *individuum*, meaning indivisible; indicating a holistic, systemic view of personality and behavior and recognizing the need to understand all behavior primarily within the larger social context(s) in which it occurs (Dreikurs, 1971; Thomas & Marchant, 1983). Adler's Individual Psychology seeks explanations to all problems by considering the interrelationship of the parts and the whole. Perhaps Adler's greatest mistake was in not labeling his psychology "Systems Psychology," while the term was still available to him.

With its emphasis on the social context and the purpose or function behavior serves for the larger system(s) in which it occurs, this systemic-holistic perspective provides a logical and consistent conceptual basis for understanding the individual, the marital dyad, the family and larger social systems as well.

Adlerian Psychology, in essence, manages to integrate both individual personality and relationship system dynamics. Thus, the marriage therapist functioning from an Adlerian perspective is able to easily move back and forth between the individual, the marital dyad and family relationships in both assessing and intervening in marital difficulties.

The perspective of the Adlerian marriage therapist might be viewed as analogous to that of a movie cameraman looking through a zoom lens. At times, the therapist moves to a wide-angle view to see the marital system within its broader context of nuclear and extended family relationships or in light of other factors that may be influencing the marital relationship such as occupational concerns or social/community relationships. While at other times the therapist may choose to zoom-in and focus upon the marital dyad itself, or upon one particular member. Intervention and change may occur at any of these levels as the interdependent or circular nature of causality between them has long been recognized in Adlerian Psychology.

In other words, change at any level will, in turn, result in change at all levels. On one occasion, the marriage therapist may choose to work on a particularly important issue of one spouse recognizing that change in the other spouse will in turn change the marital system's interactional patterns. While at other times, the therapist may focus upon changing marital interaction patterns knowing that this will, in turn, result in change in each spouse's attitudes and feelings toward the relationship.

To fully understand marital therapy from an Adlerian perspective, one needs to further recognize that Individual Psychology is firmly based in functionalism. Adlerian Psychology continually focuses upon the purpose or social function any particular behavior serves for the individual actor and the marital, familial and other social systems in which it occurs. In assessing the relative degree of pathology versus health of any behavior, the ultimate criterion will be the relative usefulness of the behavior to the growth and well-being of the individual, marital, familial and societal systems to which they belong. "The real important differences of conduct are... those of uselessness and usefulness" (Adler, 1964a, p. 78). Useful behavior was defined by Adler as being in the interest of others.

The most sensible estimate of the value of any activity, Adler stated, is its helpfulness to all mankind, present and future (Adler, 1958). In marital counseling and therapy, then, the therapist focuses upon the purposeful nature of each spouse's behavior and the consequences their actions have for one another, their marriage and the family. Dysfunctional interactions are seen as those in which the growth and development, or well-being, of either spouse is blocked. In which case, a dysfunctional interactional style is observed in the marriage wherein each spouse tries to obtain or maintain a more advantageous position vis-a-vis the other.

Relationship to other Marital Therapy Models

Given the above discussion, it is not surprising to find the Adlerian model very much compatible with most currently popular systems-based models of marriage and family therapy. Sluzki (1978) has stated the primary conceptual framework characterizing the systems approach is the utilization of transactions between people rather than characteristics of individuals as primary data. Beal (1980) has added that the systems approach places its highest priority for intervention in the interrelationship of environment and individual. Finally, Walsh (1982) suggested that the systems model to marital and family intervention conceptualizes the marriage and family as open systems that function in relationship to their broader social contexts. These statements clearly place the popular systems based models in essential alignment with the principles of Adler's Individual Psychology. Adler's principles are particularly evident in the systems-based model's focus on the social embeddedness of human behavior, emphasizing that problems exist between people rather than primarily within individuals.

In reviewing the basic assumptions of the systems orientation, Walsh (1982) has suggested a core of seven major principles. The first five reiterate the principles of Adler's Individual Psychology as developed in Ansbacher and Ansbacher (1956) and Manaster and Corsini (1982):

> **Circular Causality.** The circular nature of causality in behavior is recognized in place of one-way, linear causality. The marital dyad and family are viewed as systems, or groups of interrelated individuals, such that change in any one member affects the system as a whole, which in turn, affects each individual.

Nonsummativity. Nonsummativity reflects the view that the family as a whole is greater than the sum of its parts. Adler originally discussed this concept in relation to the individual being greater than the mere sum of one's parts and later, as noted previously, in the need to understand the part by reference to the whole and of the whole by reference to the parts. Organizational structures, patterns of interaction and shared myths and values are of central concern from this holistic, systemic perspective.

Equifinality. Equifinality refers to the idea that the same origin or stimulus event may lead to different behavioral outcomes while the same outcome may result from different origins or events. Individual Psychology has long recognized the critical importance of one's attitudes and the meaning one attaches to events as more important than the event in and of itself for determining behavior.

Communication. Communication, the transmitting of interpersonal messages, is understood as being at the foundation of all behavior. All behavior must be understood in terms of its interpersonal context. Behavioral pathology, then, is viewed as an interactional process between the intrapsychic (attitudes, myths and apperceptions) and the interpersonal.

Family Rules. Family and marital rules determine the nature of the particular relationship and provide stability to the marital system. Most current models of marital counseling and therapy, including the Adlerian approach, view marital systems as interacting in repetitious sequences or patterns based upon a small, salient set of explicit and implicit rules and assumptions. This is a logical extension of Adlerian Psychology's understanding of individual behavior as based upon a cognitive framework consisting of a set of highly salient rules, assumptions and attitudes—i.e. the Individual Lifestyle.

The marital rules and assumptions are often reflected in the myths, roles and values of the marital and family system. Each spouse brings to the marriage a particular set of myths and values from one's own family of origin. This has been referred to as the Family Lifestyle (Nicoll & Hawes, 1985; Deutsch, 1967a). Myths such as the perceived roles of fathers/husbands and mother/wives by each spouse and values such as the importance of career versus familial relationships would be incorporated in the Family Lifestyle.

The task of the new marital system is to develop a new Family Lifestyle; that is, form a separate couple/family identity which, while reflecting the respective family of origin values and myths, provide a new, distinct identity for the new marital system. Successful resolution of this task is viewed as a prerequisite, or primary developmental task, for the further growth and healthy functioning of the marital system and ultimately the family system as well. Eventually, a common perspective evolves in the relationship consisting of shared values, myths and apperceptions.

The final two basic assumptions or principles of the family systems model as discussed by Walsh focus on the issue of change over time within the family. While this issue is not specifically addressed in the Adlerian Psychology model, the concepts are quite compatible with Adler's theory. These two principles are:

Homeostasis. Homeostatic mechanisms exist within the family to maintain the stability and organization of the system. Such mechanisms maintain a steady or stable state in the marriage by prohibiting behavior deviating from normative expectations and reinforcing behavior that is acceptable.

Morphogenesis. Morphogenic mechanisms enable needed changes in family organization, rules and so forth in order for the marital system to grow and adapt to internal and external stressor events. The marital relationship is thus able to grow and change over the course of the family life cycle by altering role complexes and normative expectations of the partners.

Further Assumptions of Adlerian Marital Therapy

Equality: In addition to the above theoretical assumptions, which are maintained in common by Adlerian and other systems models of marital therapy, the marriage therapist functioning from an Adlerian framework maintains several further ideas regarding marital relationships. Foremost is the issue of equality. Functional or healthy human relationships can only exist where egalitarian attitudes based upon mutual respect are present. Equality does not imply that each spouse must be seen as the same or as having equal skills and abilities. Rather, equality implies an attitude recognizing the equal value and worth of individuals with each having unique competencies, characteristics and responsibilities which make some beneficial contribution to the relationship.

Masculine Protest: The issue of equality versus inequality between the sexes was originally discussed by Adler early in this century in terms of what he called the Masculine Protest (Ansbacher & Ansbacher, 1956). Adler recognized that our society has mistakenly placed women in a position of inferior social status. This myth, the inferiority of women and femininity, and its corollary, the superiority of males and masculinity, is so deeply rooted that it has been written into and perpetuated by our laws, folk tales, literature and children's fairy tales (Adler, 1978). As a result, both men and women manifest the masculine protest issue in their psychological development and approach to life. Nowhere is this more evident than in the marital relationship where one's ability to cooperate as an equal with the opposite sex is put to its ultimate test. Femininity has been traditionally identified with obedient, servile and subordinate behavior while masculinity has been identified with dominant, strong, victorious behavior.

For women, the masculine protest is often manifested as a discontent or resentment with the socially prescribed inferior role. For some women, this attitude may be manifested in the marriage via such dysfunctional behavior as sexual disorders, assumed disability or ineptness, rejection of household related tasks or marrying a husband perceived as "weaker" in order to overtly dominate and thereby compensating for the inferior position by controlling the relationship.

For men, the masculine protest concept is manifested in a value or attitudinal system that suggests his self-esteem/self-respect is contingent upon being, or appearing to be, "masculine"—i.e., ambitious, strong, dominating, superior and hardened against "feminine" impulses.

How the masculine protest issue manifests itself in each spouse's Individual Lifestyle, or personality style, greatly impacts upon the marital relationship. Tension may be created when the husband strives for control or dominance in the relationship or feels his position threatened by his wife's overt or covert rebellion to it. As O'Neil (1978) has noted in his work on masculinity, the issues of control, power and competence are central to the "masculine mystique." Furthermore, both males and females tend to hold this expectation of "real men." Thus, double bind situations may be created in the marital relationship wherein the male is expected by both husband and wife to be strong, dominant and in control; while, at the same time, the wife rebels against the inferior position this places her.

The more the wife feels inclined to rebel against the feminine role, as she perceives it, or the greater the husband's need to maintain his mythical position of privilege or superiority, the greater the conflict will be in the marriage. In a sense, as Adler argued, children are forced from childhood to adopt an attitude in life that is in opposition to the opposite sex. This struggle contradicts the primary requirement for harmonious, constructive marital relationships; that is, equality and mutual respect. It is, therefore, no great surprise in this time of increased female awareness of, and rebellion against, women's socially inferior position that increased difficulties are seen among people striving to successfully fulfill the primary life task of marital/intimate relationships. Marital conflict and dissolution may well be increasing largely as a result of the difficulties both males and females are experiencing in learning to live as social equals.

The masculine protest issue is of particular importance in the assessment of sexual problems or dysfunction in the marriage. Sexuality is viewed as being intertwined with one's basic personality style or cognitive system (Adler, 1978). As the early Adlerian marriage and sex therapists found, "troubles among both sexes will disappear once this senseless, coercive attitude (male superiority/female inferiority), born of an unjustifiable overevaluation of man, has been abandoned.... Sex will be able to shake off its unnatural rigidity and will develop into a more beautiful and a richer thing than it has been heretofore" (Lazarsfeld, 1934, p. 81).

Sexuality is viewed, therefore, by Adlerian Psychology not as an autonomous area of human functioning, but as an integral part of the overall psychological life. Thus, where issues of superiority/inferiority or dominance and control exist in the relationship, it should not be surprising to find both spouses using their sexuality in this struggle. Shulman (1967) has, for example, suggested at least twenty-one possible uses of sex, some of which being socially constructive (e.g. reproduction, giving mutual pleasure, expressing love and acceptance) and others socially destructive (e.g. domination, vanity and rewards for compliance). Stated simply, problems and conflicts in the marital relationship are quite likely to be expressed ultimately in the sexual behavior of the couple.

The principle of the superior/inferior dynamic in relationships and its corollary, control, has been further developed and applied to the understanding of marital discord by Adlerian marriage therapists. Indeed, this seeking of power or control—i.e., superiority over one's spouse in the marital relationship—may be viewed as the primary underlying dynamic in conflictual relationships. How this issue is dealt with or resolved will determine the success or failure of the relationship. Dreikurs stated the following:

> One would assume that no single factor can be made responsible for success or failure in marriage. Upon careful scrutiny, however, one factor does emerge as a crucial variable. More important than real events and experiences, by far outweighing the impact of any favorable or disastrous contingent, is the attitude taken by the persons involved. The same set of circumstances may permit or even produce opposite attitudes and thereby change the behavior and reverse sentiments and emotions (Dreikurs, 1968, p. 84).

While either or both partners may strive for a position of superiority or control in the relationship, the consequence will be that one partner will soon sense being placed in an inferior position. Typically, this spouse will then strive overtly or covertly to undermine the other's position of control and dominance.

This striving may be manifested in an infinite variety of ways. Some choose spouses whom they see as inferior either socially, intellectually, physically and so forth and thus avoid competition with a non-threatening spouse. Another manifestation would be the "superior" spouse attempting a Pygmalion-like relationship in which one rehabilitates or grooms the inferior for the spouse's own good. Yet another mistaken approach would be the attempt by either spouse to obligate the other through an expression of love. The beloved person, by the mere fact of being loved, is thus seen as obligated to act as the "loving" spouse desires or dictates. Failure to do so often results in a victimized or martyr-like response by the obligating spouse.

Similarly, individuals who have learned through their early development to obtain a position of superiority or control by putting others in their service and to be the center of attention will employ similar tactics in the marriage. Such closet tyrants are doomed to eventually meet with resentment and resistance from their spouses. Or, such individuals may create such a romantic ideal that they consistently find their spouses wanting and inadequate and they express this in some way to their spouses.

Sexual dysfunction often results from this striving to obtain a superior/controlling role or to avoid the inferior/controlled position. The female's sexual problems may be an unconscious way of saying, "no, I will not submit"; while for males, such issues as impotence may be a passive resistance to his wife's perceived demands upon him or, a manner of avoiding perceived failure in living up to the Masculine Protest issue of proving himself a "real man" and "winner" sexually. Thus, the sexual dysfunction, in Adlerian Psychology, is often viewed as symptomatic of a deeper relationship issue involving the individual's mistaken views of self and attitudes toward the opposite sex.

Marital Styles: Central to the Adlerian Psychology approach to counseling and therapy is the concept of Style of Living (Adler, 1958). Adler originally adopted his term, Individual Lifestyle, to refer to the patterned, consistent approach to life and relationships adopted by the individual (i.e. personality style). The Individual Lifestyle concept is very much related to Max Weber's (1946) concept of the Collective Lifestyles referring to the shared values and perspectives on life found within various ethnic and cultural groups. Deutsch (1967a) and Nicoll and

Hawes (1985) have applied this concept of style, or consistent patterns of relating to life and others, to the family system as well.

Similarly, in working with the marital relationship, it is important to recognize the marital, or relationship style, which has developed between the spouses. This style will reflect their shared outlook on life, their values, their shared apperceptions and, consequently, their patterned style of interacting with one another. Of central importance to this marital style is the issue of power or control reflecting the ability, or inability, of the couple to develop an egalitarian relationship rather than one based upon a superior/inferior dynamic. The latter style being manifested in the problematic or dysfunctional marriage.

Tobin (1975) has suggested several common styles in which the issue of superiority/inferiority or control/dominance is manifested in marital relationships. It is important in the early stages of marital therapy to ascertain how this issue is dealt with in the relationship. Possibly the most common style is the relationship in which one spouse controls and one acquiesces. The control may be exercised in a non-coercive, non-obtrusive manner with both partners appearing to accept this situation or, in a more coercive, dictatorial manner wherein the subordinate spouse expresses one's feelings of discomfort, powerlessness and futility in the relationship.

Caution, however, must be exercised by the therapist in assessment; the more active, outwardly dominant partner may not always be the controlling spouse. The outwardly appearing "controlled" spouse may, in actuality, exercise complete control vis-a-vis one's dependence and avoidance of responsibility for decisions. This style of relationship has sometimes been humorously referred to as the "trucker and dumper" marriage where the passive spouse "dumps" all responsibility on the "trucker" who must handle it all.

Another common marital style noted by Tobin is that where one spouse controls and one resists. This relationship style differs from the one above in that the spouse in the inferior position overtly and actively fights against being controlled or dominated. Moreover, this spouse becomes extremely sensitive and reacts to any situation in which there is the slightest suggestion of control. Tension and conflict characterize the marriage. Somewhat similar to this situation would be the marriage in which both spouses actively strive for dominance. Both view their appropriate role in the marriage as being decision maker/senior partner. Fighting, arguing, sarcasm or sullen withdrawal may be used in the pursuit of subjugating one another.

Yet another common relationship is that of neither spouse fighting for control and yet, neither relinquishing it either. In this marriage, an unspoken rule functions whereby each is allowed to remain autonomous, avoiding situations in which mutual cooperation and effort is necessitated. Unfortunately, the price each must pay for autonomy is that of genuine intimacy and affection. Often such couples lead largely separate lives, both socially and occupationally. Another variation on this style would be where there is a fairly rigid adherence to segregated conjugal roles and norms and a stress on emotional control. In this manner, threats to control posed by intimacy, spontaneity and sharing between husband and wife may be avoided.

One final common dysfunctional marital relationship style is that in which both spouses seek to relinquish or avoid responsibility and control. In this mutually dependent relationship, each spouse seeks to maneuver the other into a controlling, decision-making role so as to avoid personal responsibility for the marital relationship. Indecision may characterize the marriage. Ironically, it is the spouse who succeeds in relinquishing control who ultimately controls such a marriage.

The healthy/functional marital relationship style, from an Adlerian perspective, occurs when the issues of superiority/inferiority and control are eliminated. Each spouse respects the other as an equal partner and actively seeks to give and to share within the relationship assuming responsibility for contributing to the growth of self, spouse and the marriage. Such a relationship, based upon trust and mutual respect and free of dominance and manipulation, has, unfortunately, all too often proven difficult for couples to achieve. The relative health and stability of the marriage will be determined by the extent to which the couple can successfully achieve this egalitarian marital relationship style. For only in this latter relationship style, wherein neither spouse seeks to control the other, but rather, seeks to contribute to and work cooperatively, will the relationship and each individual be able to develop and grow.

Communication: Communication within the marital dyad is understood within the context of the marital relationship style and the concepts of superiority/inferiority versus equality and mutual respect. That is, the communication pattern which emerges between the partners will reflect the nature of the overall marital relationship style. Communication within the marital dyad is understood as based upon each partner's apperceptions of the other's goals and intentions for the relationship (Dreikurs, 1959). Both husband and wife are seen as working cooperatively to reach the final pattern of interaction or communication style—be it positive/constructive or negative/destructive to the marriage.

Generally speaking, these patterns between couples evolve in three communication patterns. The first is positive/constructive communication in which each is seen as striving to enhance one another and the relationship. The second is negative/destructive communication where each spouse perceives the other's words and actions as part of the struggle for power, control and dominance, placing one in an inferior position. Finally, there is miscommunication in which the intent or meaning of one partner is misinterpreted by the other.

However, it must be recognized that the consequences of misunderstanding or miscommunication will depend upon the predominant attitudes of each spouse toward the other and the marriage (Dreikurs, 1959). If it is based on respect and concern for one another and the marriage, efforts will be made to clarify the messages—i.e. move toward positive/constructive communication. However, where mistrust, hostility and antagonism are hallmarks, the miscommunication will feed into and escalate the negative/destructive communication process between them.

In the functional marriage, communication will be characterized by positive and constructive interactions, both verbal and non-verbal with misunderstandings resolved in a friendly, cooperative manner. Empathy, respect for one another's views and honesty of feelings characterize the communication process. Each spouse is able to see, hear, feel and understand events from the other's perspective. Both feel encouraged to express their views and feelings without threat to their sense of value, self-worth or status in the marital relationship. Problems and decisions are handled by actively encouraging the input and participation of the other, seeking solutions acceptable to both.

In working with the dysfunctional marriage, the marriage therapist must initially seek to disrupt the existing negative/destructive communication pattern. Then, the therapist can gently assist the couple in recognizing the purpose and consequences of their communication patterns. The therapist may at this point seek to teach the skills of positive communication based upon an attitude of mutual respect using appropriate negotiation and problem-solving skills. The focus for each spouse in the communications process shifts from one of what is best for me to what is the problem and what can be done about it which would be in the best interests of all.

Attitudes Toward Marriage and Social Interest: The attitudes and apperceptions of each spouse, referred to as their Individual Lifestyles (Ansbacher & Ansbacher, 1956), and their relative fit are also of central concern to the Adlerian marriage therapist. The attitudes adopted by each spouse regarding marriage and the nature of the relationship is considered the single crucial variable responsible for success or failure in the marriage (Dreikurs, 1968). Consistent with the systemic principle of equifinality, Adlerian marital therapy accepts that favorable or disfavorable life circumstances, may be met with different and even opposite attitudes leading, therefore, to different emotions and behaviors.

Attitudes consistent with maintaining a functional marital relationship are reflected in the Adlerian perspective on mental health. Adler (1964) offered the concept of gemeinschaftsgefuhl, meaning a community or other-oriented feeling, as a definition of mental health in individuals. This concept has been referred to as Adler's most distinctive, yet most difficult, concept—the cardinal personality trait reflecting each individual's attitude toward and relationship with one's social environment (Ansbacher, 1968).

While many authors have attempted to better define the concept of gemeinschaftsgefuhl, or social interest as commonly translated in English, we might summarize it as an attitude or process of being interested in and valuing the interests of others. It implies a merging of one's own interests with those of others, such as one's spouse in a marital relationship, resulting in a basic harmony and mutual affirmation. The development of one's mental health, or social interest, therefore involves an increased sense of belonging and contributing in relationships based upon a sense of acceptance of one another as equal and valued individuals. The individual with sufficiently developed social interest, or mental health, will be seen as being tolerant of others, reasonable, understanding, able to empathize and identify with others' views, relaxed, having a sense of humor regarding oneself and life and able to contribute and participate in the marital relationship in a give-and-take manner.

What occurs ultimately in the course of Adlerian marital therapy is the growth of social interest within each spouse. This involves not only a change in attitudes but the development of new behavioral skills consistent with these new attitudes as well. The therapist assists the couple in becoming aware of the wide range of behavioral choices available to them which may prove more satisfying for their relationship than the present rigid and destructive behavioral pattern in which they are engaged. By so doing, the marriage therapist restructures the marital, and often the family, system so as to make it more conducive to the fostering and maintenance of attitudes consistent with social interest.

To the degree that the social interest of either or both spouses is inadequately developed, cooperation in the marriage will be limited. In such a case, competition for a superior personal position will characterize the relationship rather than a cooperative focus on encouraging one another and mutual problem-solving. Such a situation can cause problems for the larger family system as well. The nature of the marital relationship is viewed as setting the tone for all relationships within the nuclear family. "Where the marriage is unhappy, the situation is full of danger for the child" (Adler, 1958, p. 132).

Where social interest is lacking or insufficiently developed in the parental dyad, the skills of understanding, empathy, cooperation and responsible contribution will be inadequately modeled for the children. Instead, a relationship style based upon competition for control and power will be modeled. Consequently, all too often the entire family system becomes characterized by overt and/or covert conflict and competition as each member strives for control or a superior position in the constellation of family interrelationships. It is important, therefore, to consider the marital relationship style and the issues of equality and mutual respect versus competition and superiority whenever discord and conflict among the children is the presenting issue in family therapy.

Ultimately, Adlerian Psychology views the functional marital relationship as one in which each spouse feels worthwhile, respected and irreplaceable. Each spouse must feel valued, wanted and needed by the other and respected as an equal partner and true friend. This directly parallels the Adlerian perspective on optimal parent/child relationships. The marriage needs to be based upon equality expressed in mutual respect and cooperation between the partners (Adler, 1978). Equality, as previously noted, refers not to sameness but rather to being of equal value albeit with different skills, interests and abilities. Equality in the marital relationship requires that both partners have an attitude of being more interested in the other than in oneself—i.e. sufficient social interest.

Mate Selection: The degree to which attitudes consistent with the concept of social interest are present in the relationship can often be ascertained by assessing the issue of mate selection in the formation of the marital dyad. As Dreikurs stated, "A better understanding of the mechanisms of attraction may lead to a clearer perception of the process of rejection" (Dreikurs, 1968; p. 85). We make our marital choice on the basis of our personal bias regarding ourselves, our relationships with others and our goals in life. Individuals decide to marry when they sense a sufficient degree of congruence between their respective Individual Lifestyles—i.e., their respective outlooks on and approach to life and relationships. Following our unique apperceptions regarding ourselves, life and relationships, we take on certain roles and seek out, albeit at a level of unawareness, individuals whose roles supplement our own.

The previously discussed issue of superiority/inferiority versus equality in each spouse's Lifestyle is often reflected in the marital choice. In the dysfunctional marriage, the desire to obtain a preferred position relative to one's spouse may often serve as the primary attraction. One may seek an individual who is viewed as inferior in terms of, for example, physical attractiveness, intelligence, skill or maturity so as to avoid competition in those areas important to one's self-esteem. Others, especially women who may have been socialized into inferior roles in our society, may seek someone who appears superior only to then use their assumed weakness and inadequacy as a tool of control and manipulation, thus placing themselves in the superior/controlling position. Still others may choose to marry someone who will bring pain and dissatisfaction in order to obtain the morally superior position of martyr.

There is also usually some degree of common ground between husband and wife, be it in interests, backgrounds, values, preoccupations or shared outlook on life and the world. This common bond or outlook between the partners may in some instances involve seemingly identical attitudes toward life, such as idealism, pessimism, certainty of failure or intellectual or moral superiority which unites them as two against the world. Eventually, each may begin viewing the other as a part of that world which they disclaim. Or one spouse may experience a change in outlook and find a sudden lack of commonality with the other.

Those same traits which initially attract us to our spouses frequently end up as the same traits that lead to conflict. To understand this concept, one must recognize that any human quality or characteristic can be viewed in a positive or negative light. Thus, the problem is not so much the behavior but rather the changed attitude toward that behavior or trait on the part of the spouse. For example, the wife who was attracted by the husband's decisive, self-assured manner may later view him as opinionated, rigid and self-centered. Thrifty may become cheap; decisive becomes opinionated and pre-occupied; generous becomes extravagant; and strong becomes domineering. In the course of treatment, the marriage therapist needs to assist couples in identifying where they have negatively relabeled characteristics of their spouses previously viewed as positive with more negative terms.

Based upon these forgoing principles and assumptions outlined in the chapter, the Adlerian marriage therapist assesses present marital functioning and develops therapeutic goals. The breakdown of the marriage typically occurs when one or both spouses fails to cooperate and work to create a mutually satisfying relationship. Rather, each begins to wait for the other to initiate change and thereby to receive the perceived benefits of that change (Dreikurs, 1946). The marriage therapist, therefore, keeps in mind that a fundamental prerequisite to resolving marital problems is the recognition by each spouse that the only point at which either can start to change the marriage is with oneself. As Dreikurs stated (1946), "When we muster our courage and try to think in terms of 'What can I do to improve the situation?' then we are on the right track" (p.189).

Marriage Counseling Process

The process of Adlerian marital therapy follows from the systemic-holistic epistemological perspective and the principles and assumptions discussed previously. Specifically, the process encompasses what may be described as four distinct stages (Dreikurs, 1959): investigation, insight, reorientation and re-education.

It is important to note, before proceeding further, that although these are discussed as distinct phases in the overall therapy process, from intake or termination, all four stages maybe operating at any given time—i.e., in the course of any given single session. The four stages are probably best understood as analogous to Erikson's eight stages of psychosocial development (Erikson, 1963). While all the stages are active at any single point in time, one stage generally dominates during a given period in the developmental process in a predictable sequence and is the central issue, but by no means does it negate or exclude the issues involved with the remaining stages. The four stages of counseling/therapy fit with the previously discussed levels of understanding behavior in Adlerian Psychology as illustrated in Figure 1.

Stage One: Investigation

In the initial stage of the marital therapy process, the therapist seeks to understand what is presently occurring in the marriage and in the lives of each spouse. This understanding begins with the identification and investigation of the presenting issues, concerns or problems each spouse brings to therapy, as well as discovering how each spouse feels about the relationship. These issues, in turn, must be understood in their larger context, which encompasses for each spouse one's stage of development as well as how each one is handling and feeling about each of the major life tasks (see Chapter 2) in their personal lives.

Secondly, at the marital system level, it is important to investigate how long the relationship has existed, its history and where it is at the present. The marriage, in turn, must be placed in context of the larger systems to which it belongs and within which it functions including the family systems (both nuclear and extended) and the ethnic/cultural heritage (Collective Lifestyles) of the respective partners.

Figure 1

The Counseling Process

Dysfunctional   Functional
Behaviors   Behaviors

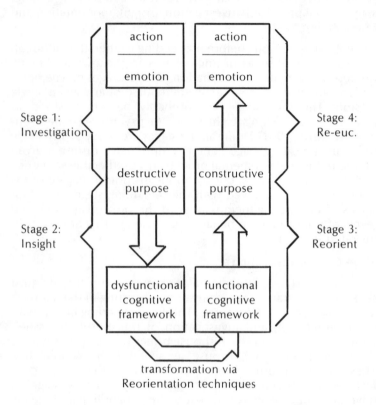

Stage 1:   Stage 4:
Investigation   Re-euc.

action   action

emotion   emotion

destructive   constructive
purpose   purpose

Stage 2:   Stage 3:
Insight   Reorient

dysfunctional   functional
cognitive   cognitive
framework   framework

transformation via
Reorientation techniques

Thus, the marriage therapist gets to identify the couple's current Family Life Cycle (Carter & McGoldrick, 1980) and how normal developmental issues associated with the Family Life Cycle stage are being handled. It is also appropriate to investigate the marriage in the context of the extended families to which it belongs by inquiring about relationships with each spouse's respective family of origin. Throughout this stage, the therapist endeavors to get a clear picture as to what is occurring, through overt behavior and emotions, in the lives of both husband and wife as well as what is occurring in the marital relationship and

---

the larger systems within which the marriage exists. From this data, the marital therapist begins to formulate tentative hypotheses regarding the purpose or function of the dysfunctional behaviors discussed as presenting issues bringing the couple to therapy.

Stage Two: Insight

As the therapist more clearly understands the current life situation of the couple, it becomes important to move toward still deeper understanding. Thus, the therapist strives in the second stage to gain further insight into the purposes that the presenting problem behavior serve both for the respective spouses as well as for the marriage. Also, at this stage, the therapist begins to gain insight into the individual logic system—i.e., Individual Lifestyle (see Chapter 3)—of both husband and wife as well as the rules, values and myths upon which the marital and family relationship systems operate—i.e., the marital relationship style.

As noted earlier in this chapter, much like a cameraman, the therapist views the marriage through a series of varying lenses. At one time, the therapist may choose to zoom in to understand the cognitive framework of one spouse and that person's life situation. Later, the therapist may select a wider angle lens and observe the relationship patterns and how the rules governing them operate in the marriage system. Still, at other times, an extreme wide angle lens may be necessary to observe the marriage within the total context of the nuclear and extended family systems.

During the insight stage, a variety of assessment techniques will be employed by a therapist depending upon the issues identified and area of investigation—individual, couple or family—involved. Adlerian marriage therapists frequently employ the Individual Lifestyle assessment technique (see Chapter 3) to gain insight into the cognitive framework by which each spouse approaches the marriage and the other's behaviors. By using the Individual Lifestyle assessment technique in marital therapy, not only the therapist but both spouses obtain a clearer understanding of how they view themselves, their lives, their marriage and their family relationships.

Both positive/constructive and dysfunctional/destructive attitudes, expectations and beliefs of each spouse are identified as well as areas of relative fit and predictable conflict between the husband's and wife's personality styles. Techniques such as

Early Recollections of the relationship, dream interpretation, guided fantasy and personal priority identification, as well as other projective instruments and techniques, may be utilized by the marriage therapist to gain a deeper understanding as to how each spouse approaches life and intimate relationships.

It is also important to directly assess the marital relationship itself regarding the relationship rules, values and myths accepted by the couple which dictate behaviors as well as form the couple's particular identity. These rules, values and myths—i.e., marital relationship style—are frequently ascertained by noting the rather salient and predictable patterns of interaction which occur between the couple. The therapist attempts to make overt the covert rules, values and myths upon which the marriage is based. Requesting the couple to describe typical conflict sequences and decision-making processes or the "last time you felt that way," may assist the therapist in understanding the couple's interaction patterns and the rules which govern it.

The marital relationship style resulting in conflicts will most often revolve around one of the superior/inferior or control patterns discussed earlier in this chapter (e.g., one controls/one acquiesces, both seek control/dominance). This style of relating in the marriage will, in turn, set the tone for all relationships in the family. Thus, as noted earlier, sibling problems and parent-child conflict may often prove to be a reflection of the mistaken or dysfunctional marital relationship style adopted by the parents.

It frequently becomes useful to assess the marital relationship within the context of the larger systems to which it belongs. Thus, the therapist may choose to look at the couple through a "wide-angle lens," taking in not only the couple but the respective families of origin or extended families out of which it developed. Both husband and wife come to the marriage expecting to recreate, albeit with some selected improvements, their own family of origin's style of relating. Each spouse may then strive, overtly or covertly, to gain pre-eminence for one's particular Family Lifestyle (Nicoll & Hawes, 1985).

The initial developmental task of the couple is to synthesize their respective Family Lifestyle expectations into a new, unique couple identity satisfactory to both husband and wife. This may be a relatively stormy and difficult process which is never fully resolved. The characteristic values, interaction patterns and role expectations of past generations for each spouse will have a significant impact upon the myths, values, interaction patterns and role expectations of the new couple and their family system. One technique for identifying such family-of-origin "baggage" issues has been described by Nicoll and Hawes (1985). By combining an Adlerian interpretive process with the family genogram technique, an effective insight technique results enabling both the therapist and the couple to better understand the dynamics of their relationship, including family values and myths within the context of their extended families.

Stage Three: Reorientation

As the marriage therapist gains insight into the Individual Lifestyles of husband and wife, their marital relationship style and the larger Family Lifestyles influencing this relationship, the therapist begins to understand the total dynamics of the presenting issues. The therapist understands what is occurring (actions and emotions) in the marriage, the purpose such behaviors serve and the cognitive frameworks (e.g., rules, myths, values, and shared apperceptions) upon which the purpose and behaviors are based. The therapist and the couple, through interpretation and confrontation techniques, now begin to recognize the congruence between the how, what for and why of the presenting problems and conflicts brought to marriage therapy by the couple. Therefore, in stage three the central concern is to challenge dysfunctional attitudes and apperceptions and assist the couple in developing new, more functional attitudes, perceptions and expectations in their relationship.

This stage requires a great deal of skill, timing and tack on the part of the therapist. The therapist not only tries to interpret the more significant themes identified in stage two (insight) that contribute to the tension, conflict or disappointment experienced by each spouse, but also must offer alternatives. Direct and indirect confrontation techniques, normalizing and catastrophizing techniques and reframing and relabeling techniques are among the tools which might be used by the therapist to reorientate the couple's relationship style as well as the respective Individual Lifestyles. As this reorientation occurs, the couple begins also to recognize the dysfunctional purposes their previous behaviors served, making such behavior more distasteful to them. (This experience is often referred to as "spitting in the client's soup.")

The persuasive influence and skills of the therapist are critical to the successful transition from stage two (insight) to stage three (reorientation). Confrontation and interpretation must be combined with the encouragement of each spouse and the couple system. Noting the important positive contributions of each spouse to the marital relationship can be useful in switching from a focus on problems to strengths. Reorientation may involve assisting the couple to view some problem behaviors in a more positive light—i.e., reframing or relabeling. This might involve, for example, rethinking how each spouse defines and experiences love and affection. The wife who saw her husband as unexpressive and overly involved with work, yet providing materially for her and the children, may be assisted in recognizing and relabeling his behavior as the only way in which he has learned to express affection. For him, providing materially for his wife and family may be the only safe way he knows to say "I love you."

Reorientation is also the stage of therapy when the therapist begins to help each spouse develop beyond a predominantly self-orientation and toward greater concern for what is best for the other spouse, children and/or the marriage itself. When conflict has persisted for some time, the individuals involved begin to view the relationship with an increasingly narrow perspective, focusing only upon the personal concerns, hurts and injustices inflicted upon them. Both husband and wife can present a good, sound argument for their positions and justify their feelings and actions in the marriage.

What the individuals fail to see is how they contribute to the maintenance of the presenting problems. Each must be assisted in assuming responsibility for changing one's own behavior rather than demanding that their spouses change. By changing one's own behavior, the dysfunctional interaction patterns occurring will be disrupted. Only then can new patterns of relating be developed which will prove more beneficial to both husband and wife as well as for the marital and family systems. A synergic effect occurs when the couple learns to combine what is best for each individual with what is ultimately best for the relationship, so that as each spouse grows, the relationship grows, and conversely as the relationship grows, each spouse grows also.

Stage Four: Re-education:

The fourth and final stage of the therapeutic process involves the teaching or education of the couple in new relationship skills. Again, it must be emphasized successful maintenance of new skills is not likely if dysfunctional attitudes that generate dysfunctional behaviors have not been identified and reorientating the couple in more productive and constructive attitudes toward one another and the marriage has taken place. However, as reorientation occurs, the couple will begin to seek new methods of interacting and handling their relationship. The old behaviors will no longer be consistent or congruent with their new perceptions and goals. It is here, then, that the marital therapist will begin to focus primarily upon the teaching of constructive relationship skills.

Such communication skills as "I feel" statements, maintaining a relationship log, listening and feedback skills and the couple council (see Chapter 4) may be taught. It may also be appropriate to teach conflict resolution skills and negotiation skills (especially in divorce mediation) and to develop a new contract between the couple regarding responsibilities and expectations. Some couples may need to learn how to build quality marriage time into their schedules and/or how to enjoy one another's company. With issues involving sexual dysfunction, skills for enabling closeness and intimacy, demonstrating affection and meeting one another's psychological and sexual needs may need to be directly taught to the couple (see Chapter 6).

To monitor the couple as they test out and attempt to use their new skills, role playing and practice sessions may be used in the therapy session during their reeducation stage. Later, homework between sessions may be assigned, directing the couple to use these new skills in their daily lives. It is often important to have the couple begin slowly by using their skills in situations that are less emotionally charged. In this way, the couple will be encouraged by initial success. Negotiating skills, for example, may be used first for deciding a weekend's itinerary rather than for resolving a major marital conflict issue.

As the couple becomes more proficient in each skill, they can apply these new skills to more stressful and conflict laden issues. It is frequently found beneficial to have the couple structure into their weekly routines practice sessions which each new skill. For example, they might first practice the couple conference (see Chapter 4). While this may at first feel stilted and artificial, it is important to point out to the couple that learning any new skill—e.g., learning to ride a bicycle—at first feels awkward and uncomfortable. However, when the use of a new skill is not structured into one's routine for a given period of time, there is a tendency to fall back into old habits—i.e., dysfunctional interaction patterns.

In concluding this discussion of the process of marital therapy from an Adlerian Psychology perspective, it must again be stressed that while the process is described here as occurring in four distinct stages, this is not to imply that marital therapy be approached in a rigid, step-by-step manner. Rather, this process model is intended as a way to conceptualize the total process for teaching purposes. Given one's immediate goals, the marital therapist may use interventions and techniques associated with any of the stages at any point in the overall therapeutic process. New communication skills, for example, may be taught as assigned as homework in one of the initial sessions in order to create a release valve for tension and conflict in the marriage.

Taken as a whole, however, the counseling process will reflect an essential movement through each of the four stages with the short-term, mediating goals of each stage designed to eventually lead the couple to the long-term outcome goal of developing a positive/constructive Marital Relationship Style—a style of relating which promotes the well-being and enables the growth and development of both husband and wife as well as the marital relationship.

Chapter 1 References

Adler, A. (1958). *What life should mean to you.* New York: G.P. Putnam's Sons.

Adler, A. (1964a). *Problems of neurosis.* New York: Harper Tourchbooks (original work published 1929).

Adler, A. (1964b). *Superiority and social interest.* H. Ansbacher & R. Ansbacher (Ed. & Trans.), Evanston, IL: Northwestern University Press.

Adler, A. (1978). *Cooperation between the sexes: Writings on women, love and marriage, sexuality and its disorders.* H. Ansbacher & R. Ansbacher (Eds. & Trans.), New York: Anchor Books.

Ansbacher, H.L. (1968). The concept of social interest. *Journal of Individual Psychology, 24(2),* 1310-149.

Ansbacher, H. & Ansbacher R. (1956). *The individual psychology of Alfred Adler.* New York: Harper & Row.

Beal, E.M. (1980). Teaching family therapy: Theory, techniques, supervision. *Psychiatric Annals, 10(7),* 33-44.

Carter, E.A. & McGoldrick, M. (1980). *The family life cycle: A framework for family therapy.* New York: Gardner Press.

Deutsch, D. (1956). A step toward success. *American Journal of Individual Psychology, 12,* 78-83.

Deutsch, D. (1967a). Family therapy and family lifestyle. *Journal of Individual Psychology, 23(2),* 217-223.

Deutsch, D. (1967b). Group therapy with married couples: The pangs of a new family life style in marriage. *Individual Psychologist, 4,* 56-62.

Dinkmeyer, D. & Carlson, J. (1984). *Time for a better marriage.* Circle Pines, MN: American Guidance Services.

Dreikurs, R. (1946). *The challenge of marriage.* New York: Hawthorn Books.

Dreikurs, R. (1959). Communication within the family. *Central Stages Speech Journal, 11,* 1.

Dreikurs, R. (1968). Determinants of changing attitudes of marital partners toward each other. In S. Rosenbaum & I. Alger (Eds.) *The marital relationship: Psychoanalytic perspectives.* New York: Basic Books (pp. 83-103).

Dreikurs, R. (1971). An interview with Rudolf Dreikurs. *The Counseling Psychologist, 3,* 49-54.

Erikson, E. (1963). *Childhood and society.* New York: W.W. Norton.

Hawes, E.C. & Hawes, R.G. (1986). *Couples growing together.* Sechelt, BC: CCMC.

Knopf, O. (1932). *The art of being a woman.* Alan Porter (Ed.) Boston: Little, Brown.

Lazarsfeld, S. (1934). How woman experiences man. In Karsten & E. Stapelfeldt (Eds. & Trans.) *Rhythm of life: A guide to sexual harmony for women.* New York: Greenberg.

Manaster, G.J. & Corsini, R.J. (1982). *Individual psychology: Theory and practice.* Itasca, IL: F.E. Peacock Press.

Nicoll, W.G. & Hawes, E.C. (1985). Family lifestyle assessment: The role of family myths and values in the client's presenting issues. *Individual Psychology, 41(2),* 147-160.

O'Neil J. (1978). Male sex role conflicts, sexism and masculinity. *The Counseling Psychologist, 9(2),* 61-80.

Papenek, H. (1965). Group psychotherapy with married couples. In J.H. Masserman (Ed.) *Current psychiatric therapies, vol. 5.* New York: Grune & Stratton.

Pew, W. & Pew, M. (1972). Adlerian marriage counseling. *Journal of Individual Psychology, 28,* 192-202.

Shulman, B.H. (1967). The uses and abuses of sex. *Journal of Religion and Health, 6,* 4.

Sluzki, C.E. (1978). Marital therapy from a systems theory perspective. In T.J. Paolino & B.S. McGrady (Eds.) *Marriage and marital therapy: Psychoanalytic, behavioral and systems theory perspectives.* New York: Brunner/Mazel.

Thomas, C. & Marchant, W. (1983). Basic principles of Adlerian family counseling. In O. Christensen & T. Schramski (Eds.) *Adlerian family counseling* (pp.9-26). Minneapolis, MN: Educational Media Corporation.

Tobin, J. (1975). An application of Adlerian principles to problems of control in marriage. *Individual Psychologist, 12(2),* 3-7.

Walsh, F. (1982). *Normal family processes.* New York: Guilford Press.

Weber, M. (1946). *Essays in sociology.* H. Gerth & C. Mills (Trans. & Eds.) New York: Oxford University Press.

Chapter 2
The Initial Interview
by
E. Clair Hawes and Roy M. Kern

The Adlerian marriage therapist must always bear in mind that no marriage can ever be understood from the outside. Hence, from the first contact, the therapist's prime objective of all interactions is forming an alliance with the couple. The process of developing this alliance involves several steps on the part of the therapist:

- making a clear statement about the role of the therapist;

- winning a position as an active, trusted element within the marital dyad;

- influencing that dyad to define and redefine realistic goals;

- using the right combination of knowledge and therapeutic expertise to obtain these goals;

- then removing the presence of the therapist without tampering with the growth and development that has taken place.

Marriage is the term being used throughout this book to describe any intimate, committed relationship between two people, whether or not they have a marriage license. It may pertain to couples who are cohabiting and have made a conscious choice not to legalize the arrangement, to couples who are experimenting with the relationship with a view to possibly marrying later, to lesbian couples, and to gay couples. The terms *counseling* and *therapy* will be used interchangeably throughout the text.

The First Contact

The therapist's first contact with the couple is often indirect and is with the source of referral, which may be a physician, lawyer, clergyperson, friend or relative of the couple, other clients, or the Yellow Pages. All but the latter may provide the therapist with a data base. However, information regarding the nature of the problem, as it is communicated by any of the above sources, is rarely reliable for various reasons. With the best of intentions, physicians often interpret problems from a paternalistic viewpoint, lawyers from an adversarial viewpoint, clergypersons from a moralistic viewpoint, and friends and relatives from a sense of the impending loss of their own relationship with the couple. On the other hand, the information can provide a tentative sense of direction for the therapist, as well as a common source of interest on which to establish rapport with the couple. The therapist, though, should not assume that this data is accurate information.

A telephone call from one of the partners to arrange the appointment is generally the next contact and is the first opportunity for establishing the alliance. This call creates the atmosphere for the first session. Therefore, whenever possible, the therapist or a specially trained receptionist should talk with the partner who phones. Usually the caller is anxious and requires specific information as assurance that the therapist can provide the product that the potential client, as a consumer, is requesting. In one approach, the therapist can suggest that the couple make one appointment, then decide if future counseling is warranted.

Concomitantly, it is most important that the therapist is clear about the objectives of counseling. Typically, the therapist might say, "I cannot guarantee you anything, but I will tell you about the process we will go through. I will see you both together at the first session for one and a half hours, and ask and answer questions. At the end of that time I will provide you with a diagnosis and tell you what I am prepared to offer you. Then you can decide what you wish to do." During that first phone contact with the potential client, it is important to agree clearly that *both spouses will be present* during the initial session.

As discussed earlier, the marriage relationship is a whole that is greater than the sum of the parts—in this case each partner. Thus it is essential that both partners attend the first session. If one comes alone, there may be an underlying agenda of building a case against the other partner. Counseling only one partner, when the issue is the marriage relationship, may lead to hostility and subsequent separation and divorce, for that partner will often interpret the supportive nature of the counseling session as tacit permission to be morally superior and to find fault with the other partner rather than to investigate alternatives for working out the conflict.

If, however, only one of the spouses shows up for the appointment, it is helpful, as an Adlerian therapist, to begin to assess the purpose of this change in agenda. Is the client attempting to gain power over the other spouse to validate that "divorce is the only choice?" Or was the spouse so discouraged as to be afraid to ask the other partner? Could it be that the only partner to show up is fulfilling the dynamics of a lifestyle goal to take on the role of victim, pleaser and so forth?

If power is an issue in that initial interview, the therapist might assess this dynamic by observing how resistant the client becomes when the therapist suggests calling the absent spouse to persuade that person to come to a session. Or the therapist may simply indicate that since the agreement was for both to be present, this first meeting will only be used to discuss fees, insurance forms, potential convenient meeting times, and some suggested readings that might be helpful for the couple if therapy continues over a period of time. The therapist should make it clear that since it is couple's counseling, it is not appropriate to discuss marital issues without "both spouses being present."

If power is an issue with the spouse who is present, these interventions will provide the therapist with more than adequate information to validate this hypothesis. If, on the other hand, the spouse is just very discouraged, wishes to please, acts the victim, or lacking some basic skills interpersonally, the therapist can use the foregoing interventions to start the encouragement process with the partner who is present. If the latter issues are the major reason for the "no show," the therapist may also discuss effective ways to entice the other partner to attend an exploratory session.

If the therapist is already working with a client individually, but decides with the client's permission, that marital counseling is needed for additional therapeutic growth to occur, the therapist and client must then reestablish the alliance to include a third person. The individual could invite the partner, but is often hesitant to do so. Behavioral rehearsal with the therapist can help prepare the client to include the partner. If the client is still reluctant to ask, or the partner refuses to come, the therapist, with the client's permission, may call and invite the other partner. If the client is in the office at the time of the call, it can allay the anxiety about what the therapist might tell the partner. Generally, a comment such as, "We have now come to a point in counseling where having you join us will speed up the process as well as probably enrich your relationship" will suffice. If the partner is reluctant, that person can be asked to come for only one session without a commitment for continued counseling, then decide on a course of action.

In addition to enticing both partners to participate in counseling, the therapist must initially address the logistics of the counseling process. Many beginning practitioners have experienced the couple who arrives at the first session and are appalled at the fee or the amount of time they are going to have to invest. When the referring person is someone in a salaried position, such as a clergyperson or a physician to whom visits were covered by medical insurance, it is often assumed that the cost of counseling will be minimal. Therefore, any discussion of fees, insurance coverage, and methods of payment should be made clear at or before the first session.

In summary, the essence of the initial contact with the couple is that nothing is left to chance or open to misunderstandings. All of the logistics are a part of the interaction between the therapist and the couple and are just as open for discussion as any other concern. The following is a detailed description of how the first session with a couple may evolve.

Initial Sessions

The initial session as described here may take two or more sessions, depending on the complexity of the issues and the trustful nature of each of the partners.

At the initial counseling session any remaining business is discharged at the beginning so that the focus can then be on the counseling. Business includes reading and filling out the financial policy, which conveys all of the basic logistical information such as fees, additional charges, missed appointments, telephone contact, and a contract for payment. Figures 1(a) and 1(b) provide a sample of one financial policy. A copy is kept in the couple's file, and another is kept by the clients for reference. The General Information form (Figure 2) provides pertinent data that can be filed separately for access by office staff when information is needed and the therapist is not available. No other data is requested at this time because the Adlerian therapist will make the gathering of information an integral part of the assessment process.

The tone of all future sessions is established with the first physical contact between the therapist and the couple. Many theoreticians (e.g., Broderick, 1984; Beutler, 1983) have argued that the relationship between therapist and client is the essential ingredient, rather than the theory used or technique applied, for a successful therapeutic experience. The way the therapist greets the couple immediately models that this is to be a mutually respectful relationship. Methods of demonstrating respect include not keeping the couple waiting, greeting them with a handshake, introducing oneself, and allowing the couple to enter the counseling room first.

The manner in which the couple enter the room and seat themselves is observed as a part of the nitial assessment. However, knowing that the couple will be anxious, the first task of the therapist is to create a comfortable, caring, and supportive atmosphere for the couple. Whitaker (1984) stated that the couple will deliberately take on the role of being "one down" when they ask for help, and that, methodologically, it is possible to separate the therapeutic experience of the interview into two components. The first few minutes and the last few minutes can be structured so that it is clear to the couple that the therapist is employed by them. This can be accomplished by an introductory few minutes about the real world, be it weather, traffic, or anything else that pertains to the life of all. Whitaker maintained that this kind of offering makes it clear to the couple that the therapist respects them as people.

To make the transition from the social to the therapeutic, however, the therapist may wish to use a statement such as, "Before we begin talking about our concerns, are there any questions about me or the counseling process that would help

Figure 1a
(Name of Agency)
(Names of Counselors)

(Address and   **List of Counseling**
Phone Number)   **Specialties**

Financial Policy

Office Visits

For payment on the day of service unless other arrangements are made:

- with one therapist, per 50 minute session $ _____
- with co-therapist, per 50 minute session $ _____

Additional Charges

Every time a statement must be prepared, an additional $ _____ will be charged.

Missed Appointments

Missed appointments which have not been cancelled within twelve hours of the scheduled time, and which are not due to unusual circumstances, may be charged for the full appointment time.

Phone Sessions

Any conversation of a brief nature over the phone between the counselor and a client are included in the routine charges for the office visits. If prolonged or repeated phone conversations are required, then a fee appropriate to the time involved may be charged.

Insurance Companies

We will be happy to provide the information you need for filing your insurance, and will provide you with a statement showing all the activity on your account. If we are required to fill out your forms an additional charge will be made. Some insurance companies have such extensive requirements that we may have to assess an hourly charge for our time in complying with their requests. We will discuss this with you if it becomes necessary.

Please be aware that your medical records are becoming less and less confidential. Almost all insurance companies require that we make a standard diagnosis from a specific manual, and you may wish to consider whether you want to have the diagnosis in your company file.

General

We encourage you to discuss the above financial matters with us at any time. The payment of the fee for therapy is part of our interaction and should be just as open for discussion as any other concern.

Figure 1b
FINANCIAL INFORMATION

Information by the person who signs as responsible party.

SS NO. _____

INSURANCE _____
Company   Policy Number

I understand that I am financially responsible for the payment of all charges rendered to me, or to any members of my family, and that payment is expected at the time service is rendered, unless alternate arrangements have been made at described below, regardless of any insurance coverage I may anticipate. I further understand that travel time for any school, home, or other visit that my therapist makes at my request will be billed on the basis of my therapist's regular hourly rate.

I understand that there will be a charge for appointments not cancelled 12 hours in advance.

I understand that (NAME OF AGENCY OR CENTER) does not file insurance claims. The receipt provided at each session is sufficient for filing my own insurance. If further information is required from your insurance company related to professional services, the (Center) will be more that willing to provide the additional information with your written authorization. Routine responses to insurance companies will be made by the (Center) without charge. There will be a charge for duplicate receipts, itemized bills, or copying of records.

I understand that, should any legal action be necessary to collect any amounts owed by me, I will be responsible for all costs for such action.

Alternate Arrangement: _____

_____

I have read and understand the above statements, and I have received a copy of this agreement.

_____
Signature of Responsible Party

Figure 2

(Name of Agency)

(Names of Counselors)

(Address and   List of Counseling
Phone Number)   Specialties

Information on this form is not confidential; office staff may have access to it.

Please Print   Date _____

Name _____ Birthdate _____

Mailing Address _____ Phone: Work _____

_____ Zip Code _____ Home _____

Employer _____
                    Name   Address   Phone

Financially
Responsible Party _____
(if other than client)Name   Address   Phone

Employer _____
                    Name   Address   Phone

In case of
emergency contact: _____
                    Name   Address   Phone

Referred by: _____

Family Doctor _____ Medications _____

If client is a student: _____
                    School Attending   Grade   Teacher

Please list all members of your household:

Last Name	First Name	Birthdate	Relationship

both of you feel more at ease?" The therapist must be prepared, however, to handle some occasional "zingers," such as, "Have you ever had an affair?" In such a case, the therapist may use these questions to an advantage by first assuming there must be some valid reason for the questions. It is best to assume that the zingers are due to the couple's discouragement or that the couple is attempting at some unconscious level to check out the therapist's competence under duress.

Whatever the reason for the zinger, the situation presents an opportunity for the therapist to establish control of the session by gently confronting the potential purpose of the zinger, stating something like, "I am wondering hy the question is important to you?" A moment of silence at this point in the interview any times will allow the client to disclose the purpose of the question. The therapist might wish to escalate the confrontation by saying, "It sounds like it might be more helpful for you if I had experienced some problems that could come up in our sessions," or "What would you think of me if I were to answer 'yes' to your question?" Remember these zingers may be employed by clients to test the therapist's acceptance level during the alliance process or competence in handling toxic issues. The therapist must be careful not to become defensive, thereby hindering the alliance process.

Other methods the therapist may use to reinforce the alliance process consist of clear delineation of counseling procedures and comments about notetaking, confidentiality, and personal biases. For example:

> I would like to tell you about the way I work. Today I am going to be asking you some questions so I can better understand why both of you are here. By the end of the session, I will discuss what I am prepared to offer you, project some short-term and long-term goals, and indicate how long it may take to accomplish the goals we establish. However, I want you to know, and you will probably detect this very soon, that I have a bias toward marriage. Being married happens be the choice I have made for living out my life as long as it continues to be a mutually satisfying and fulfilling relationship. But this kind of partnership takes constant working together. At the same time I realize that being married, or being mar-

ried to a particular person, is not everybody's choice. I don't know yet what is going on in your relationship, but I will assure you that whatever informed choices you make, I will work with you to accomplish your goals. And if your own goals differ, we will direct our effort to determining acceptable mutual goals.

Taking notes during the session and a discussion of confidentiality may be handled in a similar fashion, such as:

You will notice that I will take some notes. This is because I do not want to forget any of the details we discuss today. Also, the way my memory works, once I write something down, I rarely forget it. These notes, and your file, are totally open to each of you if you ever wish to see them. Nobody else will. Your file is locked away in my filing cabinet. The only way someone else will have access to the notes is if I am subpoenaed by one of you. In the eyes of the courts in this state, there is no confidentiality between therapist (psychologist) and client. However, you are the ones who have the power over such a decision. If I am ever requested to release information about you to another professional, I must have from you a signed "release of information" form completed prior to the transaction.

In conclusion, then, forming the alliance with the couple must take precedence over the immediate needs of the couple, which is to "get started with the relationship problem."

Presenting Problem

Once the preliminary proceedings of fees, notetaking, time parameters, and personal counseling style issues are addressed, full attention can then be given to the couple and their presenting concerns. From an assessment perspective, how the couple tells about their problems is more important than the content. The couple needs assurance that they have been fully heard, that they have been given the opportunity to completely express their individual views of the problems, and that the therapist truly understands the profundity of their concerns.

The therapist begins by asking both partners at the same time, "Why are you here today?" "How can I help you?" One partner will begin; the therapist's questions will be for clarification only and any comments will be to confirm that the person is being heard. The therapist will also physically give the presenting partner total attention. If the other partner breaks in with another version, the therapist may wish to establish further guidelines by use of blocking intervention (Minuchin, 1978) as follows:

> I want to thoroughly listen to both of you. It is unlikely that you will tell it in the same way. Let's imagine that we are putting the problems on the table, and one of you will describe it, then the other one will. When one of you is talking, the other must not interfere. You will both get equal time. I assure you that I can accept different versions from each of you and see yours as being the reality for you at this time.

For the couple to gain confidence in the therapist and nurture the sense of alliance, they must view the therapist as being strong enough to withstand their barrage of interruptions and complaints, as well as competent enough to sort out the critical impasses n the relationship. Thus the therapist must demonstrate this ability by prohibiting either partner's attempts to violate the guidelines established and at the same time be supportive and give feedback on the information being presented.

In addition, while listening to each of the partners' "immaculate perception" of the problem, the therapist should constantly be assessing what purpose the issues presented by the clients serve in each individual's Lifestyle within the relationship. For as Manaster and Corsini (1982) stated, "everyone operates in terms of one's biased apperceptions and Lifestyle...everyone attempts to reach private goals and manipulates others so that they will react to them in coherence with these goals" (p. 179).

Dreikurs (1968) went one step further by stating that this attitude (i.e., Lifestyle) will determine the degree of cooperation between partners. He stated, "All people cooperate fully with each other. There is merely a distinction between constructive and destructive cooperation" (p. 94).

The interplay of individual Lifestyles in the relationship, which may account for destructive cooperation, happens rather gradually at times. For example, a spouse, who at the beginning of a relationship was seen by the other mate as possessing excellent organizational skills and rational abilities, could ten years later be portrayed by one's mate as being "cold and too picky."

Therefore, it is the major task of the therapist to explore ways of assisting the couple in solving the puzzle of marriage so that the individuals can cooperate in their relationship in ways that will complement each mate's Lifestyles.

Even subtle discouragement of interactions that are related to each of the partner's Lifestyles can result in problems in the couple's relationship. An informational or formal assessment process will help the therapist identify these problems.

The Assessment Process

The assessment process may take two directions: informal clinical observation or a more objective procedure related to psychometric instrumentation.

The informal assessment process begins with the first contact with the couple. At every stage thereafter the therapist will be hypothesizing, "What's going on here?" Gradually a jigsaw picture puzzle will emerge; all of the pieces are there from the beginning, but the therapist will have to search for them. Some will be seen as the right shape immediately, while others will take time to fit into place. It is unlikely that all pieces of the puzzle will ever be found, but the general picture will emerge. Later, we can liken the successful counseling process to turning a kaleidoscope; most of those puzzle pieces will still be there, but some will be put aside and new ones will be added so that a new relationship may be formed from the old pieces.

Beginning with the first time they are seated in the waiting room, the therapist can tentatively look for pieces to the puzzle. Are they sitting together or across from each other? When they greet the therapist, does each communicate timidly, confidently, or with a sense of control? When they seat themselves in the office and begin talking, does one defer to the other? Does one wait for permission to talk? Does one override the other? Who is dominant and who is submissive? Who is most willing to accept the guilt and who is most willing to point the finger? Important questions that must be addressed in the assessment process, and that might also provide the therapist with clues to the foregoing questions, might focus on a brief medical history, health concerns, use of drugs and alcohol, former marriages, nutritional habits, exercise routines, previous counseling experiences, and current contact with other mental health professions.

Through these exploratory questions, the therapist not only will set the tone of the relationship, but also will accumulate valuable information on how best to approach the problem assessment stage of the interview. At the conclusion of this period, the therapist will know who talks more, who interrupts, who is the "guilty one," and who the therapist might ask to begin the discussion of particular issues in later sessions.

This assessment time is also a time when the therapist can mitigate the tendency of the partners to blame one another by asking each, "What is it in yourself that disturbs you at this time?" The answer does not have to be discussed at any length, only clarified and left with the couple to ponder. In this way, the point is made, however subtly, that there is going to be an emphasis on personal responsibility and that the counseling setting is not a forum for heaping vindictive feelings on one another.

After the therapist has completed the informal history-taking survey and ruled out situations related to alcoholism, drug abuse, or medical problems, the Adlerian therapist then begins to investigate life tasks.

Life Tasks

The Adlerian therapist uses life tasks as a guide to evaluating how effectively the couple functions, both in their relationship and in other areas of their respective lives. Understanding the concept of life tasks is essential to assessing the marriage from a holistic point of view and to determining the dynamics of personality in terms of the intertwining of the individual with the social milieu. Adler identified three tasks that he variously described as "the three great problems of life" (1919) or "the three main ties that make up reality for each individual" (1931). The satisfaction of almost all conceivable needs depends on the solution of problems of cooperation in these three areas, traditionally classified into the problems of occupation, social relationships, and intimate relationships (Adler, 1956; Kern, 1982). The complexities of today's society have prompted subsequent Adlerian theorists to suggest, in addition to the original three major life tasks, four minor life tasks:

- self-worth (Dreikurs & Mosak, 1966);
- meaning in life (Dreikurs & Mosak, 1967);
- nurturing (Ferguson, 1976; Hillman, 1981); and
- leisure (Pew & Pew, 1972)

All questions of life can be subordinated to the life tasks; these questions arise form the inseparable bond that of necessity links people together for association, for the provision livelihood, and for the care of offspring. None of the three major problems of life can be solved separately, because each demands a successful approach to the other two (Adler, 1956). Nor can these problems ever be solved once and for all, but instead demand from the individual a continuous and creative movement toward adaptation (Way, 1961). If one of the life tasks is evaded, difficulties will sooner or later be experienced in fulfilling the others.

The *occupation* task may be defined as any kind of work that is useful to the community. It is by no means restricted to work which is remunerated by a wage, but is characterized by the value it has for other people and is undertaken as a regular responsibility nd obligation (Dreikurs, 1953). Membership in the human race, the *social relationships* task, is the second tie by which people are bound. It refers to Adler's belief that human life is so limited that humankind can carry on only if we all pull together.

The way in which an individual established relationships with a few people expresses that person's attitude to the whole community (Dreikurs, 1953). This concept carried further means that an interest in the well-being of other people leads one to make efforts to understand universal problems that unite large groups of people. As this task is being met, a concomitant advance toward the solution of occupation task is also made. "It was only because men learned to cooperate that the great discovery of the division of labor was made, a discovery which is the chief security for the welfare of mankind" (Adler, 195, p. 132).

The third task refers to the fact that the human being is a member of one sex and not of the other. Fulfillment of this *intimate relationship* task means a close union of mind and body and the utmost possible cooperation with a partner. Because this relationship involves such intimate contact between two human beings, it tests their capacity for cooperation and destroys the distance that can always be preserved in the occupation and social relationship tasks (Dreikurs, 1953). Adler (1919) stressed that the same lack of concern about others that is responsible for social and occupational maladjustments is also responsible for the inability to cooperate with the other sex. Dreikurs, as early as 1933, predicted that until the goal of equality of rights is achieved, and thus the rivalry between men and women eradicated, it will be impossible to achieve success in the intimate relationships task.

In marital assessment, a delineation of the problems is achieved through an understanding of how well each partner is functioning in the above three major life asks. Through incorporating an assessment of four minor tasks as well, the therapist obtains further supporting data about the couple's marital well-being. *Self-worth* seen as judging one's adequacy in relation to one's perception of the worth of others. Essentially "man must cope th himself" (Mosak, 1979, p. 47). Such coping is achieved through interaction with others while pursuing the three major tasks, thus bringing to one a realistic sense of self-worth (Manaster & Corsini, 1982).

Finding *meaning in life* refers to the idea that human beings must deal with the problem of defining the nature of the universe, the existence and nature of God, and of how one relates to these concepts (Mosak, 1979). The *nurturing* task may include biological reproduction, but further entails teaching and giving of one's self to the young, to the needy, and to the parenting of one's parents as this becomes a necessity. Finally, leisure refers to the ability to use unstructured time in a satisfying manner.

Working through the process of assessing the relationship dysfunction through an analysis of the life tasks, the therapist must always keep in mind that it is the conclusions a spouse draws from the partner's behavior, rather than the behavior itself, that constitutes the primary problem. Therefore the therapist will often ask of each partner "and how is that for you?" The life task of occupation is a good one to begin with because it is generally less threatening. For example:

Therapist:
I want to get a more rounded picture of what goes on in your relationship, so I'm going to ask you some brief questions. For example, what kind of work do you do, Bill?

Bill:
I'm an engineer and I have my own consulting firm.

Therapist:
How do you feel about your job?

Bill:
I've been very successful because I've worked hard. We have contracts for sewage disposal systems for several surrounding communities.

Therapist:
How do you feel about it?

Bill:
I enjoy it very much.

Therapist:
Joan, how do you feel about Bill's work?

Joan:
I could understand him being so involved years ago when he first began, but I fail to see why he has to stay at the office until after 7:00 almost every night at this point in his career.

Therapist:
How do you let him know about your resentment?

Joan:
I used to complain. Now I am resigned to it and we have a late dinner or if I am going out he attends to his own. But it certainly does intrude on our marriage and it still really gripes me.

Therapist:
What kind of work do you do, Joan?

Joan:
Up until two years ago, I worked part-time as a lab technician, then I began full-time and two months ago I became chief technician.

Therapist:
And how do you feel about your work?

Joan:
I really love it. I am so happy when I am there.

Therapist:
Bill, how do you feel about Joan's work?

Bill:
It's great that she has found something that is so fulfilling.

Therapist:
But how do you feel about it?

Bill:
The household isn't as organized and I have to do more of the driving of the kids, so I guess I resent the way it has changed our lives.

Through investigating this one life task, the therapist notes the irritants and mentally questions the extent to which they interfere in the relationship. If this is the only area in which dissension exists, then the couple can probably cope with it. But if occupations is one of many problem areas, there is probably much tension created that will be reflected generally. The therapist also notes the ways in which partners respond to questions. In this case, when asked about feelings, Bill responded with a cognition until pressed about the emotional quality. this may indicate his reluctance or lack of skill in emotional expression.

The therapist will continue to question about the other life tasks in a similar manner:

Social Relationships: What about friendships? Do you have couple friends? Are those close friends? Do you each have separate friends? How close are they? How do you like the other's friends? How do your friendships end? What do you find satisfying in your friendships and community activities? What do your friends value in you?

Intimate Relationships: How is your sexual relationship for you? Is orgasm ever a problem? If so, how do you feel about it? Is premature ejaculation or impotence ever a problem? At what times is it likely to occur? Many couples, in spite of a seemingly enlightened attitude toward sex in society today, have never discussed their intimate relationship with anyone else in a forthright manner. If there are obvious problems, it is most important that the therapist reassure the couple they will return to this issue later.

Nurturing: What are the ages and sexes of your children? Were there miscarriages or children lost at childbirth or infancy? Were there other pregnancies for either of you? How do you feel about one another's effectiveness as parents? Do you plan to have children? Do you want more children? A typical discussion of a life task, using nurturing as the example, would be as follows:

Joan:
We have two boys, Doug is ten and Jeff is eight. Bill has a daughter, Becky, who is 15.

Therapist:
There seems to be an emphasis on the "we."

Joan:
The one child of Bill's, even though she doesn't live with us, takes up more time than our own two put together.

Therapist:
You sound angry.

Joan:
Angry? Well I guess I really am. I have tried to create a warm relationship with her, but it has never worked. We just seem to be getting along well as a family, when Becky gets herself in trouble and creates havoc for us all.

Therapist:
How do you view Bill as a parent?

Joan:
With the boys he is great. He is like putty with Becky; she can manipulate him and always gets her own way, which means our boys, and I, are ignored. (Because the purpose of these questions is for assessment, the therapist will resist the impulse at this time to respond to these loaded statements.)

Therapist:
How do you view Joan as a parent, Bill?

Bill:
She is really super even though she works full-time. I know I spend a lot of energy on Becky, but I have always felt so guilty about not being a better father to her.

Therapist:
With your boys, in what areas do you disagree with the other's parenting?

Bill:
Joan has taken so much of the responsibility, but at times I think she is too harsh.

Therapist:
And what do you do when you perceive her as being hard on them?

Bill:
I don't know?

Therapist:
Is it possible that the firmer she is, the softer you become?

Bill:
I suppose so.

Therapist:
And Joan, do you find that the easier he is on them, the more you have to tighten up?

Joan:
They will get away with murder if I don't.

Therapist:
You are moving in two different directions, and creating distance between yourselves. It would seem that you two are in competition when it comes to establishing discipline.

Bill:
I don't like the way it sounds when you put it that way, but I guess that it's accurate.

Therapist:
We will be coming back to this dynamic when we have completed this assessment. I have a number of other things I want to ask you about first. Were there ever any other children?

Self-worth: How do you feel about yourself as a person? Generally, how adequately do you feel you are functioning in your life right now? The importance of this life task to marriage is being underscored as it becomes more evident that marriage may be an evolving institution that requires self-actualization skills not previously essential in marriage.

Meaning in Life: Is there a religious or philosophical basis to your life? Do you have a sense of being a part of the cosmos? Is there a sense of spirituality that gives meaning to your life?

Leisure: What do you do to relax and have fun together? What do you do to relax and have fun separately? Do you structure your leisure time in a way you find fulfilling?

Extended Family: Although this entails a combination of life tasks, it is explored separately. Questions about extended family should focus on how each partner gets on with one's own family of origin, adult children and their families, as well as with the other partner's family, including parents, siblings, former marriage partners and their families, and other significant people. The therapist seeks to determine the degree to which the extended family serves either as a supportive network or as a divisive faction. The therapist is also looking at the success with which the couple has gained independence from their families of origin, as well as from their offspring.

Exploration of the life tasks gives an overview of the couple's relationship, including insight into areas of strength and weakness. Assessment, however, is an ongoing process, and after this initial session will most likely focus on Lifestyle issues as discussed in Chapter 3, priorities as discussed in Chapter 5, and particularly on an evaluation of the couple's progress from session to session. For this latter evaluation, the therapist will look at the degree of commitment indicated by actions rather than intentions, covert sabotage wherein one partner is provoked into particular types of behavior by the other then accused of alliance, and more overt sabotage, such as agreeing to a certain action then consistently not carrying it through per the agreement.

By the end of this stage of the interview, the therapist has acquired an excellent base of relevant information on life tasks, informal background history, and sense of commitment to work on the relationship by the couple. For those therapists who may wish to assess the couple's concern in a more objective fashion for research or personal choice needs, use of psychometric instruments in therapy may be appropriate.

Psychometric Assessment Options

A number of marital assessment techniques abound, and the therapist's choice of these will undoubtedly reflect one's theoretical perspective and training. Typically, efforts have been directed at the measurement of overall marital satisfaction through global self-report questionnaires (Margolin & Jacobson, 1982). One drawback to such research, and subsequent assessment techniques based on the empirical data, is the implied analysis of marriage, when it is in fact, the individuals who reside in the marriage who are being studied (Spanier & Lewis, 1980)

more serious drawback when employing psy-
tools for marital assessment is the constant problems
ility and validity. Haynes and Jensen (1981) state that
iew self-report marital satisfaction inventories satisfy even the minimal criteria of reliability and validity studies required for sound research or generalizability. Though reliability and validity is a continuous problem with assessment instruments, the authors have chosen to include a representative sample of scales that have been employed extensively in the field of marriage and family therapy, as well as to include scales that might best fit the needs of therapists using an Adlerian approach to the assessment process.

Instrument Description

The *Locke-Wallace Marital Adjustment Scale* (1959) appears to be the most quoted in the literature. This instrument, according to the authors, has been found to be internally consistent and an accurate discriminator of distressed versus nondistressed couples. The instrument is designed to assess overall couple satisfaction in eight areas, ranging from sexual compatibility to decision-making. The advantages for the Adlerian therapist using this instrument are that it is short and in many ways may provide a thumbnail assessment of how the couple is functioning in the life task areas.

Another frequently used instrument that may have less appeal for the Adlerian therapist, is the *Spouse Observation Checklist (SOC)* developed by Weiss and Patterson (1973). It consists of an eight-page listing of each partner's pleasing and displeasing relationship behaviors. Examples such as spouse appearance and mealtime behavior are types of behaviors assessed by the SOC.

The *Dyadic Adjustment Scale* by Spanier (1976), next to the *Locke-Wallace Adjustment Scale*, appears to be the second most frequently cited marital assessment instrument in the literature. The questionnaire consists of 32 items, some of which are extracted from the *Locke-Wallace* and other instruments. A total score on the instrument ranges from 0 to 151 and claims to assess agreement by couples on such dimensions as career decisions, recreational preferences, and philosophy of life.

Though as psychometrically sound as any of the instruments in the field, this instrument contains some items of questionable importance. Sharpley and Rogers (1984) and other researchers claim that as few as six items from the instrument are adequate enough to measure marital satisfaction. Because the instrument includes such general information, Adlerian therapists may find other instruments more relevant to the assessment process.

Some recent assessment instruments are more promising. The *Area of Change Questionnaire* (Margolin & Jacobson, 1981) is designed to assess marital satisfaction in terms of the amount of change a couple desires to take place in their relationship. Each partner takes the instrument and identifies those areas in which one would like the other to change as a result of counseling. Though the reliability and validity information needs expanding, this instrument holds promise for helping the Adlerian therapist in the assessment process because it focuses on the need for behavioral change in each partner and it gathers specific information that might help the Adlerian therapist begin to assess purposes of behavior.

Possibly of even more relevance and functional use for the Adlerian therapist during the assessment process are two recent instruments: the *Marital Satisfaction Inventory* (Snyder, 1981), and the *Personal Assessment of Intimacy in Relationships Inventory* (Schaefer & Olson, 1981).

The *Marital Satisfaction Inventory (MSI)* consists of eleven different scales, including one that measures global distress. The instrument contains 280 true-false items and the scale scores are reported on a profile format similar to that of the *MMPI*. This instrument holds great promise for the Adlerian therapist because the categories measured by the *MSI* parallel many of the toxic issues that evolve in troubled relationships. In addition, the eleven scales can in many ways yield a more specific description of problem areas related to the life tasks. A sample of the categories are: conflict over child-rearing, role orientations, disagreement about finances and sexual dissatisfaction. Alan Gurman stated, "...overall, the *MSI* looks like a very promising instrument with an increasing amount of validation evidence being accumulated" (1983, p. 68).

The final couples instrument that may be useful for the Adlerian therapist is the *Personal Assessment of Intimacy in Relationships Inventory (PAIR)* by David Olson. The *PAIR* provides systematic information on emotional, social, sexual, intellectual and recreational dimensions of the relationship. The author claims the instrument is easy to administer and score and is an excellent tool to get couples talking about their expectations of each other within the relationship. Other advantages are that it appears to be relevant as a pre- and post-assessment instrument and that it could also be employed for couples seeking enrichment rather than therapy. The authors would propose the *PAIR* and the *MSI* as valuable tools to employ in accordance with the *STEP, Active Parenting, TIME,* or *Couples Growing Together* programs (see Chapter 5).

Other marital adjustment inventories not included in this survey may be valid and reliable, but they do not appear to provide the assessment data most relevant to the Adlerian perspective.

Diagnostic Hypothesis

The diagnostic hypothesis which may be based on the informal or formal assessment data, includes the therapist's summation of the problem, a prognosis and a proposal for working with the couple. It is presented in terms of forming an alliance, where in each partner is a specialist on one's own problem and the therapist is a specialist in relationships and how to make them work. The therapist makes it clear that the couple will be expected to carry out homework, give feedback on their progress between sessions and generally work hard. The counseling may require the couple restrict temporarily some of their activities so that their full attention and energy can be given to the marriage. It is also made clear there is no guarantee of success in marriage counseling, but that the therapist will work to the utmost to help the couple attain greater marital satisfaction.

The therapist's prognosis should include an encouraging element if such is at all appropriate. Many couples feel desperate about their situation and depend heavily on the therapist's assessment in order to regain faith in their own ability to bring about change. Often they have been so caught up in laying blame and in what is going wrong that they are oblivious to their strengths. However, encouragement must be sincere and based on the actual evidence provided by the couple. Sometimes this is very difficult and may be limited to, "The fact that you decided together to seek counseling is some indication of your ability to make mutual decisions."

The diagnostic hypothesis will outline what is included in Lifestyle analysis if that is recommended (see Chapter 3), the skills the couple needs to attain, and, briefly, how the therapist proposes to teach these. The couple is asked to meet weekly, usually for one and a half hours for a given number of weeks. At the end of this time, the therapist and couple will mutually evaluate their progress and either terminate counseling, decide on an alternative course of action, if necessary, or renegotiate a certain number of future sessions.

Establishing Commitment

Commitment to counseling may be evident before the end of the first session. If it is not, it must be addressed before the couple leaves the office.

It is essential to determine clearly that the goals of the therapist and of each partner are congruent, even if on a short-term basis. As mentioned earlier, if the therapist's and the clients' goals are not aligned, resistance is inevitable. Often couples are reluctant to make a long-term commitment to working on their relationship because they cannot foresee that the changes will be sufficient or satisfying. Even in the most painful relationships, if a couple takes the first step of coming once for counseling, they are likely prepared to make a commitment to work together for at least one week. If they are not, then counseling for separation may be a more appropriate goal for discussion.

> **Therapist:**
> *We have taken a brief look at your relationship and I have given you a current interpretation of what I see is possible for you both. Before I can go any further, I need to clearly know your positions about your commitment to working on your marriage. Joan, how do you feel about this? Are you prepared to make a commitment for counseling to make your relationship more fulfilling?*
>
> **Joan:**
> *I think I do, at least right now, although I wasn't so sure when I came in here today.*

Therapist:
Would you be prepared to really work on your marriage for one month (or one week if that is more appropriate)? That means that after four weekly sessions we would again discuss whether or not you are open to continuing marriage counseling.

Joan:
Yes, I'm prepared to do that.

Therapist:
And Bill, do you wish to work on this relationship?

Bill:
Definitely. That is why I'm here.

Enabling the couple to hear each make this commitment, no matter how short ranged, clearly provides some hope to each partner that counseling may take a positive direction. Lack of commitment invites sabotage of any assigned tasks to be completed outside of the office setting. Even where the relationship is in greater jeopardy than seems to be the case with Joan and Bill, once the couple has made any degree of commitment, the therapist knows what direction to take.

To ensure that there is continuation of any gains made in counseling, and that the focus is on improving the relationship throughout the time between counseling sessions, homework is strongly advised (Hawes, 1982). The type of assignment will be made according to its relevance to what has transpired during this first session and, in fact, may have been assigned earlier if a commitment to counseling had been obvious then. Chapter 4 presents many choices for assignments to improve communication and build problem-solving skills. Several of these assignments arise naturally from the content of the sessions. If there has not been a spontaneous opportunity earlier in the session, the Couple Conference (see Chapter 4) is often an appropriate choice, as it allows the couple to clear the air of the tension they have created.

In the event that there is not an agreement to proceed with marital counseling, either or both spouses may be referred for individual counseling. On occasion, individual counseling can be valuable during marital adjustment, separation or divorce. If either of the latter two have been chosen or are strong possibilities, the therapist may advise the couple of mediation alternatives (see Chapter 7).

Wrapping Up

To end the session on as encouraging a note as possible, each partner is asked to face the other and to complete this sentence: "One thing I appreciate in our relationship is...." There is no further discussion, even if tears are evoked, just an acceptance of each other's offering.

Once the couple is ready to leave, the same kind of social peership that was set at the onset can reinstitute the respect the couple deserve for themselves and the respect the therapist has for them as individuals. One way of doing this is to leave the next interview scheduling open to them. To assume that the therapist is in charge of when they want to come back institutes a kind of artificial dependence that can be degrading to the couple (Whitaker, 1984). Another way is to walk the couple to the door and discuss a safe issue of possibly mutual interest to all, such as "It's Monday night and you still have time to catch the last half of the football game."   Chapter 3 on lifestyles and relationships will provide the reader with a more intense analysis of the couple's relationship and how each of their lifestyles compliments or hinders their abilities to deal with the presented problem in the initial interview. The reader and perspective therapist must keep in mind, however, that the lifestyle interview should be employed when the therapist has properly assessed that the couple is extremely discouraged, as opposed to a couple that is simply experiencing normal adjustment issues in their marriage or relationship.

Chapter 2 References

Adler, A. (1919, 1969). *The science of living.* Garden City, NY: Anchor Books.

Adler, A. (1931, 1958). *What life should mean to you.* New York: G.P. Putnam's Sons.

Adler, A. (1956). *The individual psychology of Alfred Adler.* H. Ansbacher & R. Ansbacher (Eds.), New York: Basic Books.

Beutler, L.E. (1983). *Eclectic psychology: A systematic approach.* New York: Pergammon Press.

Broderick, C. (1984, February). *Bridging the gap between theory, research, and practice in family relations.* Paper presented at the conference on family competence: Learning from prior relationships, Arizona Association of Marital and Family Therapists, Phoenix.

Dreikurs, R. (1933, 1953). *Fundamentals of Adlerian psychology.* Chicago, Alfred Adler Institute.

Dreikurs, R. (1967). *Psychodynamics, psychotherapy and counseling.* Chicago: Alfred Adler Institute.

Dreikurs, R. (1968). Determinants of changing attitudes of marital partners toward each other. In S. Rosenbaum & I. Alger (Eds.), *The marriage relationship: Psychoanalytic perspectives* (pp. 83-103). New York: Basic Books.

Dreikurs, R. & Mosak, H.H. (1966). The tasks of life I. Adler's three tasks. *Individual Psychologist, 4,* 18-22.

Dreikurs, R. & Mosak, H.H. (1967). The tasks of life II. The fourth life task. *Individual Psychologist, 4,* 51-55.

Ferguson, E.D. (1976, August). *Basic Adlerian theory.* Paper presented at the International Congress of Adlerian Summer Schools and Institutes, Vienna.

Gurman, A.S. (1983). Assessing change in the clincial practice of marital therapy. *The American Journal of Family Therapy, 11*(2), 67-70.

Haynes, S.N. & Jensen, B.J., et. al (1981). The marital intake interview: A Multi-method criterion validity assessment. *Journal of Consulting and Clinical Psychology, 49,* 379-387.

Hawes, E.C. (1982). *Couples growing together: A leader's guide for couples study groups.* Wooster, OH: The Social Interest Press.

Hillman, B.W.(1981). *Teaching with confidence: How to get off the classroom wall.* Springfield, IL: CHarles C. Thomas.

Jacobsen, N.S., & Margolin, G. (1979). *Marital therapy: Strategies based on social learning and behavioral exchange principles.* New York: Bruner/Mazel.

Kern. R. (Speaker). 1982). *Lifestyle interpretation.* (cassette.) Coral Springs, FL: CMTI Press.

Locke, H. & Wallace, K.M. (1959). Short marital adjustment and prediction tests: Their reliability and validity. *Marriage and Family Living, 21,* 251-255.

Manaster, G.J., & Corsini, R.J. (1982). *Individual psychology: Theory and practice.* Itasca, IL: F.E. Peacock.

Margolin, G., & Jacobson, N.S. (1981). Assessment of marital dysfunction. In M. Hersen & A.S. Bellack (Eds.), *Behavioral assessment.* New York: Pergammon Press.

Minuchin, S. (1978). *Families and family therapy.* Cambridge, MA: Harvard University Press.

Mosak, H.H. (1979). Adlerian psychotherapy. In R.J. Corsini (Ed.), *Current psychotherapies,* (pp.44-94). Itasca, IL: F.E. Peacock.

Pew, M.L. & Pew, W.L. (1972). Adlerian marriage counseling. *Journal of Individual Psychology, 28,* 192-202.

Schaefer, M.T. & Olson, D.H. (1981). The pair inventory. *Journal of Marital and Family Therapy, I,* 47-60.

Sharpley, C. & Rogers, H. (1984). Preliminary validation of the abbreviated Spanier Dyadic Adjustment Scale: Some psychometric data regarding a screening test of marital adjustment. *Educational & Psychological Measurement, 44,* 1045-1049.

Snyder, D.K. (1981). *Marital satisfaction inventory manual.* Los Angeles: Western Psychological Services.

Spanier, G.B. (1976). Measuring dyadic adjustment: New scales for assessing the quality of marriage and similar dyads. *Journal of Marriage and the Family, 38,* 15-28.

Spanier, G.B. & Lewis, R. (1980). Marital quality: A review of the seventies. *Journal of Marriage and the Family, 42,* 825-839.

Straus, M.A. & Brown, B. (1935-1974). *Family measurement techniques: Abstracts of published instruments.*

Way, L. (1961). *Adler's place in psychology: An exposition of individual psychology.* New York: Collier Books.

Weiss, R.L., Hops, H. & Patterson, G.R. (1973). A framework for conceptualizing matital conflict. In L.A. Hamerlynck, L.D. Hardy & E.J. Marsh (Eds.) *Behavior change: Methodology concepts and practice.* Champaign, IL: Research Press.

Whitaker, C.A. (1984, January/February). The family is always one down. *Family Therapy News,* p. 3.

Wills, T.A., Weiss, R.L. & Patterson, G.R. (1974). A behavioral analysis of the determinants of marital satisfaction. *Journal of Consulting and Clinical Psychology, 42,,* 802-811.

Chapter 3
Lifestyle of a Relationship
by
Maxine Ijams

Marriage therapy can be described as the examination by husband, wife and therapist of the tapestry the couple has woven from the threads each spouse brought to the marital loom. The therapist helps the couple identify the designs they value and want to strengthen as well as the discordant threads they want to remove. Together they examine the unique "Relationship Lifestyle" of the couple—i.e., the characteristic way that each deals with the other and with life, as developed from a functional, holistic, teleological framework. Throughout this process, the Adlerian therapist asks, "How are heredity and environment being used by these two people?" (Mosak & Dreikurs, 1973).

The interactions of these two individuals' Lifestyles leads to inevitable differences within the marital framework, thus providing great potential for dissension. In troubled relationships, the partners usually hold widely disparate views of life, reflected in the expectations each has of people, self and situations. In fact, Dreikurs (1946) wrote that the root of all marital problems can be found in the personalities of the individuals and in the subsequent ways they deal with each other. He felt, however, that differences could endanger a relationship only if the differences were used to devalue the other (Dreikurs, 1946). Thus, couples who seek marriage counseling generally demonstrate very clear patterns of intolerance for these differences. As a result, the discomfort level in the relationship increases while the mutual nourishment level decreases.

This chapter will address the gathering of early childhood information, including family background, descriptions of self, siblings, parents, other family members, family values, birth information, favorite childhood fairy tales and early recollections. A synthesis of this information and how it is employed in therapy will also be included.

During the formative years, children observe the behavior of those around them, interact with others, interpret and draw conclusions about these observations and interactions, and make decisions about self, others and the world. These decisions are typically made outside of conscious awareness and are carried into adulthood as expectations and demands on self and others (Mosak & Dreikurs, 1973).

When a group of adults is asked to remember how they got their own way as children, there is typically a flashback to childhood scenes wherein such behaviors as pouting, withdrawal, crying, temper tantrums or unresponsiveness were used to manipulate others. When further queried as to the current use of these methods in their present lives, there is recognition of the carryover of these learned behaviors, even though they may no longer be appropriate or successful. Even in the face of frustration, individuals tend to retain the old patterns and expectations formed in childhood (Manaster & Corsini, 1982).

Gathering Lifestyle Information

The rationale for gathering the Lifestyle information in the presence of the other spouse is that it provides opportunity, often for the first time, for each partner to hear and understand the formative elements in the other's development. The Lifestyle questions provide a seemingly innocuous introduction to therapy. In fact, basic inquiries about the number of siblings and ordinal position may already have been made of each partner in the first counseling session. Although during the initial assessment, Adlerian therapists may vary in the formality they employ in gathering Lifestyle information, ranging from the use of a very structured form to an informal weaving of the information-gathering into each counseling session, the final summation will be similar.

In the process of Lifestyle analysis, information is gathered about each partner's childhood and nuclear and extended family. Specific areas of expectations formed as children are examined and projective techniques focusing on early memories are employed. Gathering Lifestyle information is always in the service of the therapeutic needs of each spouse; therefore, therapeutic intervention is also an active part of the information gathering.

Each partner is first asked for a description, as remembered from childhood, of mother, father, grandparents and other significant adults. If grandparents were deceased at that time, the partner is asked, "What did you hear about them?" From these descriptions the expectations of "what is a man" and "what is a woman" emerges, as well as what "a Jones man is" or "what Phillips women are." A recalled description of the marriage relationships, and uncles and aunts, often provides relationship role modeling for the current couple.

The behavior modeled for and subjectively perceived by the child is not necessarily adopted as an adult, but rather becomes an issue for the adult to accept or reject. An individual coming from an emotionally nondemonstrative home may incorporate that stance in adult behavior or, on the other hand, may decide to be more warm and loving than the models were.

Bandura (1969) noted that formation of much of a child's behaviors and attitudes in the early years is based on modeling or observational learning. Even though adults are not always aware of why they act as they do, imitating behaviors is one of the subprocesses of observational learning (Bandura, 1969).

If the role model is perceived by the child to be powerful, a source of nurturance to the child or of the same gender as the child, a greater impact on the internalization of the modeled behavior is found (Bandura & Huston, 1961; Bandura, Ross & Ross, 1963). Significant adults in a child's life usually fulfill one or more of these requirements. Therefore, examination of the impact of modeling during childhood on the current relationship is monitored throughout the therapy sessions.

Baggage of Supposed To's

Each partner brings "baggage"—i.e., unexamined expectations into the marital relationship. This baggage, which is identified during Lifestyle analysis, refers to the convictions that each individual has developed early in life to help organize, understand, predict and control experiences. These convictions are conclusions drawn from the individual's perceptions and, of course, are biased apperceptions. Hence decisions become expectations or "supposed to's" relating to how things are supposed to be. Some theoreticians might argue that there are only facts to address in therapy, whereas the Adlerian therapist believes there are only interpretations. The interpretation of any given circumstance by the individual becomes that person's reality and it is that reality the therapist addresses.

Family Atmosphere

The "supposed to's" encompass not only the role of modeling from significant adults in the partners' childhoods, but also conclusions drawn about what an appropriate family atmosphere should be—e.g., punitive, distant, sharing, discordant, rejective, fun-loving or democratic. This emotional climate is usually set by the parents' attitudes and relationship and becomes a critical factor for the future marital happiness of their offspring.

An example of how expectations of family atmosphere can cause conflict was demonstrated by Sara and Jim:

> Sara's father had been extremely critical of her mother and the children, but no one was allowed to respond to his comments. He treated his wife with disdain and demanded that the children be seen and not heard. Jim had grown up in a household with a democratic atmosphere, where everyone had a voice in decisions and was treated with respect. He was extremely frustrated that the entire burden for family decisions and family guidance fell on his shoulders. Sara not only offered no input for decisions, but also shrank under what she perceived as his criticism of her inadequacies.

Successful Adulthood

Just as children form concepts about what defines an appropriate family atmosphere, so do they conclude what parents expect from them in order to be considered well-functioning adults. It is useful to question both spouses in therapy about what they had respectively concluded that their parents required of them to be "successful adults." In the process of the examination of old parental injunctions, many personality facets of each spouse can be uncovered. If an individual decides one must be strong and self-sufficient, that individual may find it difficult to be close, to take risks and to trust, fearing this will lead to vulnerability and thus to weakness. "Be strong" is an injunction perceived by many males, such as in Tony's case:

Tony was a paramedic who had reluctantly accompanied Pat for counseling. His mother had died when he was four years old, and his father had left him and two much-older siblings in the care of their crippled grandmother. The family home was on the outskirts of a small rural town, and Tony spent many hours virtually alone. Grandmother had continually emphasized "boys are strong." He reported an early memory of digging a hole by a back fence, covering it with tin, and spending many hours there alone. His reported decision that he had to be self-sufficient served him well in his paramedic role, but his ability to relate to his wife and children was seriously impaired.

Another perception leading to difficulties in adulthood is an early major decision resulting in an exaggerated investment in the judgments of others. Subjugation to the subsequent marital partner will often then occur, with accompanying resentment toward that partner:

Mary Jane was the middle of three sisters, whose mother had been the dominate influence in Mary Jane's youth. Mother had stressed, "Remember you are a Jones!" Mary Jane was repeatedly reminded, "Neighbors talk," "Mind your manners," "What would your grandmother say?" Mary Jane's behavior with her husband was mostly obsequious, as she constantly sought his opinion or apologized for speaking. Under questioning, she acknowledged her capitulation to his control as well as the resentment she secretly harbored. This resentment surfaced in subtle but destructive ways, such as forgetting things that were important to him.

Awareness developed in the therapeutic analysis of how the environment is manipulated by each partner provides opportunities, often for the first time, for each spouse to choose to change faulty belief systems and unsuccessful approaches to others.

Marriage is a place where...

Rewards expected from the marriage relationship are typically modeled by those significant couples observed by the spouses as children during their formative years. One's parents generally provide the strongest modeling, although this does not always follow:

> John treated his wife and children with disregard for their feelings and requests, then found it difficult to identify with their discomfort. In examining his description of the personalities and relationships of his parents and grandparents, there was no evidence of this kind of modeling as an antecedent for his behavior. An off-hand remark about a friendship developed with an older neighbor man when he was twelve years old, however, led to a similar description of the male behavior he was now following.

Children likewise perceive parental attitudes toward the marital state, then many times incorporate these attitudes in their own expectations of marriage. The marital institution may be viewed as a haven, where perhaps needs are met and happiness found, or as a burden where one spouse is subservient to the other or where there is nothing but hard work and lack of joy. For example:

> Paul described himself as a long-term depressive when he and Polly began counseling. He was discouraged in his belief that they could ever find happiness in their marriage and he was seriously considering leaving the relationship to live alone. He had no specific complaints, just a general melancholic outlook toward marriage. When asked what he perceived as his parents' view of marriage, he visualized his father slogging through the mud and snow on their Iowa farm, shoulders bent, head down, and dour-faced. He pictured his mother standing on the back stoop, looking at the grey horizon with a hopeless, tired expression on her face. "Marriage," Paul offered, "was nothing but never-ending hard work and no real happiness."

Affection

Affection "supposed to's" are particularly meaningful in marital relationships. Each spouse is asked to examine the parental dynamics in this area of interaction. The couple is questioned about who moved toward whom with affection. Each spouse is asked to describe the mode employed, such as words, hugs or touching. A second question determines how the offering was received—i.e., passively, joyously or with rebuff. The rebuff could have ranged from subtle cues to vicious reactions. Once again, the interpretations and expectations formed by each spouse are examined for the impact these conclusions have on the present relationship. For example:

> Steve and Beth were both attractive and verbal, with each complaining that the other was not affectionate enough. Questions about their childhood memories of the affection interaction of their respective parents brought answers from each resulting in great hoots of laughter. Steve's mother had always made the overtures of affection to his father, who had been very accepting of them. On the other hand, Beth's father had been the initiator of overt gestures of warmth. Both Steve and Beth had been hungry for affection while each waited for the other to make the expected moves.

Another example of observational learning and modeling behavior was that of Sam and Angie:

> Angie slapped her forehead in dawning and under-standing as the concept of modeling was explained to her and Sam. She complained that Sam seldom hugged her, but always hugged the other women at church. As she listened to the explanation of his ob-servational learning, she remembered all the times she had seen Sam's father hug the women at church, only to be later brushed off by Sam's mother at home. At this point Sam interjected, "I didn't think wives liked to be hugged."

The sexual functioning in a marital relationship is often closely related to the comfort level in the exchange of affection be-tween the spouses.

Sexual Relationship

The sexual area is often heavily laden with taboos, regardless of the age level of the couple. Information about current sexual at-titudes is gleaned through an informal questioning of each partner as follows:

> *"As a child, did you ever see your parents in the nude?"*

"If so, what was your parents' reaction?"
"What was your conclusion?"
"Did you ever see your parents in a sexual activity?"
"If so, what was your parents' reaction and your con-
clusion?"
"Did adults ever catch you involved in sex play?"
"If so, how was that handled by the adult and what
did you conclude?"

The acquisition of information about menstruation for both
spouses is also examined.

Often, what emerges at this juncture is a hitherto suppressed
negative childhood sexual experience. Such an
unacknowledged trauma typically affects the sexual relationship of the couple in therapy (see Chapter 6).

> Don and Penny were both upset over Penny's grow-
> ing relationship with another man. She was angry
> and frustrated about the inactive sexual relationship
> she had with Don for the last five years. As the sexual
> history of each was explored, a very uncomfortable,
> early memory surfaced for Don. He and several other
> seven-year old boys had been playing in the play-
> house-sandbox of a neighbor boy. As small boys will,
> they began to dare each other to take off their
> clothes, and began to tug and pull at each others'
> penises. The mother of the neighbor boy looked out
> the kitchen window with an expression of horror on
> her face and began screaming at them. The small
> boys grabbed their clothing and fled from the yard.
> From this incident, the fear that he was homosexual
> had grown through the years, but he had never ex-
> amined or talked about his concerns with anyone.
> Subsequently, this fear had interfered with his ability
> to relate sexually with his wife, although he had had
> no further experiences that could be considered
> homosexual. The relief Don felt at uncovering and
> dealing with this long-suppressed trauma and the
> understanding and support he received from Penny
> increased Don's willingness to be vulnerable in their
> relationship.

In a lighter vein, the examination of some family traditions can
be helpful to the couple.

Holidays

Although of seemingly trivial nature, holidays and how they are observed are the vehicle by which valued family traditions are handed down to following generations. Each spouse wants the children to have the "right traditions." Christmas, in particular, and how it is celebrated can therefore become a divisive issue in the marital relationship. Some families traditionally put up the tree, exchange gifts and have a large dinner on Christmas Eve. To the individual whose family marked Christmas Day as the time for gift exchange, feasts and gathering, the celebration on the eve of the holiday would be a travesty. An examination of options and agreement to negotiate is often helpful with this type of problem.

The relative importance of birthdays is another source of potential friction. If one mate was reared in a family where the individual's birthday was treated as a royal day, and the other's family basically ignored birthdays, there is often fertile ground for disappointment and dissension. The problem is further exacerbated with the arrival of children with their recurrent birthdays.

Money

Money handling is often a source of conflict. Responsibility for the distribution of finances can be handled by the husband, the wife or both, with varying degrees of comfort for each. A child observing the practices of parents can grow into adulthood expecting to follow the same practices in one's own marriage. This arrangement can work smoothly only if the expectations of the spouses are congruent. For example:

> George was raised in a family where Dad handled all the finances. He earned it and deposited it. While he perhaps allowed Mother to push the cart in the grocery store, he paid the cashier. Every family purchase had to be checked with him. Susie, on the other hand, grew up in a home where Dad handed Mother the paycheck. She then paid the bills, saved for purchases and gave Dad and the children their weekly allowances. George and Susie's first shared payday ended in a big blowout when Susie met him at the door with a request for the money. It would be

a mistake to interpret the conflict that followed as simply a battle to see who was going to wear the pants in the family. Instead, it is an example of each moving in the direction of expectations.

Private Time

Many children, especially only children, grow to adulthood with a strongly developed need for quiet and private time. This can easily be misunderstood by the mate who was prepared by experiences with siblings for a very different kind of time and space sharing. For example:

> Bert and Brenda were accusing and labeling each other in their first counseling session. Bert was a part of a large, extended Italian family who had always shared each other's homes without benefit of invitation. On the other hand, Brenda, an only child, felt she could not continue to have her home and privacy invaded with no warning and was demanding they have large segments of time that would be off-limits to his family. He said she was selfish and she labeled him inconsiderate. The root of the problem was probably neither of these things, but rather the collision of their expectations about the way family life should be conducted.

Conflict Management

How anger and disagreements were handled in the family-of-origin typically has an impact of what individuals do as adults when faced with an anger-loaded situation. Using anger to control may be part of the behavioral repertoire of one or both spouses. Withdrawal from confrontation or avoidance of arousing displeasure in others are other manifestations of parental conflict management for example:

> Mamie, as a child, had watched her mother's temper explosions with great discomfort and had been afraid of her older brother's lack of anger control. As an adult, she constantly placated her husband, fellow workers and friends in an effort to avoid the discomfort of confrontation. This had led to great frustration on her part and confusion for her husband about her authentic feelings.

Many circumstances experienced in childhood, such as conflict management and illness, were emotionally charged areas for most people. Examining these childhood episodes and the conclusions drawn often provide clear pictures of expectations operating in the present relationship.

Illness

Because slight or serious illness is a part of all growing up, it provides another important source of "supposed to's." Many children interpret their worth from the perceived quality and amount of care received, typically from their mother, when they are ill. This attitude, brought into adult interaction, can be the trigger for conflict in marriage. For example:

> Betsy, a beautiful woman, was the only girl in her family. She had been Dad's "little girl" as well as Mother's pride and joy. When she had been ill as a child, all family activity came to a halt and Dad would even stay home from work. He and Mother would spend hours by Betsy's bedside, reading to, massaging and entertaining the child. Betsy's husband, Randy, was the eldest of three brothers. His family's practice was to have the ill person retreat to the guest house, in order not to inflict the illness on the rest of the family. One morning Betsy called to state she was divorcing Randy. She had been ill and he had taken the children to her mother's, brought Betsy orange juice, the radio and telephone and then had gone to work. She stated she could not continue to live with such an uncaring man. He, of course, felt he had gone the extra mile.

Just as long-lasting strong feelings exist about how one should be treated by a spouse when one is ill, so do we find other "baggage" areas of varying importance, such as what foods are acceptable to each spouse, how leisure time is to be spent, what dinnertime activities are appropriate, the place of animals in family life, and socializing, religious and childrearing practices.

Evaluating these childhood decisions in light of the impact on the marital relationship, looking at other options and negotiating adjustments and compromises is part of ongoing marital therapy. Change is always possible, but it is similar to learning a new sport in adulthood—i.e., it is difficult but attainable with practice.

Sibling Relationships

The sibling relationships experienced by each partner are further examined for possible displacement of old feelings to the present relationship. For example, the man who experienced constant putdowns from a bossy, older sister, may be married to a woman who was the oldest sibling of five. She may unknowingly interact with her husband in a manner that rekindles his feelings of inadequacy and anger.

Self

A childhood description of self offered by each partner gives a glimpse of current self-esteem levels and often the reason for these feelings. This description should include information about the client's origin in the world. The questions asked are:

> *"What do you know about your own birth?"*
> *"What have you heard about your conception?"*
> *"Your mother's pregnancy with you?"*
> *"Your delivery?"*
> *"What did your parents' think when they first saw you?"*
> *"Were you the sex they wanted?"*
> *"What kind of an infant were you?"*
> *"Where did your name come from?"*

The therapist should always ask for the individual's conclusions about the information, even when the client denies having made any conclusions.

When a person cannot remember hearing anything about one's own arrival in the world, it is often helpful to determine what was heard about the birth of any sibling, and then to ask for conclusions about sibling information being available when none is available about self. Further questions may include information about baby pictures and baby books and subsequent conclusions.

There is a strong relationship between negative origin information and low self-esteem versus positive information and high self-esteem. For example:

> George and Martha came for counseling after a serious argument about their teen-age son. George appeared depressed and as Martha sat down she said she was frightened George would try to commit suicide again. Subsequent questioning revealed that

he had made several attempts at suicide beginning when he was a young boy and continuing after their marriage. George had been born three months prematurely and had spent a long time in a hospital incubator. He reported that his family had thought he wouldn't live and he had vivid memories from childhood of hearing this tale over and over. Under questioning he revealed that he had early concluded that the way to control people and circumstances was to threaten not to live.

Another example of the long-lasting effects of birth information can be seen in the case of Jane and Phillip:

The identified problem in Jane and Phillip's relationship was Phillip's taking her for granted. She had been a long-awaited second child and the prettiest of the two daughters. Dad had left no question that she was his favorite, telling her constantly that she was a beautiful baby. She was so special that he would come home on his lunch hours to feed and play with her. His pet name for her was "Princess." Jane's expectations of the significant male in her adult life reflected these early experiences and the conclusions she had drawn from them.

Fairy Tales

Adler described all behavior as movement (Ansbacher & Ansbacher, 1956). The individual's law of movement can be understood from the opinion of self and from the decisions made about what has to be done in order to meet one's goals. If an individual's goal is to avoid vulnerability, for instance, the movements (behaviors) will be in the service of self-protection.

A functional tool for divining the movement the partners manifest is to ask each to retell a favorite story or fairy tale from childhood. In this manner, it is often disclosed how each moves toward, away from, with or against another person. A verbatim recording should be made of each report. For example:

Anne, in retelling Cinderella, clearly exposed her expectations. Cinderella lived with her stepmother and stepsisters, who got to go to the ball while Cinderella had to stay home and do all the work. Suddenly, a Fairy Godmother appeared and asked her if she wanted to go, too. When she arrived, the Prince noticed her and asked her to dance. She dropped her slipper when she left, and the next day the Prince went out into the city looking for her. When he came to her house, he tried the slipper on the sisters, then asked if anyone else lived there. He went into the back room, found Cinderella, put the shoe on her foot, then took her back to the castle to live.

Anne's expectations that she had to contribute nothing and that others were supposed to seek her out was reflected in her narcissistic behavior with her husband, Hank. Hank's story:

Hank remembered Jack and the Beanstalk as a rough-and-tumble adventure story. Jack threw some beans out of his window and from them a huge vine shot up into the clouds. Jack climbed it and found a lot of gold. He grabbed it and started down the vine just as a giant came roaring after him. Jack got to the bottom, grabbed an ax and chopped the vine down, killing the giant.

A rakish attitude and the grabbing of what he wanted, with disregard for others, was characteristic of Hank's interpersonal behavior. Anne and Hank's marriage was characterized by Hank's insensitivity to Anne's needs or wishes and his self-centered following of pre-marital routines of time schedules, bar-hopping and leisure activities.

Early Recollections

The final phase of Lifestyle information gathering is the sharing by each spouse of five to seven early childhood memories, including the earliest incident that can be recalled. The individual's basic conceptual framework will be reflected in these memories. Alfred Adler wrote, "Among all psychological expressions, some of the most revealing are the individual's memories" (Ansbacher & Ansbacher, 1956, p. 351). The memories the individual holds in the retrievable memory bank are frames of reference for the manner in which the world is viewed at the present time. The memories will reflect the way it is hoped life will be and, conversely, the fears that person maintains.

An early recollection is a unique, specific event that gives generalized information about how an individual views self, others and life (Davis-Evans, 1980). The recollections reflect decisions made during the formative years that define the person's basic conceptual framework. In the sharing of early recollections, the subjective reality of the individual becomes available for scrutiny. The memories represent the "life story," which is used by the person to interpret, organize and control experiences. An example of this is a person who sees one's self as a victim, who maintains a conviction of victimization by reviewing memories of exploitation and hurt. This person would find it difficult to sustain a sense of being victimized if memories of success and being-in-charge were reviewed instead.

As the general study of human development has grown, interest in human's contributions to their own creation has grown. Allport (1962) discussed a person in the process of becoming as one who uses memory of the past to help organize and construct the present. The research in the area of memory has been well summarized by Davis-Evans (1980). According to that discussion, the reproduction of simple stories was significantly influenced by the frames of reference held by the subjects, demonstrating that active construction in the present is part of memory recall. The subject's attitude distorts the recognition and memory when the memory is inconsistent with the present attitude. The relationship of affect in memories to present levels of security feelings was demonstrated in results of Maslow's Security-Insecurity Test (Ansbacher, 1947).

In completing the Lifestyle analysis in couples counseling, early recollections are therefore gathered to clarify the positive and negative expectations each has carried into the marital relationship. The recollections are examined not only for content, but for movement as well. Is the individual who is reporting the recollection the observer, doer, interactor or receiver of the action? Clearly divergent personality patterns emerge between individuals who report recollections wherein they are the doers of the action as opposed to being either the receivers or observers of the action. The persons remembered in the incident are also meaningful as generalized views of men, women, authority figures and peers. The recalled feeling state of the individual as well as the conclusions drawn are also significant facets of each early recollection.

A pattern, or theme, of the feelings the individual has about self, others and the world emerges from the memory material. A key life statement can typically be drawn from the recollections. Danny's behavior was an example of how an archaic decision can nearly destroy a marriage.

> Danny and Kate had reached a breaking point in their relationship when they came for counseling. She said she was no longer willing to live with Danny's long faces and depression. Under questioning, Danny reported a memory that was congruent with his present behavior. In Danny's words, "I was seven or eight years old. Mother, my brother, John, and I had gone to the store to get John a coonskin cap, which he needed for a Davy Crockett play. John picked the one he wanted and Mom started for the cash register. She looked back at me. I guess I was looking sad, just staring at the coonskin caps. She melted and asked me if I wanted one too. The feelings I had were envy because John always got what he wanted, sadness because I wanted one too, and gratification because I got what I wanted."

With Danny's new awareness that he was attempting to manipulate Kate's behavior with his depressed demeanor, he asked her for help in recognizing when this occurred. His sense of humor assisted him in seeing the absurdity of "coonskin cap situations."

A clear example of movement and a key life statement is reflected in Bill's childhood memories of being reared on a farm as the youngest child of a large family. After detailing a memory of resisting the directions of an older sister, he stated emphatically, "I did exactly as I pleased and nobody told me what to do." This stance was clearly reflected in the difficulties present in his two-year old second marriage.

In order to elicit from each spouse a specific, unique early memory, the therapist can give the following instructions:

> "Please go back into your childhood, before the age of eight years, and find the earliest memory you have. Look for a single event, an incident that took place one time. Close your eyes and visualize the scene: Who is there? Where does it take place? What is happening? Is there anything else that happens?"

The individual can then be asked to explore the affect, or aura of feeling, around the memory and then to answer the "because" of the feeling. The "because" will reflect the individual's fears or hopes, thus giving clues about how the individual views life and what is expected of that person.

Conflicting spousal expectations can be disclosed by the use of early recollections as demonstrated in the analysis of two memories offered by Barry and Carol. Carol was a sparkly, spontaneous young woman with many friends and a large convivial family. Her habit of impulsively sharing her time and possessions with others had led Barry to question his decision to marry her. He was an up and coming real estate developer who carefully considered every move before he made it. Carol reported:

> "It was my birthday and I had just received a lot of presents. The family next door was a large, poor one with six children. I saw Sarah looking through the fence at all of my presents. I went over to the fence and gave her my new tea set, and she was really happy. I felt good and happy and proud because I had shared my things with someone and made her happy."

Barry reported:

> "Dad took me for a walk, I was about nine years old, and he told me to always watch my step. Dad was a very serious and successful businessman. As Dad said this, I felt apprehensive and anxious because I knew I mustn't take chances; I would have to be cautious."

Carol demonstrated her early decision to feel happy and proud through spontaneous sharing, which came into direct conflict with Barry's early decision that it was imperative not to be impulsive, but to be cautious in his moves. This couple was encouraged to discuss options and consequences before any choices were made. Barry was asked to take small risks in spontaneous behaviors and Carol was to reduce her impulsivity by waiting 24 hours before committing herself to a generous action.

The relationship of Ellen and George provides an additional illustration of current conflict being reflected in early recollections. Ellen felt starved for warmth and closeness and complained that George had no feelings. His complaint was that she was too emotional and demanding. Her memory was:

> *"I was about eight years old and was sitting at the dining room table doing homework. I was stuck and asked Mother for help, which she at first ignored. I asked Dad and he said he had to go somewhere. I went into the kitchen and asked Mother again and she got mad at me and said to stop bothering her. I had a temper tantrum but it didn't change anything. I felt unimportant, hurt, rejected and mad because no one had time for me or cared about me."*

George's story was:

> *"I was about four years old and I was running away from Dad, who was scolding me. I ran into Mother's room and told her, 'Don't tell him I'm in here,' and dove under the bed. He came into the room and said 'Where is he?' She didn't say anything, but the next thing I saw was his face peering at me under the bed. I felt ratted on and betrayed, because she didn't care about me; she didn't protect me. I couldn't trust her."*

Ellen's expectations that significant others in her life would fail to meet her emotional needs were borne out in her interactions with George, who at a very early age had concluded that others couldn't be trusted. Consequently, George allowed no vulnerability to develop with Ellen. The more angry she became at him for his "unfeelingness," the more convinced he became that he had to protect himself.

It was suggested to Ellen that she offer warmth and affection to George rather than demanding it, and George was asked to take some small risks by exposing his feelings to Ellen, beginning with one-sentence notes responding to her offerings. This later included his telling her of his appreciation and then asking her to meet his emotional needs. They were also asked to give each other one positive feedback each day and to offer spontaneous touching to each other. This gradually met her need for assurance of his caring and provided a safe environment in which he could risk vulnerability.

In Summary

Out of the material gathered in the Lifestyle analysis, the faulty belief systems and approaches are discerned and listed. Through helping individuals change their faulty beliefs, movements toward a goal will be altered and opportunities can be created for more constructive interactions. Insight into the faulty logic behind the behavior, as well as comprehension that current behavior is often built on an inaccurate childhood decision, often leads to a decision to risk a change in attitude and behavior. The introduction of new options by the therapist serves to increase the spouses' optimism that through practice changes can occur. Reinforcement by the partner is encouraged.

When the Lifestyle information has been completely gathered, each section is evaluated for possible key elements. The description of adult females and males often provides clues to the individual's expectations of the way women, men and relationships should be. The childhood self-description provides insight into expectations of the adult self, and the family values section provides valuable information about what motivates the individual in the present.

A most valuable source of insight is furnished by what the individual knows of one's own origins in the world. If that beginning was unwanted, resented, or negative in any way, the individual typically has a very different feeling about self, than does the person whose birth was heralded. These feeling very much color the individual interactions on a daily basis.

The fairy tale, evaluated for movement of one figure with others, suggests the possible way the individual expects interactions to move in the present. The early recollections complete the evaluation with the entire analysis being examined for possible faulty belief systems (e.g., that women in general cannot be trusted), and for strengths (e.g., resourcefulness or honesty) as reflected in the disclosures.

The possible faulty belief systems of each spouse are examined in light of the declared difficulties each spouse is experiencing, and the strengths are called upon by the therapist to assist in the changes each spouse wants to make.

The Relationship Lifestyle Analysis can be viewed as an exciting, creative opportunity to enlarge one's knowledge of self, others and options for changes in attitudes, feelings, and behaviors.

The chapter Therapeutic Intervention in the Marital Relationship to follow is intended to provide the reader or therapist with some additional strategies one may employ that will complement the information gathered in the chapter related to the Lifestyle concept.

Chapter 3 References

Allport, G.W. (1962). Psychological models for ounseling. *Harvard Educational Review*, 32, 372-381.

Ansbacher, H.L. (1947). Adler's place in the psychology of memory. *Journal of Personality*, 3, 197-207.

Ansbacher, H.L. & Ansbacher, R.R. (Eds.). (1956). *The individual psychology of Alfred Adler*. New York: Basic Books.

Ansbacher, H.L. & Ansbacher, R.R. (Eds.). (1978). *Cooperation between the sexes*. New York: Anchor Books.

Bandura, A. (1969). *Social learning theory of identificatory processes. Handbook of socialization theory and research* (pp. 213-262). Chicago: Rand-McNally.

Bandura, A. & Huston, N.B. (1961). Identification as a process of incidental learning. *Journal of Abnormal and Social Psychology*, 63, 311-318.

Bandura, A., Ross, D. & Ross, S.A. (1963). A comparative test of the status, envy, social power, and secondary reinforcement theories of identificatory learning. *Journal of Abnormal and Social Psychology*, 67, 601-607.

Davis-Evans, Carol. (1980). Self written early recollections. Unpublished Ph.D. dissertation, University of Arizona.

Dinkmeyer, D.C., Pew, W.L. & Dinkmeyer, D.C., Jr. (1979). *Adlerian counseling and psychotherapy*. Monterey, CA: Brooks/Cole.

Manaster, G.J. & Corsini, R.J. (1982). *Individual psychology*. Itasca, IL: F.E. Peacock.

Mosak, H.H. & Dreikurs, R. (1973). Adlerian Psychotherapy. In R.J. Corsini (Ed.), *Current psychotherapies* (pp. 35-83). Itasca, IL: F.E. Peacock.

Mosak, H.H. (1977). *On purpose: Collected papers*. Chicago: Alfred Adler Institute.

Part II:
Therapeutic Interventions

Chapter 4
Therapeutic Interventions in the Marital Relationship
by
E. Clair Hawes

Adlerian Psychology is comparable to other interpersonal and systems theories in its emphasis on social and interpersonal dynamics and its stress on the individual's responsibility for one's own behavior (Kern, Matheny & Patterson, 1978). However, Adlerian Psychology differs from other perspectives in the degree to which Adler believed this responsibility contributes to the individual's well-being in the social environment. To facilitate healthy coexistence in the social environment, which includes marriage as a basic element, the individual must have an intimate awareness of one's own needs and priorities. The Adlerian perspective stresses that such self-knowledge and awareness determines those perceptions and behaviors that affect the individual's and the couple's functioning.

During marital counseling, the recognition and understanding of these perceptions and behaviors by both partners is examined through an assessment of their Lifestyles (see Chapter 3). The therapist and the couple then work together on revising those mistaken beliefs that have led each spouse to use ineffective behaviors. Concomitantly, communication skills are taught through building on the strengths of the Lifestyles. The husband who has felt a need to control through creating emotional distance learns to risk giving up some control and sharing his feelings in order to move closer to his wife and thereby to receive her warmth. The wife who has learned she only gets what she wants through manipulation discovers how to ask for what she needs, directly and without guilt. Thus, communication skills must be built before the couple can begin to change their behavior.

All behavior is purposeful and hence communicates useful information within the context of the dyad. Therefore, the therapist also investigates each partner's behavior. Further, as Margolin and Jacobson (1981) have pointed out, it is often the conclusions that spouses draw from their partner's behavior, rather than the behavior itself, that constitute the primary problem. Such interpretations may be based on mistaken apperceptions, which can be identified during the Lifestyle assessment.

Interventions presented here are structured to re-educate the couple so they can move through the reorientation stage. Most problem-solving techniques will be useless unless each partner has adequate interpersonal communication skills (Weiss, 1978), for the couple will not be able to negotiate if they cannot communicate clearly about their desires.

Teaching the couple communication skills and, later, problem-solving skills, is considerably more difficult than specifying the optimal content of the couple's interaction. Jacobson's (1977c) explanation still holds today in which he stated that:

> This is because the technology of *how* to implement behavior procedures is primitive; skillful behavioral clinicians can help couples change using their procedures, but a substantial portion of factors operating in the treatment milieu, in addition to the hypothesized "active ingredients," become abstracted from the procedural descriptions which appear in the literature... few procedural descriptions have been sufficiently elaborate to allow clinicians to implement the procedures on the basis of reading the article (p. 20).

This chapter is presented to help the clinician directly apply specific intervention techniques to the particular couple situation.

Part I: Building Communication Skills

Communication has been defined by many authors. Basically, it is the process by which information is either changed from one state to another or moved from one point to another point in space (Steinglass, 1978). Satir (1972) viewed communication as a huge umbrella that covers and affects all that goes on between human beings. It is the largest single factor determining the kinds of relationships one makes with others. She went on to point out that all communication is learned and that individuals can change their communication skills.

A broad range exists in quality of communication. In fact, a familiar axiom in family and marital therapy stated that "a person cannot not communicate" (Satir, 1967; Lederer & Jackson, 1968; Steinglass, 1978). Many theoreticians believe good communication is the key to family interaction as well as the lifeblood of the marriage relationship (Andes, 1974). For example, over 20 years ago, Satir (1964) observed the increasing recognition of the positive relationship that exists between marital adjustment and a couple's capacity to communicate. Over the intervening years it has become commonly accepted that open, honest communication is a major factor in satisfying marital relationships.

Breakdown in marital communication is considered an early sign of warfare long before overt acts of hostility erupt. Therefore, from the first counseling session, the therapist attempts to reestablish communication and mutual understanding as a means of reconciliation (Dreikurs, 1967).

Teaching Communication Skill Building

Dreikurs (1968) labeled all dysfunctional communication as a "game" in which the partners unwittingly try to demonstrate how wrong the other is. Instead of realizing the psychological basis for disputes, the couple remains on the logical level, with both partners finding new proofs for their respective positions. Dreikurs then set out to help the couple take the first step toward resolving conflicts by assisting them in the mutual respect that is the essence of improved communication. The goal of the communication intervention techniques presented here is to develop mutual respect through emphasizing that clear and functional communication is the responsibility of both the sender and the receiver of the message.

These techniques are ordered so that communication and problem-solving skills are acquired in a step-by-step process. Each new skill builds on concepts previously learned. The most fundamental skills will be reintroduced throughout counseling, both to reinforce the skills and to help the couple assimilate new learning into their repertoires in a familiar, comfortable and natural way. The basic scheme, then, is a progression from building couple trust, to teaching effective communication skills, to applying these skills in problem-solving, to having the couple spontaneously integrate these skills when dealing with issues of conflict and intimacy. The net result is that the couple replaces inappropriate and ineffective interactions with new learning. All techniques are not appropriate for all couples, so the therapist will select and tailor each intervention.

Most intervention techniques are first taught to the couple in the counseling session; then a related assignment is given to them for homework. As L'Abate (1977) has ascertained, the use of homework assignments pertaining to dyadic communication is an effective therapeutic technique and a useful adjunct to couple counseling. Repeated practice in the natural environment makes couples more comfortable in using newly learned skills, and the effect of the counseling process is extended throughout the intervening interval. When assignments focus on positive feelings and experiences, they can effectively encourage each partner. There is also a strong connection between regularly completed homework assignments and the degree to which a couple's relationship improves (Liberman et al., 1980). If couples do not have certain tasks to pursue, their expectation may be that some kind of magical transformation will occur in the counseling setting (Paul & Paul, 1975).

Each of the following techniques is very structured, and the guidelines must be followed when the couples do the exercises at home. When couples are not given very specific instructions, they tend to fall back on former ineffective or possibly destructive methods of interaction. The more dominant or controlling of the partners will often exert pressure to change the method, which results in resentment for the other. Such interactions will perpetuate the dysfunction that already exists.

Following a structure set out by a trusted third person may be the first step in establishing mutual respect, as the emphasis is on completing the task and checking out how they feel about one another rather than competing for being right. To further assure compliance with the guidelines, the therapist may simultaneously write out all homework instructions while giving the oral directions. In later sessions, the couple will be asked to assume more responsibility for taking instructions by writing such directions themselves.

Skills for Effective Communication

"Discuss It." This technique can be incorporated into the counseling session at any time and can be used repeatedly. Perceptive and articulate couples will soon integrate it into their discussions, both at home and during counseling. Other couples will find it more difficult. The technique can be given as a homework assignment once the therapist has ascertained that the couple has adequately mastered the structure. One approach is to assign a brief period per day when the couple discusses any topic, using this method of interaction.

Implementing "Discuss It" at the first session when the couple is explaining the presenting problem can help both the therapist and the couple assess the degree of communication dysfunction. For example, how well each partner is listening to the other, the clarity of the message sent, the extent to which the partners respond from their private logic, their ability and willingness to follow directions, and above all, the degree of mutual respect can quickly become obvious to all involved.

Much guidance and coaching is needed as "Discuss It" is prescribed by the therapist:

> *"I want you to discuss your problem with decision-making with one another instead of telling me. Please turn and face each other so that you can establish and maintain eye contact. Joan, you were telling me how Rob makes decisions about your time. I want you to tell him first how you feel about it and to own the problem by keeping your statements as much as possible in the 'I' context. Also, keep your statements as short as possible. Rob, you are going to have to repeat this back to Joan before we go further with the discussion. Go ahead Joan."*

As Joan begins, the therapist listens and watches for any sense of blaming, points it out, prohibits it, then models how to rephrase by changing the pronouns. Particular attention is paid to vocal quality and body language, such as whining, finger pointing, folded arms and rigid posture. Interpretations of what such behavior may convey are communicated to the couple. Pronouns are stated as "I" wherever appropriate so that Joan can own her problem. Mind reading and making assumptions are prohibited. The focus is on the communications process rather than the content. If Joan's message is too long or involved, the therapist asks her to stop. When she is finished, the next step is described by the therapist:

> *"Rob, will you please show Joan that you understand what she is saying by stating in your own way what she has just said to you? You may find you are repeating her own words, but that is okay because then she will know that you were truly listening. When you are finished, she will tell you if you are correct. It is possible that even if you use the exact words, she may say that is not her message. Don't worry about it, because it may mean that as she hears you, she realizes that what she said is not exactly*

> *what she means. What is important is that you both*
> *begin to truly hear each other. There will be no dis-*
> *cussion about one of you being right or wrong."*

With the therapist's careful monitoring, Rob paraphrases Joan's statement, and she in turn decides whether what he said is what she meant. If it is not, she gives her message again, and Rob paraphrases it again. This continues until his feedback meets with her satisfaction. It helps to point out to the couple that this process precludes the listener planning a response and/or defense rather than paying close attention to the speaker. With some couples this process may take many attempts before it is satisfactorily completed. The therapist can then keep encouraging the couple by demonstrating to them the confusion in their communication that must constantly exist and assuring them that this is the first step in obtaining clarity. They must work at this process until they feel progress.

Once Rob has received confirmation that his feedback is correct, he will make his statement to Joan which she paraphrases until he confirms that she is correct. As they work at becoming proficient and comfortable with "Discuss It," the therapist keeps the discussion in the present tense, makes sure they do not become stuck by rehashing the past, and emphasizes that the focus be on feelings rather than content.

Once the therapist is confident that the couple will follow the structure, a related homework assignment is made: The couple is to set aside a half hour each evening for a week to have a discussion using this technique. Most couples need it reemphasized that following the structure will protect them from falling back into their dysfunctional communication process.

"I'm Done." A simpler exercise, related to "Discuss It," is to have each partner talk for as long as needed, without interruption from the other, and when finished to say, "I'm done." Then the other speaks until done, and so forth until some resolution is felt by both people.

The Talking Stick. This technique, another variation of "Discuss It," was developed by the writer in desperation during a session with a highly volatile husband and his angry, distressed wife. Neither would let the other complete a statement, even when the therapist physically intervened. At the time, the offices were being renovated and the room was shared with a physician who had left tongue depressors on the desk. The therapist picked up a depressor, dramatically stripped off the paper wrapping, held it out between the partners, and made a statement that has been repeated with great success many times since:

> "Here in the Northwest, our native Indians have a tradition of discussion during conferences between tribal elders—people who are equal to one another. When a person is talking, that person holds a 'talking stick' and no one can interrupt the person with the stick. When finished, the stick is passed to the next speaker. Here is your talking stick. When one person holds it, the other must stay silent."

Relationship Highlights. When a couple is very discouraged, and the outlook for their relationship seems bleak, they may need help in looking back over their years together to recognize that it was not always so. Most likely they are choosing to pinpoint the negative aspects of their history together rather than to focus on what they have built together. This choice is at a level of unawareness, but may have as its purpose the living out of Lifestyle themes that indicate an expectation of being unsuccessful or of suffering. Another possibility is that one or both partners are depressed, and one aspect of depression is a negative view of the past, present and future. To counteract this negativity, couples are given the assignment of making a list at home of the twenty highlights of their relationship—times that were not necessarily major events but during which they felt very close to one another. The number of items can be varied but should be large enough so that the individuals have to spend time searching over their history together. The items are not to be shared before the next counseling session.

At the following session, the couple is asked to alternately share their highlights with one another using the "1-2-3 Interchange" (given below), as the "highlights" technique helps teach the interchange with a positive focus. Once the therapist feels assured that the couple knows how to do the sharing, they are assigned homework to each share five of the remaining highlights per day, using the "1-2-3 Interchange."

Sara and Dan, for example, came for counseling after Sara discovered that Dan had been having an affair with a mutual friend. In spite of her hurt and anger, Sara came up with a list that had as its first three items their wedding ceremony, Dan's method of cleaning the bathroom tiles, and purchasing their first house. Although Dan was feeling very defensive and was only committing himself to work on their relationship on a week-by-week basis, the first three items he chose to share were coming home to Sara after a long business trip, the purchase of their first home, and the subsequent moving day, which revealed the disbelief of their friends who were helping that they had so many possessions. The exchanges were punctuated by both uncontrollable tears and spontaneous laughter as they recalled events that were the building blocks of their relationship. The barrier of estrangement was broken through, and both were able to respond to each other with a genuine warmth that had been absent for a long time.

1-2-3 Interchange. In almost every troubled marriage, the spouses speak to each other but neither "hears" what the other says. Lederer and Jackson (1968) originally developed the prototype of this 1-2-3 Interchange exercise to counteract the "hearing" problem by exaggerating the emphasis on every communication, no matter how small. The purpose is to make each partner more aware of the lackluster nature of their daily interaction and to have them focus on one another. Both partners commit themselves to complete all communication in a minimum of three steps for two weeks as follows: 1) The first speaker makes a statement; 2) the recipient must acknowledge having heard the statement through making a response; and 3) the speaker must acknowledge the acknowledgement with a related response.

Example 1:

Rob:
Would you like a cup of coffee?

Joan:
Not right now, thanks.

Rob:
Maybe I'll have one later instead.

Example 2:

Joan:
I plan to visit my mother on Saturday.

Rob:
Say "hello" to her for me.

Joan:
Okay.

Example 3:

Rob:
The Celtics are playing the Lakers tonight.

Joan:
Maybe I'll sew.

Rob:
Perhaps you could do your sewing in front of the TV.

Couple Conference. This highly structured technique for discussing sensitive or volatile issues was originally developed by Corsini (1967). The Couple Conference has a built-in test of good intentions toward the marriage—i.e., if both partners make a appointment to confer and then do so, this expresses good intentions. If one of the partners does not keep the appointment, that person may not be serious about making the marriage work and can be confronted about this possibility.

Although it is a particularly appropriate exercise to assign at the first session for couples who are living together in hostile silence, the couple conference can be equally effective with couples who are unable to have mutually respectful discussions, who do not make time to talk together, or who stay with safe topics when they do talk. The purpose of the couple conference is to allow the couple to express literally anything they wish to at a time when they are not in conflict. Once these issues have been aired, they are more likely to be able to deal with current concerns.

It is essential that the therapist write out the instructions for the couple while also explaining the technique, so they have written tailor-made guidelines during the conference.

Therapist:
I am going to outline a Couple Conference. You will take two one-hour time periods. In each, one of you will speak for half an hour, while the other only listens—that is, makes no response at all. In the second half hour, the other speaks and the first listens. This means, of course, that the second person has an opportunity for rebuttal. However, in the second one-hour conference, the second speaker from the first conference will speak first. The topics may include anything you want—how you feel about life in general, the past, the future, what is currently going on—anything.

Joan:
I couldn't talk for a whole half hour.

Therapist:
You don't have to talk all the time. Silences are okay. How often have either of you, through your whole relationship, had the opportunity to say anything you want to say, knowing the other person is prepared to listen?

Rob:
We always seem to be competing for time when we do talk. We jump in and contradict each other.

Therapist:
Now you have a chance to think about how you want to phrase it. If you say something and as you hear yourself you realize, "that is not what I intended to say," you can take the statement back and change it around.

Joan:
But what if I say all I want in the first ten minutes?

Therapist:
You two have not been communicating effectively for a long time. So once you have dealt with the first issues, ask yourself, "What have I wanted to say to Rob over the years?" Think about it. My experience with couples is that they fill up the silences pretty quickly. It is essential that you do not cut the time short; take the full half hour each, or make it longer if you mutually agree to do so. Often the person who is more reluctant to talk will change the time rule and the other is afraid to express a need. Some other guidelines are important: set up a time when there will be no interruptions, unplug the phone, be sure your children are sound asleep or arrange a babysitter and go out, and do not have the conference while you are driving.

The therapist continues to write every detail of these instructions on the notepad. Couples have greater success with their conference when they have these tailor-made guidelines developed just for them, rather than a handout.

Rob:
This is beginning to sound interesting.

Therapist:
I expect that you will enjoy it. Another guideline is that you begin each appointment by standing and facing each other, touch hands or arms, and give each other a bit of verbal appreciation—share something you like about the other. Then sit back to back. You are both so used to misreading each other's body language and facial expression that for now I want you to concentrate on listening and talking. When you come to the end of the hour, STOP! Stand up again, touch each other, and acknowledge something you appreciate about the other. Change your activity and do not discuss any of the conference topics at any other time. Are you prepared to do this twice in the next week?

Joan:
Yes, it sounds good. We have nothing to lose.

Therapist:
What about you, Rob?

Rob:
Absolutely.

Commitment from the couple for action is always clearly elicited. If the couple is asked to do the Couple Conference immediately after they have committed themselves to working on their relationship (see Chapter 2), they will inevitably agree to do this exercise. If one partner disagrees with using the Couple Conference, the therapist should investigate the resistance. From the Adlerian perspective, resistance indicates that the therapist and the couple do not have congruent goals.

Therapist:
Let's now set up two conferences for the coming week. You are, in effect, making appointments with one another that are as important to keep as the ones you make with me. If you find you have to change the time or place, make the specific arrangement with your partner and write it down. When will you have the first conference? It's a good idea to have several days between them. (The time, date and place for each conference is discussed and noted on

the therapist's written instructions, which are then handed to the couple.) If there are any complications or misunderstandings after the first conference, please call me so we can clear up difficulties immediately.

Couple Conferences invariably clear the air for both partners and are effective in giving each the sense that one has been thoroughly heard. When the couple returns for the next session, the first item is to check out the conference. Upon hearing that it was successful, the therapist proceeds:

Therapist:
You will find that by having the courage and wisdom to surrender to your partner's point of view, while not giving up the importance of your own perspective, you may have begun your joint victory. Instead of continuing a power contest, you can now engage in the phenomenon of mutual accommodation, appreciation and resolution.

The Couple Conference is only a tool. It has limited use, but when it is the technique you need, it is possibly the only one that will do the job. It is not unlike the city map in your car that you only use occasionally, but is indispensable when you need to know how to get to where you are going. Joan, if Rob ever calls a Couple Conference, would you agree to it?

Joan:
Of course.

Therapist:
Rob, if Joan ever calls a Couple Conference, would you agree to it?

Rob:
Certainly.

Therapist:
At this moment, you both have committed yourselves to responding to the other's request for a Couple Conference. Whether you use it or not will be up to you. Here are further guidelines: The person who calls the conference speaks first, always leave a few hours between calling a conference and holding it, so the other can prepare, and set up the time and place exactly as we did here.

"I Feel...." This exercise is based on work in sexual communication developed by Beryl and Noam Chernick (1977). It addresses the emphasis in Adlerian marital communication training on separating affective statements from cognitive statements. Basically, feelings are the catalyst between thoughts and behavior and logically result from the thought content (McKay & Christensen, 1978). One can take responsibility for one's thoughts, evaluate them and revise them according to their appropriateness. Then the feelings will follow the thoughts. Thoughts, then, give rise to action.

When focusing on a discussion of feelings, the couple is taught to suspend all value judgments and to acknowledge that emotions cannot be right or wrong. Individuals own their own feelings, and although they may seem inappropriate to others, the feelings belong to the partner and are to be respected. The explicit purpose of the "I feel..." exercise is to provide a method for taking responsibility for these feelings. However, the implicit purposes are to be self-disclosing in an atmosphere that is nonthreatening to expresser and receiver, to provide ownership of a problem, to open communication, to allow the receiver to pay full attention to the content of the message, and to create warmth between partners (Hawes, R., 1984). Essentially, the purpose of an "I feel..." message is simply for one partner to tell the other how one really feels, and why, with the expectation that the other will truly hear the statement.

The "I feel..." interaction is best taught to a couple if it can be modeled by the therapist and a co-worker. However, with careful directions, it can also be modeled by one therapist and one of the partners.

The first step in teaching the "I feel..." technique is to give each partner a set of five pictures torn from a magazine, with the picture side face down. Years of clinical experience have proven that even the most perceptive couples have great difficulty learning to discuss their feelings if they begin with their own spontaneous emotions. Thus, the pictures provide security in revealing feelings while the exercise is being learned.

The "I feel..." technique has the following steps and, as a result, is highly structured. First, the partners decide who will be "A" and who will be "B." "B" holds the set of pictures face down, then lifts the top one so that "A" can see it but "B" cannot. "A" looks at the picture, then they carry out steps 1 through 5, following this structure exactly:

Step	Partner	Content of Message
1	A	"I feel: __(emotion)__:."
2	B	"Tell me about feeling: __(emotion)__:."
3	A	"I feel: __(emotion)__: because ... (several sentences)."
4	B	(Feeds back the information given in Step 3)
5	A	"Yes" (affirms, if feedback considered correct), or "No" (denies, if feedback not considered correct).

If "no" is given, the process starts again at Step 2 and continues until a "yes" is achieved. The partners alternate being "A" and "B," discussing each picture in the same way. A number of points about the structure must be taught to the partners. For example, Step 1 provides only for the statement "I feel..." and then a one word emotion. If either says, "I feel that," it is a clue that that partner has expressed a thought rather than a feeling. If agreement is made that both partners will use the exercise, the two words "I feel..." will later act as a signal that partner "A" is going to use the "I feel..." technique. In accepting this arguing technique, the partners agree that when one says, "I feel...," the other will stop whatever is happening, will listen carefully for the emotion that will follow, and will then proceed with the rest of the exercise. Couples are reminded that it may take from ten to thirty seconds for "A" to actually label the emotion once the "I feel..." message is given.

Step 2 is likewise very structured. The wording is purposefully specific and designed to create a sense of invitation and caring. It is an invitation that indicates "B" would like "A" to share a concern, as well as assures "A" that "B" is prepared to listen fully.

The content of "A's" statement about why one feels this way, and the feedback provided by "B" in steps 3 and 4 will vary with the couple. If "A's" statement is too long in Step 3, the memory of most "B" partners will be overloaded. Thus, the explanation in most cases should be short. Some partners have difficulty remembering several sentences if the content is involved or emotionally charged, whereas others can handle statements of much greater length.

Step 5 requires careful listening by "A," who has to concentrate on what "B" is feeding back to see whether the message has been heard correctly. "A" also has to display the courage to say "no" if there is a sense that the partner has not fed back correctly.

It is very common in the beginning stages of "I feel..." training for "A" to neither affirm nor deny the feedback and at the same time to feel uncomfortable and unheard. "A" will often state satisfaction when only part of the original message is fed back by "B." Careful therapist supervision is needed to show partners that accepting only part of the original message as the whole during feedback is in itself a block to good communication. Accepting incorrect feedback is reported to leave a sense of distance and incompleteness in the partners (Hawes, R., 1984). Repeatedly not receiving feedback or allowing incomplete feedback tends to discourage couples from using the technique.

Once the couple becomes competent in using the "I feel..." structure (and most have to be reassured that it is far more complicated than it appears), they are assigned homework of sharing five pictures each per day until the next session, and they are not to use the technique at any other time. At the following session they are asked to commit themselves to incorporating "I feel..." into their repertoire of communication skills as explained above. That means that whenever one hears the phrase "I feel...", there is a preparedness to stop whatever is going on and focus on following through with the structure. It is once again emphasized that feelings are not for evaluation or resolution.

Therefore, all that is being asked is for the partner to hear the other and demonstrate caring. Trying to solve a problem for the other when not asked to is demonstrating superiority, and thereby inequality, by assuming that the partner cannot solve one's own problems. The next assignment is for each partner to use at least three "I feel..." messages per day in the context of everyday living for one week. Continued monitoring from the therapist helps couples incorporate feeling statements as one of their communication skills.

"May I?" This skill, which was derived from W.L. and M.L. Pew (Personal Communication, May 1975), can be used independently, or for "B" to follow up on an "I feel..." message.

Rob:
The "I feel..." messages are really working for us, but sometimes I do have some answers that I think will help Joan.

Therapist:
Then ask for permission to give her an answer by using "May I?" Don't assume you can impose your suggestion on her. You might say, "May I tell you what I think about that?" or "May I give you a suggestion?" This gives her an opportunity to accept your input without feeling ineffectual or bankrupt of ideas.

An example of how this worked for me was when my husband was teaching me to play golf. I would look forward all week to spending Friday afternoon with him. Then by the time we were on the third tee, I would feel an incredible urge to wrap my driver around his neck. What we discovered was that every time I prepared to take a shot, he would freely offer advice. This did not allow me the opportunity to work out for myself the best strategy or form or to demonstrate to myself what I had learned. Once we agreed to follow the Pews' directive that he would ask, "May I make a suggestion?" I had a number of choices. I could ask for his advice because I wasn't feeling overloaded with it, I could say "yes" and learn needed improvements, or I could say "no" and later have the freedom to say "now please tell me."

No Questions. A two-line poem attributed to Lois Wyse stated:

"Marriages are killed by two things, Questions and answers."

This verse becomes the basis for a communication technique wherein couples make an agreement to suspend all questions for one week (Hawes, E.C., 1984). Instead of questions, all inquiries are made through statements about the self, such as "I'm wondering what happened that made you late." Although interaction without questions is almost impossible to maintain for this time period, Powers and Hahn (1977) stated that this exercise lessens the number of defensive responses, decreases hostile reactions, and makes each partner aware that the other is truly working at changing dysfunctional communication. It also has an added benefit of eliciting creativity and humor.

Written Communication. Many writers recommend that couples be taught to communicate through writing as an adjunct to other methods (L'Abate, 1977; and Hawes, 1982). The purpose of the written communication can be to explain a point of view, to bring up a delicate subject, or to express encouragement to a mate. It allows the writer time to clarify one's thoughts, freedom from the pressure of having to respond immediately, a longer time element between interchanges so that the sting is relieved from conflict, and it can inject a playful note into verbal exchanges.

Couples may have ongoing relationship journals in which one writes an observation and then leaves the journal in an obvious place for the other to respond when ready. One couple with a bookcase headboard on their bed agreed that the partner who had just written would leave the journal above the pillow of the other partner. The time interval between entries varied from a few minutes to two weeks. Another couple left the journal in one another's underclothing drawer after an entry. This is a particularly appropriate intervention to recommend when the couple's history reveals that letter writing was an integral part of their courtship or when both obviously have writing strengths.

Couples can also be encouraged to write notes to one another, both to stimulate closeness and to stop nagging. Once a note has been written, the partner knows the statement has been made and is encouraged to leave the topic alone. One couple who worked shifts would leave notes of endearment on each other's pillow. A humorous note on a steering wheel asking the other to fill up the gas tank acts as an effective reminder. When a partner discovers a note that states, "I look forward to seeing the movie with you tonight," it both confirms their arrangement and expresses a desire to be together.

Summary of Communication Skills

Few couples actually incorporate the complete structure of these exercises into their relationship in an ongoing, spontaneous manner. What they do learn is to integrate the spirit of the exercises, which leads to expressing their own feelings and point of view concretely and openly and to being receptive to the partner's problems and sharing. Mutual respect, the essence of improved communication, can be achieved once the competitive nature of verbal interchanges no longer has a place in the relationship and once appropriate skills are learned. Mutual respect occurs when each partner experiences the sense that together they have created an atmosphere where there are neither winners nor losers.

Part II: Building Problem-solving Skills

Conflict within a marital relationship results from the spouses' attempts to experience an egalitarian relationship without having the necessary skills and background to treat each other as equals. Adler (1931) recognized the dynamics of marital conflict and stressed that both partners must strive for equality as the only standard for the mutually respectful relationship that is a prerequisite for a successful marriage. Whenever one partner tries to become elevated above the other, the relationship is tenuous because the partner in the inferior position will always attempt to reverse the situation (Dinkmeyer, Pew & Dinkmeyer, 1979).

This can be demonstrated to a couple during the discussion of conflict as the therapist balances a pen on a finger to represent a see-saw. When one end is moved up, the other automatically moves down; so it is with marriage. The person in the superior position must work hard to stay there by keeping the other in an inferior position, and at the same time, the person in the lower position will seek to rise and "unseat" the higher person. Neither position is comfortable.

The therapist may demonstrate the fallacy that a relationship can be fulfilled when one person tries to control the other through another technique. The therapist asks the more controlling partner to extend a palm, with fingers outspread, over a waste basket. The therapist then fills the client's hand with foaming shaving cream, having paper towels on hand. As long as the person does not try to impose control, the individual can move that hand around with much freedom, and the shaving cream stays in place. Once the person attempts to control through tightening one's fingers, all of the cream is lost. An accompanying monologue pertaining to the specific problem under discussion effectively demonstrates to the couple how they are, in fact, losing control, which is just the opposite of what they want to achieve through their current method of conflict-solving.

Intramarital fighting, it must further be pointed out to the couple, not only does not lead to a solution of the problem, but it also lays the groundwork for the next conflict. Thus the couple is forever in a state of competition that is either active or latent. Dreikurs (1946) pointed out that human beings act cooperatively as long as fear does not frustrate their natural inclinations. "The desire to cooperate is curbed only by a feeling of inferiority which produces a compulsion toward self-defense" (p. 102). Dreikurs further stated that a misconception exists with regard to human cooperation:

> ...a belief that resentment can lead to improvement or that it is even a prerequisite for actions directed toward improvement.... The husband will gladly adjust himself to his wife's desires if he feels fully accepted by her. But he may drive in the opposite direction if he senses her resentment and rejection (pp. 103-104).

The challenge for the therapist in teaching conflict resolution skills is to demonstrate that neither partner has to lose, has to be on the lower end of the see-saw, or has to feel squeezed out.

The Adlerian marriage therapist deals with marital conflict by following Dreikurs' four principles of conflict resolution (1967):

1) showing mutual respect;
2) pinpointing the issue;
3) reaching a new agreement; and
4) participating in decision making.

Every marriage conflict involves a violation of one or more of these principles. By being aware of each principle, the therapist is provided with guidelines for beginning, developing and then concluding successful conflict-resolution techniques that are appropriate to the problem being solved.

Showing mutual respect may be achieved through using such communication skills as discussed earlier. If mutual respect does not exist, all conflictual interactions will be characterized by an underlying resentment. Thus the resolution of conflict must be preceded by understanding and respecting each other's point of view.

Pinpointing the issue addresses the fact that the presenting problem is rarely the real issue. Although the complaint may center on children, lack of time together or finances, the underlying problem will pertain to some threat to personal status, to who is in control, or to who is right and who is wrong. The partners are taught to pinpoint the issue so they can discriminate between arguing and problem-solving, focus on the solution rather than talk around the topic (which most often leads to exacerbating the issue), and ultimately resolve the conflict on their own.

When couples cannot resolve the conflict, it may be that they are focusing on the content rather than on the feelings and the process. Therefore, they must feel comfortable with owning and expressing feelings and following learned skills for conflict resolution. The relevant communication skills learned earlier combined with intervention processes addressed here will make couples less defensive and more able to draw on their new learning to use it to their mutual advantage.

The therapist's responsibility during pinpointing is to help the couple systematically move from the initial statement of a problem to a viable resolution. Therefore, the therapist helps each partner state the problem in clear, concrete terms, so their conceptions of the problem will not be disparate. Through the use of clarifying questions such as "Tell me when this last happened" and "Exactly what occurred then," abstractions and deflecting behaviors are avoided. Vagueness in stating the problem leads to intellectualizing and, consequently, circumventing the real issue. The couple must focus on one problem at a time. When more than one problem is attempted simultaneously, successful resolution of either is unlikely.

The resolution of conflict is based on the understanding that when the partners are fighting, there is an unverbalized agreement to fight. Therefore, if conflict is to be resolved, **reaching a new agreement** means that each partner is stating an agreement: "This I am willing to do." Such a resolution can be reevaluated at any time and some of the intervention techniques have a built-in renegotiation time.

Participating in decision-making may by choice and agreement be either active or passive. It includes both partners assuming responsibility for those decisions that affect the other. Although one partner may be the person who carries out a specific action, it is with the support of the other. The violation of this principle reflects a lack of respect for one's partner and leads to resentment. For example, in many relationships one partner is more socially oriented. Although the husband may arrange activities for them both, he does so with the full agreement of his wife.

Skills for Effective Problem-solving

As with communication skills training, the therapist will tailor each of the following problem-solving intervention techniques to build on strengths and skills the couple already possesses.

Couple Council. Couples who already possess negotiation skills but do not use them in their marital relationship may be stuck for some reason or another. In such a situation, the couple assumes that if they love each other enough, each partner will automatically respond helpfully to the other's needs, fears, aspirations and so forth, whether overtly expressed or not. For the couple who is functioning relatively well in spite of their problems, the emergence, development or recurrence of further interpersonal dysfunction may be partially prevented through a Couple Council.

The Couple Council is a weekly or biweekly meeting during which the partners discuss the business of their relationship. It does not supersede other discussions, but does relegate the most contentious issues, plus those that require judicious decision-making, to a set time and place. The Couple Council insures that important issues will not be dealt with in a nagging or haphazard fashion. Typical matters for discussion in a Couple Council (and only a few of the myriad possibilities are listed here) include: assigning responsibilities such as researching house insurance or the purchase of a new item; deciding on vacations, social plans or home renovations; expressing concerns about children, undone chores or in-laws; and planning short- and long-range financial arrangements. Other discussion time, then, can be used more for sharing.

Many couples keep a minute book of their Council. One couple who started their Councils before marriage kept their minutes as a record of their relationship; included were decisions on birth control, educational needs, place of residence and the compromises necessitated by the partners' two professions. In addition to keeping minutes, couples are encouraged to write items on an agenda as they come up during the week. By the time of the Council, the contentious aspects of the issue may have been dispelled, so it can be handled in a more forthright manner.

Contract of Expectations. This technique, when discussed early in the counseling process, provides insight into current dynamics plus information that can be used as a theme throughout future counseling sessions. Based on a compilation of work by Mosak (Personal Communication, 1974), Sager (1976), Dreikurs (1946, 1968), and others, a Contract of Expectations essentially refers to an assumption that when problems exist, one or both partners are not living up to nonverbal expectations they had about what each is going to give and to receive within the marriage. In fact, the couple is often unaware of their explicit expectations. Hence, they are unable to rework the contract because they do not realize one exists. Instead, there is an implicit sense that one partner is not doing something one is "supposed" to do to meet the expectations of the other. The therapist must help the couple become aware of and then revise the contract to bring it in line with what is reasonable. (A similar task may have been incorporated in the Lifestyle assessment, in which case this intervention will be redundant.)

The therapist may introduce the Contract of Expectations when, in discussing a current problem, it becomes evident that hidden agendas may be operating. For example, when Anne and Paul had been married for four years, they entered counseling to explore a growing irritation that was being expressed through back-biting. This was the second marriage for both, and they had four teenage daughters, two from each of their previous marriages. When they married, Paul left his business, which though successful he had never liked, to enter a less demanding, self-employment venture. Their overt agreement was that he would oversee the girls' activities and would take on the main responsibility for their home. This would leave Anne free to attend to her medical practice without feeling overwhelmed by the pressures of home and children.

Paul:
I feel that I come second in Anne's life. We spend less and less time together and her practice always takes precedence.

Anne:
I've realized lately that as I leave my office I just drag myself to the car and feel more and more reluctant to come home. I know when I walk in the door there is going to be uproar from the kids, dishes in the sink and cereal spilled on the counter. Sometimes I will drop by the hospital to check on a patient rather than face the hassles.

Paul is a responsible person who tries to live up to his commitments. They obviously care deeply about one another; Anne has previously expressed her intense love for Paul, which the therapist has no reason to doubt.

Therapist:
When people marry, they always have expectations about how their life is going to be fulfilled by the

other. Each partner anticipates that something one does not have, or doesn't want to have, will be fulfilled by the partner. Paul, when you and Anne decided to marry and become a step-family, what did you think your new relationship would provide for you?

Paul:
We talked about this so much. I had always resented having to work and making sure there was enough money to meet the financial demands, and I never had enough time to spend with the kids and feel assured that my parenting relationship was solid. Anne's work brings in enough money that I can arrange my time pretty much as I please.

Therapist:
It would seem that you expected security from the marriage, both financially and with respect to the bonding with your children.

Paul:
Yes, I guess I did.

Therapist:
Anne, what did you expect your marriage would provide for you?

Anne:
One of the things that became clear as we discussed it was that while Paul wanted less involvement with his work, I wanted more with mine. I had always felt like a yo-yo before. When I was at work I worried about the children, and when I was at home I worried about my patients. Since he was willing to take charge of the home, I expected time with the children would truly be together time. Yet he doesn't take charge of the home.

Therapist:
I wonder if you mean he doesn't take charge of the home the way you would if you were there all of the time.

Anne:
Well, that's true. My girls really love him a lot, and most of their needs are taken care of.

Therapist:
So one of the things you were going to get out of the relationship was freedom—freedom to carry on your professional life the way you wanted to.

Anne:
Absolutely! As much as I love my children dearly, I don't really enjoy the nitty gritty aspects of motherhood. And I can't stand any mess around the house.

Therapist:
Well, Anne, I wonder what you thought you were going to give to the relationship.

Anne:
That is pretty transparent. If I brought in enough money, Paul could take as much time off as he wanted.

There is a catch in all of this for Anne. Although she wants freedom, she wants it on her terms. She wants a clean kitchen, no fighting between the children, and the freedom to pursue her career without problems from home. The security she is willing to give is mostly financial, with very little emotional outlay. Further discussion revealed that she resented Paul wanting to spend some time with her during the day. The time she was willing to spend was when there was nothing else to do professionally, so that she also determined their time together. In addition, she expected Paul to be there when she wanted him.

Therapist:
What about you Paul? What did you expect to give in order to get your security?

Paul:
You make it sound like a series of trade-offs.

Therapist:
That is essentially what your expectations were, and you may feel more reassured to know that every marriage has similar dynamics. What gets in your way is that you were never fully cognizant of these expectations. All we are trying to do is bring them to awareness so you can modify them to be more realistic and so that there is no hidden agenda.

Paul:
Well, I really want Anne to get everything she wants out of her work, but I thought she would want to include me in more of her life.

Therapist:
What is so interesting about this is that you want to give her freedom.

Paul:
Of course.

Therapist:
And freedom is what she asks for. Anne, you are willing to give security, which is what Paul asks for? So your contract does fit, except for the hooks in it. What we have to do now is straighten out those hooks, work it out so that rather than get and give expectations on "my" terms, you are doing so on "our" terms.

Following such a discussion, the therapist could then focus on helping Anne find ways to meet more of Paul's emotional security needs and to accept his standards of housekeeping and child care. At the same time, Paul might wish to modify his methods so that Anne's desire for order is satisfied.

Once the Contract of Expectations has been clearly spelled out, the therapist must help the couple determine how they can collaborate so either they begin or continue to achieve their expectations, or to mitigate their contract. Deciding on mutually satisfactory conditions may require much discussion. Successful negotiation will depend on the degree of flexibility in each other's demands. Unsuccessful negotiation may mean that one or both partners are attempting to undermine the relationship, perhaps because they want out of it but do not want to be held responsible for the marital breakdown. When negotiations become bogged down, one intervention has the couple commit themselves to meet a new demand for only one week, at which time the decision will be reviewed with the therapist. In this way, neither feels trapped by a commitment that may seem indefinite. By moving one small step at a time, both may be more open to experimentation and risk taking.

Review of First Impressions of the Relationship. The first impressions that each partner had of the other will provide an understanding of current dynamics; what disturbs each partner now is inevitably what impressed and attracted each to the other at significant points early in the relationship. The basic convictions, expectations and intentions that guide the Lifestyle are not only self-consistent but also constant. When people who once loved each other no longer want to be together, the assumption of Adlerian Psychology is that the Lifestyles of the partners have not changed, but only that those qualities that were once seen as pluses have since come to be seen as minuses (Belove, 1980).

> The factors which lead to the choice of a partner are correlated with the conflicts which later result during a marriage.... Even when former virtues turn into faults, these faults serve to maintain the once established equilibrium. Thrift in finance is seen as miserliness; generosity as extravagance; assurance as lust for domination; orderliness as exaggerated meticulousness; fondness for home life as dull domesticity (Dreikurs, 1946, p. 83).

Any significant interaction between partners, painful or not, reflects an implicit agreement and a complementary of Lifestyles with respect to convictions, expectations and intentions. Once a couple recognizes this possibility, they may be able to accept the current dilemma with less trauma, which in turn provides greater impetus to working toward improvement in problem-solving.

Therapist:
Rob, remember the first time you set eyes on Joan. What did you notice?

Rob:
My friend and I were at a Sweet Adeline concert. Her group was performing and she had a lovely smile. In fact, she was the lively leader of her group. My friend knew her and arranged for me to meet her.

Therapist:
And the next time you saw her, what did you notice?

Rob:
I was standing in her apartment lobby and she literally bounced out of the elevator. She was so confident.

Therapist:
Anything else that appealed to you at that moment?

Rob:
As we walked to the car, she chattered away. We had arranged to go to a movie, but she was excited about a group at a local club. Before we knew it, she had us organized to go there. It was a particularly good group and we had a lot of fun.

Therapist:
What is your most frequent complaint about Joan these days?

Rob:
(Oh no!) Her demands and getting everyone organized and wanting to do things when I want to be quiet and alone.

A similar discussion ensues with Joan. Then each relates the value of these early impressions to their lives at that time, and how they expected that these aspects of Lifestyle would enhance the relationship and lead to pursuit of their respective goals. With their new information, the couple can reassess and determine if they are willing to review one another from their earlier perspectives, understand and minimize past injustices, and ultimately to see the first impressions as current assets.

Written Double Dialogue. Once the therapist feels confident that the couple will complete their homework, the following exercise, developed from a concept by Powers and Hahn (1977), might be assigned. Its purpose is to enable the therapist to follow through with problems that come up but cannot be resolved during the counseling session. While still in the counseling setting, couples will learn the logistics of this exercise quickly by just going through the motions, but not actually writing.

Partners sit back to back. Each has a piece of paper and writes a statement about a specific concern. When they have both finished briefly writing out the problem, they exchange the papers without talking and write a reply to the other's statement. Papers are again exchanged and a response written to the reply to the original statement. The exchanges continue to take place until each person has written five statements on each paper. Thus, each paper will have ten statements. It is very important that there be no talking throughout the exercise, and that the couple not stop until there are ten statements, even if the basic problem is resolved earlier. When they are finished, they face and touch each other, then tell each other something each appreciates in the other.

As with all homework, the therapist must follow up on the effectiveness of the exercise. One survey (Hawes, E.C., 1984) of 32 couples who completed the Written Double Dialogue revealed that all of them rated it as 4 or 5 on a scale of 1 (not helpful) to 5 (very helpful). Several people commented that they were amazed at the power of their written statements. By the third statement, the edge was gone from the problem and by the fifth statement, the problem was completely resolved. When resolution was not achieved, it was generally because the focus was on content at the expense of feelings.

The Double Thermometer. This powerful technique has been developed from an idea by K. and B. Kvols Riedler (Personal Communication, May, 1976). The purpose is to break a deadlock for couples who feel paralyzed by their conflict, yet who desire to resolve it.

The partners stand about twelve feet apart, facing one another, on an imaginary thermometer. A pen is put on the floor halfway between them. The person who feels the most discomfort or who owns the problem begins by expressing a personal view of the issue. Upon hearing the statement, the partner has to move a distance forward, to indicate a warming or positive response, or backward, to indicate a cooling or negative response. The distance moved indicates the degree of warmth or coolness. Then the partner verbally responds, and the other person has to make a move forward or backward, according to the warmth or coldness perceived in reaction to the statement, before verbally responding. Similarly, a further statement is made, the partner moves, and so on. The objective of the intervention is for the couple to discuss the conflict openly, to give honest nonverbal feedback, and at the same time, to generate warmth until they are standing face to face. Neither is allowed to step over the pen.

This exercise may take a lot of time, but it is worth the expenditure. It also must be monitored closely by the therapist, who coaches each partner openly. When much hostility exists, the therapist may find it helpful to invite a co-therapist of the opposite sex to coach one partner while coaching the other.

Number-one Priority. An understanding of their "Number-one Priority" can help partners accept each other's uniqueness and peculiarities. Armed with new knowledge, as their perceptions change, their insight into behavior can increase dramatically. These "priorities" are thoroughly presented in Chapter 5 by

Allred and Poduska. Although these authors discuss the use of priorities in a group setting, this information can be very effective when presented to the individual couple. In fact, providing the couple with general information about priorities and reassuring them that all of us have each of the four priorities to a greater or lesser extent can demystify much of the partner's behavior.

Priority Contracts. Of the many versions of contracts that exist, the two presented here are most likely to be used by the Adlerian marriage therapist.

Brief Contract: This contract is presented when the couple is in constant dispute about who is to take care of the various responsibilities in the relationship. Couples who will benefit from this the most are those whose Lifestyles indicate a desire to control and compete, who are currently resisting making changes, and yet who express a desire to resolve conflict. The purpose of the Brief Contract is to initiate cooperation and to establish a model the couple can use in the future.

The couple is assigned the homework to each write a list of all necessary duties or responsibilities that result in arguments. Then the items on the lists are to be prioritized. At the next session, with the therapist observing, the couple begins to mesh their lists. When any item is disputed, the therapist asks them to consider any communication skills previously learned that they can apply to resolve the conflict. Once it appears that the couple can continue without guidance from the therapist, they are to complete the meshing of lists at home, then go over each item together and decide who will be responsible for that duty. If neither wants to fulfill the responsibility, the couple may decide to leave it undone or to hire somebody for the job. Any item that is still in dispute by the following session is to be brought for discussion with the therapist. After observing this process over several years, one therapist noted that rarely did a couple not resolve the issues when the alternative was to pay somebody else to complete a job.

Extensive Contract: The therapist presents to the couple the principle that when two people have an ongoing commitment to each other, their relationship also constitutes a business. Most business partnerships that work well demand that each member fully understands all aspects of the business, even though only one member may take responsibility, have greater expertise or carry out the duty. If understandings are left to chance, there may be misunderstandings. One method of reassessing all aspects of the partnership is through a contract. The contract presented here, based on work by Chernick and Chernick (1977), is enthusiastically received by couples who want to go beyond settling problems to developing working tools for enhancing their relationship. Essentially, the contract is a mutual endeavor that aids couples in stating their needs and areas of conflict and in reaching possible resolution in order to restructure their union (Hight, 1977).

Each partner independently writes a list of the specific items regarding any aspect of the relationship, such as children, life insurance, in-laws, budgeting and church attendance, that one feels needs discussion. The partners then look at each other's lists and together merge them into one list in order of priority, as they did with the brief contract discussed above. There is no argument about whether or not to discuss an item. The fact that one person wants to include it means that it becomes an item. Each item is assigned a separate page in a notebook, which is divided into four columns labeled before, now, future and renegotiation date.

First the partners share their views of how they have dealt with the item in the past and actually write down that procedure in the before column. The purpose of this is to clarify any misunderstandings or expectations about past dealings with this area. Rob and Joan chose repainting the house exterior as a major issue. In the before column they wrote, "Six years ago, Rob took most good weekends to work on it—seemed to go on forever—resented time spent when he could have been golfing. Joan was frustrated by the constant mess." Next they discussed the now column to obtain agreement about the current standing and wrote, "We are doing nothing. Paint is beginning to flake. Rob chooses to ignore it. Joan silently fumes that the house is in disrepair." These two columns will not be written in again and at later dates will be used as benchmarks.

With encouragement from the therapist to use all of the communication and problem-solving skills they have learned so far, the couple tackles the future column. After much discussion, Joan and Rob wrote, "Decide to paint trim, work together and only on Saturday mornings in good weather. Set aside money each month over the next year and hire a house painter to do the rest one year from now." In this example the renegotiation date is obvious, and they wrote "One year from today" (stating the exact date). As this couple had previously established a Couple Council, they had simply inserted a calendar in their minute book and circled the future date. Future dates can range from one week to many years, depending on the issue. If contract worksheets are filed in order of renegotiation date, it becomes a simple matter to deal with items as they "come due."

Marital Group Counseling. (Contributed by Miriam L. Pew.) The importance of marital group counseling is related to the importance of the questions and tensions that many couples have regarding the marriage relationship today. In 1946 Dreikurs wrote "...we do not know how to resolve conflicts and clashes of interest in the spirit of mutual respect—a prerequisite for living in a democratic atmosphere. Our cultural inability to live with each other as equals which we have become in fact is most painfully felt in our closest relationship—marriage" (p. v.). What he said then is just as important today.

Marital group counseling has many of the advantages of group counseling, such as:

(a) discovering a belongingness within the group as an individual and as a couple;

(b) enhancing cooperation, both between the married pair and within the group, by interacting with group members in an atmosphere of equality; and

(c) enhancing self-respect and couple-respect, leading to a feeling of encouragement (Dreikurs, 1960; Konopka, 1963).

As in any successful group (Shepard, 1964) and in marital counseling itself, goals are clear and agreed upon. In marital group counseling the specific goal is to work on intimate relationships.

Many couples can benefit from group marriage counseling, especially:

(a) those who have worked together in marriage counseling and are ready for greater social interest since their own issues are no longer all-encompassing;

(b) those who have been in individual psychotherapy and are now ready to integrate new ideas together;

(c) those who are "stuck" in some way and want guidance for conflict resolution; and

(d) those who simply want to grow and change.

If distressed couples enter marital group counseling while in the throws of rather severe conflict, they may find a group experience unsatisfactory because their desire is really to work intensively and exclusively on their own marriage. After some of the marital crises have quieted, however, marital group counseling may be helpful to encourage ongoing growth.

Couples may represent a rather wide age range, which can be stimulating and helpful to all the members. For example, couples who have survived the turmoil of the beginning years of marriage can offer suggestions and encouragement to a young couple in the midst of early marital adjustments.

What happens in marital group counseling? A couple may be interviewed by the facilitators in the style of Alfred Adler, as in Adlerian Family Education Centers (Christensen 1983; Pew & Pew, 1972), with the group participating, empathizing, encouraging and perhaps offering homework assignments. Various communication and conflict resolution tools, as described earlier in the chapter, are taught and practiced both inside and outside of the group. General group discussions might include such subjects as sexuality, money, in-laws, discipline of the children, problems of step-families, spirituality and dual-career couples.

When a couple discusses an issue in a marital group session, they discover that other couples in the group share similar concerns. Feedback is given from a much broader perspective than each couple could have figured out by themselves. Through the weekly contact of group counseling, and with the interest that is shown by the facilitators and other group members, a couple is encouraged to move toward new ways of looking at their situation or new ways of resolving the conflicts.   In common day-to-day marital interaction, partners frequently deal with a problem by resolving the crisis but not the underlying issue. The common underlying issues in marital disagreements are questions that have been described earlier, such as: Who is in control? Who is right? Who wins or loses? Who makes the decisions? Who is smarter, or who thinks they are? Whose status and prestige is threatened? Work on changing the perception of these underlying issues is what begins to change the relationship between the partners.

For example, the partner who resents having to make decisions will struggle from a one-down position until it is perceived that both partners have regained equality. Such underlying issues will surface in various kinds of disagreements. The problem is then set aside until another version of the issue resurfaces to trouble the marital pair. With weekly group counseling sessions, couples are less likely to avoid the underlying issue because the group is constantly dealing with what goes on in the relationship. This consistent checking on a couple is both confrontive and supportive. It is confrontive because the issues are continually subject to discussion until there is full resolution, and it is supportive because group members are interested in and desire that the couple have a more harmonious relationship.

Group marital counseling promotes social interest and enhances cooperation. Cooperation is necessary for all of life's tasks, and the task of marriage is more difficult than any other life task (Dreikurs, 1946). Couples in a marital group become aware of their ability to cooperate or of their propensity to block cooperation. When this happens, they can learn tools within the group setting to create better cooperation between them. It is common for a couple to believe that they are cooperating to the best of their ability, while being oblivious to how one partner's communication or behavior diminishes or discounts the other. Members of a marital group are quick to point out these kinds of inequities.

John and Sue were interviewed as part of a marital group. Sue insisted that John help her wallpaper the entrance hall of their home. John was unwilling to succumb to her demand. When Sue was gently shown by the group that she was indeed demanding rather than requesting cooperation, she approached John in a new way and found him willing to compromise with her. Although it was not on the time scale that she had demanded, it was one that was satisfactory to both of them.

During the teaching segment of each session, the greatest emphasis is placed on communication. Most of the exercises described earlier can be adapted to the group setting. Further ideas include the "sharing" technique described by Mace and Mace (1982a, 1982b), wherein sharing of the day's activities is done in a monologue fashion. It is used as a daily maintenance communication method rather than for difficult problems. Couples are also encouraged to communicate to each other within the group, while the members and facilitators listen, watch and point out to them when they are being disrespectful or when the discussion is leading to a conflict.

Facilitators who have had experience in psychodrama can incorporate role-playing as a way to get at communication issues. This is a powerful method for teaching people the experience of being the other as they exchange roles with their partners. At times, role-playing has included playing out a protagonist's family constellation, which means that the person chooses someone to represent each member of the family. It creates a live sociogram of the partner's family of origin and provides an opportunity for the protagonist to experience the role of each of these important people in the family constellation.

Facilitation of the group is often handled by a husband/wife team or by male/female colleagues. The leaders have training and experience with both groups and a marital relationship and are seen by the group members as having personal and professional expertise (Shepard, 1964).

Because the institution of marriage is experiencing a great deal of pressure in these days of high divorce rates, it is important that people have an opportunity to discuss issues related to their marriages. There is still a rather strong taboo against people discussing their marriage relationship (Mace & Mace, 1982a). When couples get together in a marital counseling group, they discover that as well as having many common questions to discuss and share, they are not alone in their marital issues and experience some encouragement in being together.

Since old autocratic values are disappearing, couples lack the appropriate traditional rules and effective models for resolving conflicts, coping with everyday tasks and finding answers to their questions regarding their relationship. Married couples need the help of others who have a commitment for continuing their marriage relationship in spite of differences that are common to all. They may find support from sharing with other couples in a marital group setting.

Summary

Once couples have been provided with skills for problem-solving and have used them successfully, the critical issue becomes whether they will choose to use their new knowledge or not to use the skills that have worked under the guidance of the therapist. When both partners choose to fight, they are, in fact, deciding to maintain the hostility that has characterized the relationship. This may be a way of saying that they wish to end the relationship without either one taking the responsibility for such an overt statement. Then it is time to explore several possibilities: Individual therapy for each partner, a contract of honor for a brief separation in order to gain a fresh perspective (Hight, 1977), or temporarily suspending therapy in order to realize how much they have depended on the therapist to be the agent of change.

Couples who do choose to use their skills for problem-solving will grow closer together and become more inspired to implement their new knowledge. These are the couples whom the therapist will help to gradually take full responsibility for themselves. Sessions with these couples will be phased out, perhaps moving to an every-other-week schedule, then monthly, then bimonthly. Most couples welcome an opportunity to meet every six months, much as they do for regular preventative checkups with the dentist.

In summary, this chapter has attempted to provide interventions with couples that would be acceptable with a therapist employing an Adlerian perspective. The remaining chapters of relationship enhancement, sex therapy, divorce mediation and remarriage are more specialized interventions related to the changing role of the therapist working with couples in today's society.

Chapter 4 References

Adler, A. (1931, 1958). *What life should mean to you.* New York: Capricorn.

Andes, D.E. (1974). An evaluation of a couples' relationship building workshop: The use of video and small group feedback in teaching communication skills (Doctoral dissertation, University of Massachusetts). *Dissertation Abstracts International,* 35, 4637B. (University Microfilms No. 755984).

Belove, L. (1980). First encounters of the close kind (FECK): The use of the story of the first interaction as an early recollection of a marriage. *Journal of Individual Psychology,* 36(2), 191-208.

Chernick, B., & Chernick, N. (1977). *In touch.* Toronto: Macmillan.

Christensen, O.C. (1983). The rationale for family counseling. In O.C. Christensen and T.G. Schramski (Eds.), *Adlerian family counseling* (pp. 3-8). Minneapolis, MN: Educational Media Corporation.

Corsini, R.J. (1967). Let's invent a first-aid kit for marriage problems. *Consultant,* 40.

Dinkmeyer, D.C. & Muro, J.J. (1971). *Group counseling: Theory and practice.* Itasca, IL: F.E. Peacock.

Dinkmeyer, D.C. Pew, W.L., & Dinkmeyer, D.R. (1979). *Adlerian counseling and psychotherapy.* Monterey, CA: Brooks/Cole.

Dreikurs, R. (1946). *The challenge of marriage.* New York: Hawthorn Books.

Dreikurs, R. (1960). *Group psychotherapy and group approaches.* Chicago: Alfred Adler Institute.

Dreikurs, R. (1967). *Psychodynamics, psychotherapy, and counseling.* Chicago: Alfred Adler Institute.

Dreikurs, R. (1968). Determinants of changing attitudes of marital partners toward each other. In S. Rosenbaum and I. Alger (Eds.), *The marriage relationship: Psychoanalytic perspectives* (pp. 83-102). New York: Basic Books.

Hafner, R.J. (1986). *Marriage and mental illness.* New York: The Guilford Press.

Hawes, E.C. (1982). *Couples growing together: A leader's guide for couples study groups.* Wooster, OH: The Social Interest Press.

Hawes, E.C. (1983). Marriage counseling and enrichment. In O.C. Christensen & T.G. Schramski (Eds.) *Adlerian family counseling* (pp. 159-192). Minneapolis, MN: Educational Media Corporation.

Hawes, E.C. (1984). A validation study of a couples' enrichment program: "Couples growing together." Unpublished doctoral dissertation, University of Arizona, Tucson.

Hawes, R.G. (1984). Testing the effectiveness of a communications exercise in a marriage enrichment program. Unpublished master's thesis. University of Arizona, Tucson.

Hight, E. (1977). A contractual, working separation. Journal of Divorce, 1, 21-30.

Jacobson, N.S. (1977a). Problem solving and contingency contracting in the treatment of marital discord. Journal of Consulting and Clinical Psychology, 46, 442-452.

Jacobson, N.S. (1977b). Training couples to solve their marital problems: A behavioral approach to relationship discord. Part I: Problem solving skills. International Journal of Family Counseling, 5(1), 22-31.

Jacobson, N.S. (1977c). Training couples to solve their marital problems: A behavioral approach to relationship discord. Part 2: Intervention strategies. International Journal of Family Counseling, 5(2), 20-28.

Jacobson, N.S. & Margolin, G. (1979). Marital therapy: Strategies based on social learning and behavior exchange principles. New York: Brunner/Mazel.

Kern, R.M., Mathney, K.B., & Patterson, D. (1978). A case for Adlerian counseling. Chicago: Alfred Adler Institute.

Konopka, G. (1963). Social group work: A helping process. Englewood Cliffs, NJ: Prentice Hall.

L'Abate, L. (1977). Enrichment: Structured interventions with couples, families, and groups. Washington, DC: University Press of America.

Lederer, W., & Jackson, D.D. (1968). Mirages of marriage. New York: Norton.

Liberman, R.P., Wheeler, E.G., deVisser, L.A., Kuehnel, J., & Kuehnel, T. (1980). Handbook of marital therapy. New York: Plenum.

Mace, D.R., & Mace, V. (1982a). Close companions. New York: Continuum.

Mace, D.R., & Mace, V. (1982b). Love and anger in marriage. Grand Rapids, MI: Zondervan.

Margolin, G. & Jacobson, N.S. (1981). Assessment of marital dysfunction. In M. Hersen & A.S. Bellack (Eds.), Behavioral assessment. New York: Pergamon Press.

McKay, G.D., & Christensen, O.C. (1978). Helping adults change disjunctive emotional responses to children's misbehavior. *Journal of Individual Psychology,* 34, 70-84.

Paul, N., & Paul, B. (1975). *A marital puzzle.* New York: W.W. Norton.

Pew, W.L., Pew, M.L. (1972). Adlerian marriage counseling. *Journal of Individual Psychology,* 28, 192-202.

Powers, R.L., & Hahn, J.M. (1977). Creativity in problem-solving: The double dialogue technique. *The Individual Psychologist,* 14, 22-32.

Sager, C.J. (1976). *Marriage contracts and couple therapy.* New York: Brunner/Mazel.

Satir, V. (1964, revised 1967). *Conjoint family therapy.* Palo Alto: Science and Behavior Books.

Satir, V. (1972). *Peoplemaking.* Palo Alto: Science and Behavior Books.

Shepard, C.F. (1964). *Small groups: Some sociological perspectives.* San Francisco: Chandler.

Steinglass, P. (1978). The conceptualization of marriage from a systems theory perspective. In T. Paolino & B. McCrady (Eds.), *Marriage and marital therapy: Psychoanalytic behavioral, and systems perspectives.* New York: Brunner/Mazel.

Weiss, R.L. (1978). The conceptualization of marriage from a behavioral perspective. In T. Paolino and B. McCrady (Eds.), *Marriage and marital therapy: Psychoanalytic, behavioral and systems perspectives.* New York: Brunner/Mazel.

Chapter 5
Relationship Enhancement Programs
by
G. Hugh Allred and Bernard Paduska

Couples' efforts to build rich, rewarding relationships are challenged by many factors: poor training in cooperation, intimacy, love and effective communication in families of birth; high mobility rates that may sever them from their extended families and long-term friendships that could give them valuable support in times of stress; and their submergence in movies, television and radio programs, and magazines. All of these factors promote transitory, many-partner relationships devoid of real commitment, intimacy and stability. The high rate of divorce, which has stabilized only in recent years, attests to the need for concrete methods to help couples improve their relationships. Such methods must go beyond the programs currently provided by a limited number of counselors and therapists.

Recent approaches designed to strengthen couples' relationships include programs that emphasize enrichment and prevention of dysfunction. These programs can often be used in premarital, marital or other couple settings and as adjunct aids to counseling and therapy. This chapter explores some of the typical characteristics and objectives of these programs, as well as their underlying assumptions. Adlerian programs are reported along with their research findings when available. This is followed by descriptions of an Adlerian open-forum couple enhancement program, number one priorities, and a unique

Adlerian approach that couples and leaders can use to diagnose problems and to train couples to improve their relationships. The three approaches are presented because they are uniquely Adlerian and could be used with almost any Adlerian-oriented couple enrichment program. Finally, some of the other well known couple enrichment programs grounded in various theoretical approaches are described, and their research findings are discussed.

The term "couple enrichment" is commonly used to identify those programs designed to enhance couple relationships. This term is used interchangeably in this chapter with the terms "couple enhancement" or "relationship enhancement." These programs are not designed to treat couples with serious difficulties; rather, they are appropriate for fairly well functioning couples who desire to improve their relationships. In an extensive review of the literature, Hawes identified five common characteristics of couple enrichment programs:

- a focus on direct, clear expressions of feelings;

- an emphasis on personal responsibility for one's behavior in marriage;

- a differentiation of feeling from thoughts and actions;

- a receptiveness to research outcome on the effectiveness of the programs; and

- a group structure that provides for more than three couples. (Also see L'Abate, 1981.)

Hof and Miller (1981) identified some of the common objectives of couple enrichment programs: to promote awareness of the strengths and potential of growth of oneself, one's partner and the relationship; to encourage the disclosure of thoughts and feelings; to promote partners' empathy and intimacy; and to improve couples' abilities to communicate, solve problems and resolve conflict. (Also, see Gurman & Kniskern, 1977.)

Probably the most pervasive assumption underlying the couple enrichment approach is that didactic approaches are not sufficient by themselves to bring about change. The most widely used and successful approaches assume that vicarious and direct experimental exercises are essential for effective change to occur. Other assumptions are heavily influenced by the theoretical ground from which the programs are structured. Adlerian theory has produced several marriage enrichment programs.

Adlerian Enhancement Programs

Couples Handbook for Effective Communication (CHEC): is a couple enhancement program developed by Allred and Graff, 1979. One of the unique features of this approach is the codification of interaction based on the Adlerian concepts of vertical and horizontal relationship styles.

CHEC is designed for six weekly sessions lasting one and one-half hours or two hours each. The program has a mix of didactic and experiential exercises. The topics covered are:

Session 1: Pinpointing destructive communication;
Session 2: Pinpointing constructive communication;
Session 3: Making the most of CHEC;
Session 4: Sending safe messages;
Session 5: Sharpening your sensitivity; and
Session 6: Enriching your relationship.

No experimental studies with husband and wife dyads have been conducted for CHEC. However, in an experimental study conducted among female residents living together in a university dormitory (Graff, 1978), the experimental group showed significant improvement in effective interpersonal communication over the control group on four of five criterion measures.

Couples Growing Together (CGT): (Hawes, 1984) is a promising marriage enrichment program with an Adlerian orientation. Hawes developed the program in response to requests from Canadian couples enrolled in an Adlerian parent study group. As a result of their experiences, these couples generated a desire to achieve more cooperative and democratic styles of interaction, not only with their children, but with one another. In addition, these couples came to understand that the interaction between themselves served as the model for their children's interaction with one another. This new knowledge became a catalyst for them to want to improve their marriages. These responses encouraged Hawes to develop the CGT (Hawes, 1984).

CGT has a heavy experimental emphasis and is designed for eight weekly two-hour sessions:

Session 1: Orientation and family constellation;
Session 2: Feelings;
Session 3: Communication and wants;
Session 4: Written dialogue;
Session 5: Conflict resolution and couple contracts;

Session 6: Couple conferences;
Session 7: Freedoms; and
Session 8: Flags, belt line, coat of arms.

Hawes studied the effectiveness of the program and found that CGT can be used as an effective approach for improving couples' marital communication and satisfaction.

TIME: A new Adlerian marriage enrichment program called TIME, an anacronym for Training In Marriage Enrichment, has been developed by Don Dinkmeyer and Jon Carlson (1984). The TIME package includes a marriage handbook, *Time for a Better Marriage*, a *Leader's Guide*, five audio cassettes, ten Leader's Outline Cards, a certificate of participation, publicity aids and a carrying case. The authors named the marriage handbook as the core of the program. TIME is geared around ten discussion sessions that follow the chapter outline in the handbook. The chapter headings are:

1. A Good Marriage Begins with You;
2. Encouragement in the Marital Relationship;
3. Understanding Your Relationship;
4. Honesty and Openness: Being Congruent;
5. Communication: Basis for an Effective Relationship;
6. Communication Skills;
7. Choice in the Marital Relationship;
8. Conflict in Marriage;
9. Conflict Resolution: Applying Your Skill;
10. Self-help Procedures for Maintaining Your Marriage.

In addition, TIME includes the following items: My PLAN forms, Marital Self-evaluation forms, Dating Focus Card, Points to Remember, Marriage Maintenance Checklist, Marriage Skills Cards and Activity for the Week.

Adlerian Open-forum Couple Enhancement Programs

The open-forum approach, a technique in which volunteers agree to participate in counseling sessions before a participating audience, was first introduced by Alfred Adler in the 1920s at his child guidance clinic in Vienna. From the time Adler first began to demonstrate the open-forum approach, it has been seen by Adlerians primarily as an effective prevention and treatment method for addressing parent-child and teacher-student relationships. As a result, the open-forum technique has now become a relatively well known technique in family education clinics and academic programs in many parts of the world.

This approach is also used in some Adlerian marriage education centers (Pew & Pew, 1972). The purposes of these programs generally, are: 1) to communicate mental health principles to large audiences; 2) to act as resources for people wishing to improve their relationships; and 3) to provide a means of training therapists (Dinkmeyer, Sperry & Dinkmeyer, 1987).

Advantages of the Open-forum Approach for Couple Enrichment: After two years of experience, we have found the open-forum method for improving couple relationships to include the following inherent advantages:

- Therapists communicate the basic Adlerian principles for achieving effective marital relationships to large audiences of couples, using minimal therapist time.

- Adlerian principles presented during the lecture/discussion portion of the class can be modeled during the counseling portion of the class.

- Participants mutually identify with the problems of couples in focus, thereby realizing they are not "alone."

- Participants use each other for feedback and as resources for alternatives.

- Couples receive encouragement and support.

- Couples in the audience learn through vicarious experience.

- There is continuous quality control over the therapy through the use of video taping and the questions class members ask about such things as information missed by the therapist, alternate hypotheses and alternate assignments.

Course Design: Our marriage enhancement course is designed primarily for those who are married or engaged. Couples are encouraged to enroll together. The purpose of the course is to present ways to strengthen couple relationships in keeping with Dreikurs' (1968) position that couples must learn to live with each other as equals, treat each other with mutual respect and trust, solve problems on the basis of agreement rather than by winning or losing, and generate feelings of belonging.

During the first class, the basic premises and principles of the open-forum approach to couple enrichment are discussed. We then distribute a form that permits students to volunteer to be counseling participants—i.e., couples-in-focus. However, the students are instructed not to fill out the form until the end of the first meeting.

We also outline to the class the procedures used when counseling with couples in the open-forum. This summary appears to help them know what to expect and thus decreases any fear they might have. We inform the couples that we first ask individuals what they would like to accomplish by way of strengthening their premarital or marital relationship through participation in counseling. We then explain that we will help them identify these goals in very precise and concrete language so that we and they can more easily evaluate how much progress they are making toward achieving them.

In addition, we advise the couples that the information we acquire through recollection of early memories, description of the composition and interaction patterns of their family of origin, and major beliefs about themselves usually enables us to help them effectively focus on behaviors they can change to strengthen their relationships. Finally, we inform the class that those who do volunteer to become couples-in-focus will be asked to commit to work on changing specific behaviors during the interim between open-forum sessions. Typically, each couple has three weeks to work on these changes, while two other couples take their turns in focus. Each couple is in focus every three weeks—a total of four times during a semester.

Selecting Volunteers: The couples to be in focus are selected from those who have marked "Yes, I am interested in being a couple-in-focus" on the form handed out earlier. After a screening interview, three couples are chosen. The screening interview provides a variety of birth position and first priority combinations and differences in the length of the marriage and family size and helps us evaluate the severity and appropriateness of the couples' problems. Due to limitations of the classroom setting, we do not select severely disturbed individuals or couples with severely dysfunctional marital relationships. Similarly, we do not deal with problems of sexual dysfunction in the open-forum setting. We have no way to know how open-forum class members may respond to explicit sexual topics, and we feel that the extremely personal and emotional nature of sexual problems makes public discussion inappropriate.

Format: The class typically meets one evening a week during the semester for two and one-half hours. The first hour is devoted to the open-forum counseling session. About ten minutes of the counseling session are spent in reviewing assignments and the couples' evaluations of their relationship since the last time they were in focus. About thirty minutes are devoted to Adlerian marriage counseling techniques. During the final ten minutes, changes are prescribed, assignments given and the session summarized.

In the first session, with each of the couples in focus in the open-forum, we gather information. Much of the information gathering centers on the couple's families of origin: data such as family position, and events related to former generational history. The genogram technique has proven very useful in obtaining this information. In some cases, we ask couples to fill out and submit Adlerian Lifestyle questionnaires, which we assess before the couples come to their next session. The results of our assessments are then shared and reevaluated during the open-forum. Early recollections of childhood and of the courtship period have also proven quite useful.

Using the information gathered in each initial session and the couple's own evaluations of themselves and their relationships, we suggest possible Lifestyles and number-one priorities for each partner. (The use of priorities will be discussed in greater detail later in this chapter). We have found that the discovery of a "common thread" or persistent theme (Dreikurs, 1968) often reveals much about how the couples' Lifestyles tend to mesh.

For example, in one couple, the wife was an eldest and the husband a younger middle child. She remembered being a "little mother" when caring for her younger brothers and sisters. During the open-forum sessions, we learned it was she who had "finally" convinced her husband to return to college to get a degree. To help reduce the stress for her husband while he was in school, the wife had "volunteered" to take over all financial affairs—income, budgets and so forth. The common theme of control over others as a means to gain and maintain a sense of belonging and significance seemed to flow through most of the wife's interaction patterns. In contrast, the husband's familiarity with a woman's taking care of him appeared to go all the way back to his relationship with his older sisters.

In succeeding sessions, we try to do several things: maximize the strengths of Lifestyle themes and minimize weaknesses, develop more effective communication and problem-solving skills, encourage greater tolerance for individual differences within the relationship, and offer more effective ways to cope with the major tasks of life.

With regard to the development of more effective communication, we have found the vertical and level communication techniques in the Couples Communication Chart (CCC) (Allred, 1976) (see Table 1 and Table 2) to be effective in improving couples' communication skills. (The CCC is discussed in greater detail later in this chapter.) We use the CCC in conjunction with such techniques as teaching the couples how to paraphrase, how to provide feedback and how to listen effectively.

There is usually a short break after the counseling, followed by lecture, discussion and practice. We discuss with class members what they have learned from the couples in focus to help them improve their relationships with their own partners. We then present Adlerian and Dreikursian principles for enriching the relationships of all couples in the class. Finally the couples practice applying the principles. The lecture, discussion and practice portions of the class period include the following topics:

1) what each person brings to marriage;
2) dysfunctional vertical communication;
3) functional level communication;
4) sexual bonding;
5) conflict management;
6) loyalty challenges;
7) crisis management;
8) financial management;
9) nurturing and managing children; and
10) use of recreation and leisure time.

Rules of Audience Participation: The members of the audience are encouraged to be actively involved with the counseling by asking questions and offering ideas for consideration. However, they are advised that their involvement will be managed by the therapists. They are encouraged to be honest, sincere and supportive when they participate; they are discouraged from such things as laughing inappropriately and from dominating the session. The following rules are reviewed before each open forum session:

●   Members of the audience are to raise their hands and wait for acknowledgment by the therapist before they make statements or ask questions;

●   Statements and questions are to be directed to the couple-in-focus and are to be pertinent to the subject being discussed; and

- Audience questions and feedback are to originate from within the framework of and be given in a manner consistent with Adlerian theory.

On the basis of our experiences of the past few years, we conclude that the open-forum approach in marriage enhancement classes can be an effective and efficient educational, enrichment and treatment tool. It is not only a resource for couples who wish to strengthen their relationships and for those who wish to work to resolve their marital problems, but it also provides a means to train student therapists in the techniques of Adlerian couple counseling and enrichment. As a result, we remain committed to the continued use of the open-forum approach for enriching couples' relationships and to the Adlerian principles upon which it is founded.

Number One Priorities

Alfred Alder (1956) was one of the first personality theorists to recognize that individuals tend to organize their repertoire of personality characteristics around what he referred to as a Lifestyle. Adler saw these four major themes, or primary methods of interacting with others, as ruling, getting, avoiding or acting useful. Kefir (1981), expanding on this concept of primary interaction patterns, has developed what she refers to as "personality priorities," such as superiority, control, pleasing and comfort (avoiding). It has been our experience that the determination of the partner's primary method of interacting with others—i.e., the partner's "number-one priority"—is one of the more useful tools in conducting a couple enhancement program.

Validating studies of the priorities concept have been conducted by John Sutton (1976) and Langenfeld and Main (1983). In one analytical review of the concept, Donald Ward (1979) proposed that an individual's priority allows that person to retain the "who" of what one is.

Superiority: According to Kefir (1981) and Dewey (1978), the person whose first priority is *superiority* attempts to avoid anonymity and to gain a feeling of significance and belonging by trying to be better than others. From the standpoint of couple relationships, this priority may manifest itself through "mothering" or "fathering" one's partner, having to be right all of the time or overindulging in self-aggrandizing behavior. Such individuals often find themselves participating in an undeclared game of one-upmanship. "How do I measure up?" "Am I as good as other members of a particular league?" The answer frequently leads to competitive behavior designed either to raise oneself higher or to push one's partner lower.

Some superiority-oriented persons will attempt to raise themselves by assuming a martyr role toward other family members. A defense of "I did it all for you" is not unusual. Others seek to be superior by being a victim rather than a martyr. In such cases, one is often self-indulgent, causing the partner to go without. In some couple relationships, both partners have superiority as their first priority. The partner who seeks superiority through consumption typically satisfies all personal wants, while the partner who attempts to be superior by assuming the role of victim fails to satisfy any personal wants.

We have found that an effective means of dealing with superiority-oriented individuals is to increase their awareness of how their first priority (superiority) affects their consumer or social behavior. They can become aware of this by reviewing the motivations behind particular buying or social habits. Increased insight into the development of comparison groups in childhood, competition with siblings and the relation of these to the person's need to feel important or loved can be helpful.

Control: For those whose first priority is control, the avoidance of ridicule seems paramount, and the attainment of this goal appears to coincide with the three primary areas of control presented by Dewey (1978): control of self, control of others and control of situations.

From the point of view of couple interaction, control of self typically translates into not giving into one's emotions. With regard to self-control, giving into impulses is frowned upon, and those who indulge in such spontaneity are often perceived as weak and are frequently criticized. In the extreme, this type of control can result in a very miserly existence with regard to the amount of feelings or thoughts shared with the partner.

Whereas control of self often assumes rather passive interaction in relationships, control of others is much more active and seems to be a far more frequent orientation for those who have control as a first priority. Typically, control-oriented people believe that only if they are in charge of others and the others are obedient will they have any significance. Frequently this need will manifest itself when one partner controls all the finances; the real intent is to keep the other partner subservient. This type of manipulation is often accomplished through control of the checkbook, credit cards and allowances. Such control is frequently converted into a position of power.

Counseling for those whose first priority is control typically includes distributing the couple's responsibilities between both partners and having control issues become a topic of open discussion. Therapists and audiences must take special care to avoid humiliating or ridiculing the control-oriented person for past tendencies. In addition, controllers can be gradually led to develop a more cooperative, democratic perspective toward finances and relationships.

Pleasing: Partners who have chosen pleasing as their first priority wish to avoid rejection (Kefir, 1981) and choose to believe that one can earn or buy the love and acceptance of others. Such individuals often tend to buy gifts for their partners in an attempt to gain recognition and affection. Similarly, pleasers find it difficult to say no to the requests of partners. As a result, they often accrue heavy debts in their attempts to satisfy their partner's every wish.

As part of the couple enhancement program, it is recommended that therapists confront pleasers with the dilemma that they can never know whether it is their gifts or themselves that are being accepted or rejected. Partners often benefit from learning that only by risking the presentation of themselves without the compensating gifts or undue services can they ever know the true basis of their relationships. Similarly, therapists put forth the premise that whether a person is happy, sad, loving or rejecting is a personal choice and is not in the power of others to generate unless it is given to them.

Comfort: According to Dewey (1978), people who have chosen comfort as their number-one priority are often those who were pampered as children. As a result, they tend to be self-indulgent and to make little or no discrimination between needs and wants. Comfort-oriented people often have a history of impulsive behavior, whereby the very desire for something is sufficient reason for attempting to obtain it. The reason behind the impulsive behavior is closely associated with the characteristic of impatience and the stress generated by the frustration of not having what is desired.

The reduction of stress, it seems, is one of the primary goals of the comfort seeker. Kefir (1981) referred to comfort seekers as the avoiders and sees them as reactors who use delay to avoid finishing tasks, resolving problems and making decisions—all in order to avoid anything that suggests stress. Usually the comfort person sees stress as something to be reduced as pragmatically as possible and at any cost. Reducing stress may mean refinancing loans or declaring bankruptcy, changing jobs or quitting school, or separating or getting a divorce. In some cases, comfort-oriented people see divorce more as a means of escaping the stress of the relationship than as a way of solving current marital problems. For a few, the "easy way out" may mean merely walking out on the marriage and setting up a relationship with someone new.

Such individuals often carry this theme of seeking immediate relief from stress to the therapist as well and frequently expect the therapist to solve in a matter of days or weeks the marital problems they have taken years to generate. It is often helpful to point out that one of the most efficient ways to reduce stress is to act responsibly. Similarly, comfort types often resist structured or limiting corrective programs; therefore, the remedial programs developed usually cannot be too rigid. Approaches that center on how to increase positive interactions rather than overemphasizing how to reduce negative interactions appear to be most effective.

In summary, we have found that coping with priorities is a valuable strategy in our couple enhancement programs. We attempt to help couples: 1) identify their priorities; 2) discover how they mesh with their partners' priorities; 3) learn of their costs and benefits; and 4) help them maximize their benefits and diminish the costs of their priorities in their relationships with one another.

The CCC: An Expressway for Enriching Relationships

Relationships are bound to communication. There is no way to relate to others without communicating with them. In fact, it can be said that relationships equal communication (Watzlawick, Beavin & Jackson, 1967). There is no way for us not to communicate and not to influence. Even saying or doing nothing carries with it a message, sometimes a powerful message. Thus, those who wish to improve their relationships with those they love must work to improve their communication.

Allred (1976) has developed the Couple Communication Chart (a modification of the Allred Interaction Analysis, hereafter referred to as the CCC) to analyze family interaction styles, and he has applied it to a program for helping people achieve skills for effective communication, emphasizing the need to move from a vertical, competitive style of interaction toward one that is level and constructively cooperative. He suggested that all people are equal in their rights to progress and develop unhindered by the vertical behaviors of others. Level individuals do not push other people down and away or treat them as inferior because of name, sex, occupation, race, nationality or economic status. In functioning levelly, there develops mutual respect for one another and relationships become free from demeaning critical comments.

The CCC was designed and developed as an instrument to codify communication into an efficient and comprehensive system. Patterned after a model developed by Flanders (Amidon & Flanders, 1963), the CCC enables couples who wish to improve their communication, and thus their relationships, to identify the dynamics of their vocal exchanges in order to pinpoint areas for improvement, and to monitor the nature of their progress toward that end.

Twelve categories make up the vocal characteristics measured and outlined by the CCC; seven categories codify the level model of constructive personal relationships and five categories codify the vertical model of destructive vocal behavior.

As shown in Table 1, the seven categories for analyzing *level behavior* are: 1) Disclosing Thoughts, 2) Teaching, 3) Seeking to Understand Meanings, 4) Negotiating, 5) Committing, 6) Encouraging, and 7) Disclosing Feelings. These categories are characterized by expressions of warmth, sincerity, empathy and respect. According to Allred's theory, the degree a couple uses level communication in their interaction with one another determines how constructive their relationship will be.

Table 1

Couples Communication Chart (CCC)
G. Hugh Allred, Ed.D.

LEVEL COMMUNICATION (must be expressed with warmth, sincerity, empathy and respect)

DISCLOSING THOUGHTS

- revealing one's own ideas or opinions regarding oneself, the other person(s) or the relationship)

- revealing one's own ideas or opinions regarding other persons or relationships beyond that which is ongoing

- revealing one's own ideas or opinions regarding things, events or places

TEACHING

- structuring for teaching
- giving facts and referencing sources, e.g., books things, events, places or people
- providing guidance or direction based on authoritative sources (the above may be presented using unstructured or structured methods)

SEEKING TO UNDERSTAND

- paraphrasing another person's thoughts or feelings in the form of a question
- asking questions to understand or to clarify or asking for a response
- hypothesizing or guessing about meanings

NEGOTIATING

- discussing alternatives, exploring or discussing their advantages or disadvantages
- disagreeing in a courteous manner
- making requests
- negotiating trade-offs

COMMITTING

- agreeing
- committing oneself to act on a decision

ENCOURAGING

- identifying, recalling and/or predicting the other person's feelings, paraphrasing the other person's feelings in the form of a declaration, making empathic statements
- making encouraging statements, e.g. recognizing the other persons efforts or contributions
- paraphrasing the other person's thoughts in the form of a declaration

DISCLOSING FEELINGS

- revealing one's own positive or negative feelings concerning oneself, the other person(s), or the relationship (negative feelings are disclosed in a courteous manner)

- revealing one's own positive or negative feelings regarding other persons or relationships beyond that which is ongoing (negative feelings are expressed in a courteous manner)

- revealing positive or negative feelings concerning things, events or places (negative feelings are expressed in a courteous manner)

When persons are **Disclosing Thoughts**, they reveal their own ideas or opinions regarding themselves, others or a relationship; they are not trying to convince others that they are right. The same is true when expressing opinions regarding things, events or places. The conversation tends to be pleasant, each person sharing about equal talk time. Examples of effective phrases would be "It seems to me...," "My perception is...," or "I could be wrong, but I think...."

Teaching is the communication of information or facts based on sources other than oneself. The one speaking may reference such things as a book, a television show or a newspaper article. "Yesterday's paper had an article outlining the steps for effective budgeting" is one example. Teaching may be accomplished by sharing ideas, perceptions, attitudes or feelings of others with regard to things, events, places or other people. For example, a partner may say, "I saw an article in the *Wall Street Journal* today that recommended we sell our gold stocks and buy silver stocks." Teaching includes the expression of the opinions or judgments of others regarding things, events, places or people. These points of view may be expressed by statements such as, "Mr. Smith stated that to achieve a happy marriage, it is essential that couples prepare a budget and stick to it." It is important to keep in mind, however, that the intent of teaching is to impart knowledge and not to criticize ignorance. The purpose of teaching is to enable the listener to acquire new knowledge, understanding or skills.

Seeking to Understand involves expression of respect and empathy for the other persons's position. To ensure greater accuracy between the speaker and the listener, the listener may paraphrase the other person's feelings or thoughts in the form of a question, ask for a response concerning the accuracy of one's own perception, or merely ask additional questions for greater clarification. In addition to these efforts, the listener may propose some hypothesis or merely guess at the speaker's meaning. Examples of typical phrases: "Could it be that you feel...?" or "What do you mean?" Negotiating occurs when partners discuss alternatives, exploring the advantages and disadvantages of each. When there is a difference of opinion, they disagree in a courteous manner, suggesting trade-offs and making requests.

Negotiating involves a sense of fairness, equality and mutual respect for the rights of others. Examples of typical phrases: "How do you see the possibilities?" "It seems that the advantages are...," or "Will you... if I...?"

Committing is making a decision, expressing one's willingness to act on it, or agreeing to work hard toward an outcome. It can take the form of agreeing with a partner's request or dedicating oneself to a particular task or effort. Examples of typical phrases: "I agree to...," "Yes, I will do...," or "As I understand it, you...."

Encouraging occurs whenever a person recognizes the efforts and contributions being made by one's partner. Encouraging involves expressing an interest in what the partner is saying or doing and includes making empathic statements or paraphrasing the other's thoughts or feelings in the form of a declaration. There is a tendency to increase the warmth and friendliness in a relationship through interest, concern and support. Examples of typical phrases are: "Please go on," "I think you're doing great," or merely "Mm-mmm." An example of a statement: "Thanks for helping with the dishes tonight."

Disclosing Feelings often involves a greater sense of risk than some of the other categories; therefore, it often tends to reflect the amount of trust within a relationship. Disclosing feelings includes the respectful expressions of both positive and negative feelings concerning oneself, one's partner, the relationship, or the relationships between others. Feelings can also concern things, events or places; again they must be expressed in a respectful, courteous manner. Examples of typical phrases are: "When... happened I felt sad," "Sometimes I feel mad when...," "I felt happy to...," and "I'm afraid...."

The second style of interpersonal interaction Allred calls vertical behavior. Vertical behavior in relationships may be viewed as movements away or against one's partner and reflects the belief that to get ahead, a person must appear superior to other people, including one's partner. As a result, relationships often reflect a dog-eat-dog existence with others. In order to prove superiority, such a person may often move into the game of one-upmanship. In addition, there is a tendency to be very critical of oneself and one's partner as well as others. The individual who suffers from feelings of worthlessness tends to measure self-worth against what is perceived as the progress of others. Consequently, tension and anxiety often develop and may be reflected in psychosomatic illnesses.

As Table 2 shows, there are five categories in the Allred Interaction Analysis for measuring vertical (destructive) behavior: soliciting attention, bossing, punishing, distancing and surrendering.

Table 2

Vertical Communication

SOLICITING ATTENTION

- bragging, parading oneself, dropping names
- talking in a pompous, self-righteous manner
- interrupting, competing for focus, drawing attention to oneself at the expense of another person
- monopolizing the conversation, talking with little or no request for feedback
- seeking service or approval from others, seeking to please inappropriately
- using a weak syrupy tone of voice

BOSSING

- justifying oneself
- fighting to/for control, talking angrily
- pushing, pounding, ordering, cornering
- lecturing or preaching in a demanding overbearing manner
- patronizing, talking down to the other(s)
- making intrusive statements or questions
- whining, crying, complaining of being ill

PUNISHING

- blaming the other person(s)
- demeaning, belittling, or ridiculing the other person(s)
- finding fault
- using sarcasm

DISTANCING

- talking in a disinterested, aloof manner, intellectualizing, talking in a robot-like manner, ignoring the feelings of the other person(s)
- using humor that creates distance
- wandering, talking off the subject, talking evasively
- refusing to reveal one's convictions, desires and so forth.

SURRENDERING

- abandoning one's own wants, wishes or desires (giving in) as the other person(s) is behaving vertically
- showing evidence of feeling fearful—e.g., heavy breathing, change in pitch of voice, as other persons are acting vertically
- agreeing when other person is bossing or punishing
- agreeing with or providing service for one who is seeking attention
- agreeing after other person has persistently used distancing

Soliciting Attention is essentially an act of self-centeredness, such as bragging, name dropping, parading oneself or putting on airs. People who solicit attention generally lack a regard for the thoughts and feelings of their partners. They tend to interrupt their partners in conversation, to finish a sentence for them, and typically, to monopolize the conversation in order to draw attention to themselves at the expense of their partners. In addition, soliciting attention can take the form of excessive flattering or catering in the hope of getting approval or recognition from their partners and others. Examples of typical phrases are: "I'm so good I even amaze myself," "I was just talking with Mrs. Smith, you know, the mayor's wife" (name-dropping), "Look what I just did—isn't it great?"

Bossing is primarily built around attempts to gain control over others, such as when a person gives orders, lectures, preaches or talks angrily to one's partner. The person doing the bossing often attempts to justify one's own behavior and convictions, tending to talk down to the partner and make intrusive statements. However, it is important to note that not all bossing takes an overt, aggressive form; whining, crying (water power) and complaining of being ill can also be categorized as bossing. Examples of typical phrases are: "Do it my way or not at all," "I can't help it," "Can't we go home now?"

Punishing statements often result in hurt feelings and a loss of self-esteem in the partner who is punished. They occur most frequently as accusations, when one partner is blaming or finding fault with the other. However, punishing statements usually go beyond mere criticism to include attempts to humiliate the partner through ridicule, demeaning comments or to belittle through sarcasm or mockery. Examples of typical phrases would be: "How can you be so stupid?" "Can't you do any better than this?" "You're really a big disappointment."

Distancing is a form of vertical communication that is often used to avoid or reduce intimacy, such as when a partner refuses to reveal one's convictions, desires and so forth; talks in an aloof, uninterested manner; wanders off on irrelevant tangents; changes the subject inappropriately; talks evasively or intellectualizes. Such conversations often take on a mechanical or robot-like quality, showing little concern for the feelings of others. Sometimes certain types of humor are also used to maintain distance. Surrendering is generally interpreted as giving up, giving in or in some way abandoning one's own beliefs and desires in deference to those of one's partner.

Surrendering is often highly emotional and it is often used by those who wish to avoid responsibility within the relationship; it is largely motivated by fear or discouragement. Fear is often manifested through heavy breathing, change in the pitch of the voice or other nonverbal cues of acquiescence such as dropping the shoulders and looking at the floor. Examples of typical phrases are: "You're right. I never do anything right," "Whatever you say dear," or "Well you know what's best." Surrendering is often manifested by agreeing when one's partner has been bossing, punishing or distancing, or by providing services for one who has been seeking attention. Here is an example:

Wife:
No, sit back and be quiet. What could you know of such things.

Husband:
I guess you're right. I always manage to mess things up anyway.

Recording Observations: For homework, the CCC Tally Sheet (Table 3) can be used to tabulate the behaviors in each CCC0 category. Typically the Tally Sheet would be used while observing one's own behaviors in interaction with one's partner. Tallying may be done best by recording on cassette tapes conversations with one's partner and playing them back when convenient. It is recommended that the conversation be recorded on the Tally Sheets by sentences according to the descriptions given in the CCC (Tables 1 & 2), and (2) marking down about every ten seconds the type of conversation that is occurring at that particular time. This approach can provide a good sample of the behaviors.

Analyzing the CCC Tallies: Simply looking at the patterns on the CCC Tally Sheet can provide couples with some valuable information about the conversation: Which categories were used and how frequently they were used, which categories were not used, and whether vertical or level categories were favored.

Percent in Each Category: Those who desire more specific information can determine the percentage of phrases or sentences used by the partners in each category by dividing the sum of all tallies in all categories for one person into the sum of tallies for each of the categories (% = sc/T). (sc represents sum of tallies in a given category; T represents the total from all categories for a given participant).

Partner's Talk-time Score: Another calculation that provides valuable information is the Partner's Talk-time Score, determined by dividing the sum of the tallies attributed to one partner by the sum of those attributed to both partners. For example, to determine the husband's Talk-time Score on Table 3, HT/HT + WT or 30/30 + 31 = 49 percent.

Partner's Level Percent Score: A third easy calculation is each Partner's Level Percent Score. To calculate a given Partner's Level Percent Score, divide the sum of one's tallies in the Level categories by the sum of one's tallies in both the Vertical and Level categories; e.g., using the wife's tallies on Table 3, 27/31 = 87 percent. The higher the score, the fewer the vertical responses in relation to the level responses. The score of 87 percent, as shown on Table 3, means that 87 percent of the wife's responses were in the level categories and 13 percent were in the vertical categories.

The Interaction Level Percent Score: A fourth simple calculation is the level percent score of the combined interaction of both partners. This score is calculated by dividing the sums of both partner's tallies in the level categories by the sums of their tallies in both the vertical and level categories; e.g., using Table 3 again, 47/61 = 77 percent. Seventy-seven percent of all tallies given were in the level categories. This score is useful for ob-

Table 3
CCC Tally Sheet

Illustration

Date _____
Topic _____
Recorder _____

	Wife			Husband	
LEVEL					
Disclosing Thoughts	|||	S _03_ % _01_	||	S _02_ % _07_
Teaching		S _00_ % _00_		S _00_ % _00_
Seeking to Understand	Ж		S _06_ % _19_			S _01_ % _03_
Negotiating	Ж		S _06_ % _19_	Ж	S _05_ % _17_
Committing	||	S _02_ % _06_			S _01_ % _03_
Encouraging	||||	S _04_ % _13_	Ж		S _06_ % _20_
Disclosing feelings	Ж		S _06_ % _19_	Ж	S _05_ % _17_
Total L _27_ % L _87_			Total L _20_ % L _67_		
VERTICAL					
Seeking attention		S _00_ % _00_		S _00_ % _00_
Bossing	|||	S _03_ % _10_	Ж ||	S _07_ % _23_
Punishing			S _01_ % _03_	|||	S _03_ % _10_
Distancing		S _00_ % _00_		S _00_ % _00_
Surrendering		S _00_ % _00_		S _00_ % _00_
Total V _04_ % V _13_			Total V _10_ % V _33_		

Total Sums _31_   Total Sums _30_
Total Time % _51_   Talk Time % _49_

Total of all Level _47_
Total of all Vertical _14_
Total of all sums _61_
Interaction Level Percent Score _77_

taining some idea of the overall atmosphere or tone of the interaction. Generally, the higher this score the more constructive the interaction.

Research findings on a structured communication training program based on an earlier version of the CCC suggests that the CCC can be used to alter significantly communication in dyads (Graff, 1978). The same research indicates that the level ratio score of the CCC can be used with some confidence as a criterion measure of effective communication. In addition, Wimbish (1980) found some support for the factorial validity of an earlier version of the CCC. The CCC has been found to have a high degree of reliability for coding interaction when using trained coders (Graff, 1978).

In summary, grounded in Adlerian theory and practice, the CCC is a unique instrument that codifies relationships. It can be used in Adlerian couple enrichment programs to help couples identify where they are in their communication with one another, what they can do to improve it, and how they are progressing in meeting their goals. The CCC, therefore, provides couples with a cognitive map for understanding their relationship and a tool for measuring it.

To Learn the CCC: The following CCC format can be used by couples and their leaders (with various time frames) to improve relationships:

- Couples memorize the names of each category of the CCC. Couples show they have done this by writing the names from memory on a sheet of paper.

- Couples learn the definitions of each category. They demonstrate this knowledge by writing them out from memory on a sheet of paper. A general response for each is often sufficient.

- Couples memorize three to five phrases for each of the level phrases. They demonstrate they have acquired this knowledge by writing them down from memory on a sheet of paper.

- Couples mentally practice coding communication of couples' interaction on television or in public places using the CCC to classify phrases and sentences.

- Partners practice mentally coding their own communication in their relationships with their partners.

- Couples record their communication on cassette tapes when they discuss such topics as finances or disciplining children and then code the interaction using the CCC tally sheets. A tally can be given about every ten seconds to get a good sample of communication. For this exercise, it is best for couples to choose a topic that is not too emotional, because intense emotions may undermine the communication training efforts.

- Couples use the completed tally sheets from the above to identify what they need to do to improve their interactions.

- Couples practice and rehearse phrases from those level categories in which they need to communicate more in order to improve their relationships.

- Couples work to avoid talk in those vertical categories they discover they habitually use.

- Partners take responsibility to continue to work to improve their own behavior (not their partner's). To accomplish this, they select one category to work on each particular day of the week. For example, those who wish to improve their encouraging skills can commit themselves to giving their partners three encouraging comments every Monday. The other days of the week are used to practice other categories as needed.

Other Marriage Enrichment Programs

In this section, several non-Adlerian couple enrichment programs are briefly presented. Their objectives, format and research findings are discussed. Inherent to the discussion are sources identified for readers who wish to explore these programs in greater depth. All of these programs encompass the spirit, although not necessarily the theoretical perspective, of Adlerian thought.

The Association of Couples for Marriage Enrichment (ACME): Two of the prominent pioneers behind the marriage enrichment movement are David and Vera Mace. They also are the chief authors of ACME, the name given to their national organization for married couples as well as to their marriage enrichment group.

The objectives of ACME are to help couples enrich their marriages, to help unite couples in a supportive group of other couples in order to plan programs for marriage, and to improve the public image that in the final analysis marriage must be seen as a relationship (L'Abate, 1981).

ACME involves very little structure. It is a flexible program that is allowed to take its clues from the needs of the group. Couples share experiences, not opinions. Partners' experiences are communicated to the group through the couples' dialogue with one another. The group attempts to understand and interpret these experiences (Mace & Mace, 1975). Mace and Mace (1974) stated a preference for a weekend retreat over weekly meetings.

Considering the large numbers of couples that have been involved in ACME, the research efforts and results have been sparse. Apparently little has been done, and the research that has been completed shows mixed results (Swicegood, 1975; Gurman & Kniskern, 1977; Confer, 1980; Peters, 1981).

Conjugal Relationship Enhancement (CRE): CRU was developed by Guerney (1977) to assist couples in replacing their dysfunctional communications with those more functional. CREE is grounded in Carl Rogers' notions (1951) of unconditional acceptance and respect for feelings and the modeling and power concepts of social learning theory (L'Abate, 1981).

The objectives of CRE are to help couples express their thoughts and feelings clearly and accurately, to accept the expressions of their partners, to evaluate their own communication skills from moment to moment, and to work constructively to resolve their conflicts (Rappaport, 1976).

At least three couples are required for each group. Two trained co-leaders assist couples in the program. There is some variation in the format, depending on the preferences of the facilitator. One format (Ely, Guerney & Stover, 1973) consisted of about ten two-hour sessions, along with homework assignments. Rappaport (1976) reported another format of two four-hour and two eight-hour sessions over a period of two months. Another format suggested weekly sessions of unspecified length continuing from week to week in an open-ended fashion (Collins, 1976). L'Abate (1981) reported that CRE is usually twenty-four hours in length with various formats.

Research on CRE has been encouraging. Jessee (1978), Collins (1977), Rappaport (1976) and Ely, et al. (1973) found significance in their studies.

Couples Communication Program (CCP): L'Abate (1981) and Wampler (1982) identified the CCP as one of the most popular and well researched marriage enrichment programs available today. The CCP was originally developed in 1968 as a structured twelve-hour program to teach couples effective communication skills (Miller, Nunnally & Wackman, 1979; Miller, Miller, Wackman, Nunnally & Saline, 1981). The CCP is designed to teach couples communication skills using meaningful dialogues. The emphasis is on the couple, not on the individual or the interaction among nonpartners in the group. Skill practice within the group and structure to encourage transfer of learning beyond the group are provided (Nunnally, Miller & Wackman, 1975).

The objectives of the CCP are to help partners acquire skills for increasing awareness of self, others and interaction; to develop more effective and satisfying relationship patterns; to develop greater flexibility between partners for coping with change effectively; and to enhance the autonomous behaviors of the partners (Nunnally, et al., 1975).

The program is guided by the book *Alive and Aware* (Miller, Nunnally & Wackman, 1976) along with a companion workbook. The first session focuses on strengthening couples' awareness of speaking for self, making statements of sense, giving interpretive statements, speaking feelings, making intentional statements and giving action expressions. The second session emphasizes teaching couples how to exchange important communication accurately. In the third session, couples are taught how to analyze for ineffective and effective ways to communicate. The fourth session is devoted to rehearsing and practicing what has been previously learned.

In an extensive review of the CCP research, Wampler (1982) concluded that the CCP is "an effective program for teaching communication skills to couples." However, she found no significant results on some of the criterion measures, no consistent follow-up findings, and serious methodological problems with some of the best studies.

Marriage Encounter: According to Doherty and Walker (1982), Marriage Encounter is the largest marriage enrichment program in the world, with over 1,500,000 couples having participated in one of its weekend retreats. Marriage Encounter began among Catholic church members in the United States and has had strong support from Protestant and Jewish couples (Bosco,

1976). There are currently two rival organizations, the National Marriage Encounter and the Worldwide Marriage Encounter (Doherty & Walker, 1982). Both organizations feature weekend retreats.

The primary objective of Marriage Encounter is to teach couples unity, a concept that is proclaimed as "God's Plan" for marriage. Doherty, McCabe and Ryder (1978) criticized unity as a concept that needs further development. The focus, as identified by Doherty, et al., is to achieve an emotional high and a spirit of oneness.

The format is a weekend retreat, free from distractions, where 20 to 25 couples are taught by leaders (two or three experienced couples and one religious leader). The main concern is the disillusionment couples go through and the "dialogue" technique that is taught to counteract the disillusionment. Partners write down their feelings about certain topics and then exchange their notes. The focus is on feelings, not on solving problems. Couples are encouraged to explore their relationships in terms of individual weaknesses, strengths, hidden hurts, dreams, disappointments, joys and frustrations. The dialoging is primarily between husband and wife; little is shared with the group.

Marriage Encounter appears to be a controversial program. Studies by Millholland and Avery (1982), Taubman (1981), Costa (1981), Dempsey (1979) and Neuhaus (1976) produced positive results. Hawley (1980) found no significant results, while Huber (cited in Hof & Miller, 1981) obtained mixed results. Lester and Doherty (1983) found some negative results they felt were significant. The reader may wish to read Genovese (1975), Regula (1975) and Stedman (1982), who defended the program and Doherty et al. (1978) and deYoung (1979), who were highly critical.

Marital Enrichment Program (MEP): Adam and Gingras (1982) based the MEP on a synthesis model of psychoanalytic, systems and behavioral models. Adam and Gingras stated that marital difficulties occur when the relationship fails to meet the partners' needs and expectations (contracts).

The primary objectives of MEP are to help couples to become aware of their individual contracts, to communicate one's contract to one's partner and vice versa, to become aware of the interaction contract, and to negotiate the interactional contract to better meet the needs and expectations of each individual.

Typically, the MEP format involves eight two and one-half hour weekly sessions with four or five couples. The sessions include didactic presentations and explore experiences of individuals, couples and the group. Most sessions have homework assignments. The first four sessions emphasize awareness and communication skills; the last four focus on negotiation and problem-solving.

Since MEP is a relatively new program, little research appears to have been reported. Adam and Gingras (1982), in their research, found evidence that MEP is effective in improving marital communication and problem-solving skills. The followup study was impressive. Experimental couples maintained their mean gain scores at one year follow-up.

The Pairing Enrichment Program (PEP): PEP is grounded in an eclectic theoretical framework. The two major objects of the program are to encourage couples to develop open, authentic communication and to improve and maintain meaningful sexual intimacy (Travis & Travis, 1975b).

Two formats are suggested by PEP. The couples meet for five three-hour sessions over a weekend. Each three-hour session is followed by the couple meeting privately for three hours of intimate encounter in their rooms. They practice suggested exercises during this time. Following the weekend, the couples continue working at enriching their relationship through activities guided by a manual. In the second approach, couples meet for three weeks using a format of six three-hour sessions, and the intimate encounters are done in their own homes. In the group sessions each couple is separated from the other couples by a space large enough to afford them a degree of privacy. In three studies (Travis & Travis, 1975a; Travis & Travis, 1976a; Travis & Travis, 1976b), the authors found significant gain scores for their subjects. Each one of the studies has serious methodological weaknesses, including a lack of control groups in two, and no follow-up testing in two.

The Systems Marriage Enrichment Program: One of the surprising aspects of the marital enrichment movement is the paucity of programs based on systems theories. With the system theorists' concern for interaction and the family, one would expect they would be at the forefront in designing and producing marital enrichment programs. A review of the literature indicated that this has not been the case, with one exception.

Elliott and Saunders (1982) suggested that the critical unique-ness of their Systems Marriage Enrichment Program is the clarity of its concepts and the experience of group leaders in the systems thinking.

The objectives of the systems program include helping couples to understand the circular, reciprocal nature of their relation-ships, to gain a greater sensitivity to process, to identify strengths and weaknesses in their interaction, to enhance their communication and problem-solving skills, and to motivate their desire to change by increasing the emotional intensity of their interaction (Elliott & Saunders, 1982). The authors at-tempted to get their couples to achieve these objectives in a five-phase format.

No studies were found in the literature on the effectiveness of the Systems Marriage Enrichment Program. However, Elliott and Saunders expressed the wish that their program would generate methodologically sound comparative studies.

Unilateral Marriage Intervention Programme: This is a unique program designed to help marriages where for one reason or another only one partner can or will attend an enrichment pro-gram (Brock, 1978).

The major objective of the program is to improve the com-munication of both marital partners through maintaining pro-fessional contact with only one of the partners. Training one of the partners in communication skills and then training this partner to change the partner's skills is a major emphasis of the program.

The program is designed for ten weeks and is in two parts. For the first five weeks, groups of up to 20 people are trained in em-pathy, self-disclosure skills and feedback skills. The following five weeks are devoted to teaching participants how to change the communication of their absent partners (Joanning, Brock, Avery & Coufal 1980).

Two studies by Brock (1978, 1979) suggested that the unilateral approach to enriching marriages can be developed as a viable approach where only one of the married partners can or will at-tend a marriage enrichment program.

Summary

Adlerians will find little to fault in most couple enrichment programs, since they tend to emphasize those very things that Adlerians hold dear, including self-understanding, understanding of one's partner, interaction, encouragement, communication, problem-solving, personal responsibility and commitment.

Like systems theorists, Adlerians are in the somewhat embarrassing position of having the right theoretical ingredients for producing well designed and theoretically sound couple enrichment programs, but of only recently entering the field with CHEC, CGT and TIME. Adlerians can band together to produce many fine couple enrichment programs. The theoretical foundation is ready to be utilized and the need is increasingly great.

Chapter 5 References

Adam, D. & Gingras, M. (1982). Short-and long-term effects of a marital enrichment program upon couples functioning. *Journal of Sex and Marital Therapy*, 8, 97-101.

Adler, A. (1956). *The individual psychology of Alfred Adler*. H.L. and R.R. Ansbacher, (Eds.). New York: Basic Books.

Allred, G.H. (1976). *How to strengthen your marriage and family*. Provo, UT: Bringham Young University Press.

Allred, G.H. & Graff, T.T. (1979). *CHEC: Couples handbook for effective communication*. Provo, UT: Brigham Young University Publications.

Allred, G.H. & Graff, T.T. (1979). The AIA a mental map for communicators: A preliminary report. *Journal of Marriage and Family Therapy*, 5(4), 33-42.

Amidon, E.J. & Flanders, N.A. (1963). *The role of the teacher in the classroom: A manual for understanding and improving teachers' classroom behavior*. Minneapolis, MN: Paul S. Amidon and Associates.

Bosco, A. (1976). Marriage encounter: An ecumenical enrichment program. In H.A. Otto (Ed.), *Marriage and family enrichment: New perspectives and programs*. Nashville: Abingdon.

Brock, G.W. (1978). Unilateral marital intervention: Training spouses to train their partners in communication skills. Unpublished doctoral dissertation, Pennsylvania State University.

Brock, G.W. (1979). Training spouses as relationship change agents. Paper presented at the National Symposium on Building Family Strengths, University of Nebraska, Lincoln.

Collins, J.D. (1977). Experimental evaluation of a six-month conjugal therapy and relationship enhancement program. In B.G. Guerney Jr. (Ed.) *Relationship enhancement*. San Francisco: Jossey-Bass.

Confer, H.P. (1980). The effects of a marital enrichment program upon spousal perception of the dyadic relationship (Doctoral dissertation, Southwest Baptist Theological Seminary, 1979). *Dissertation Abstracts International*, 41, 2507A.

Costa, L.A. (1981). The effects of marriage encounter program on marital communication, dyadic adjustment, and the quality of the marital relationship (Doctoral dissertation, University of Colorado, 1981). *Dissertation Abstracts International*, 42, 1850A. (University Microfilms No. 8122276).

Dempsey, R.J. (1979). Marital adjustment, improved communication, and greater self-disclosure as the effects of a weekend Marriage Encounter. (Doctoral dissertation, United States International University, 1979). *Dissertation Abstracts International,* 40, 4258A. (University Microfilms No. 8000246).

Dewey, E. (1978). *Basic application of Adlerian psychology.* Coral Springs, FL: CMTI Press.

DeYoung, A.J. (1979). Marriage encounter: A critical examination. *Journal of Marital and Family Therapy,* 5, 27*34.

Dinkmeyer, D. & Carlson, J. (1984). *Training in marriage enrichment.* Circle Pines, MN: American Guidance Service.

Dinkmeyer, D.C., Sperry, L., & Dinkmeyer, D.C. Jr. (1987). *Adlerian counseling and psychotherapy.* Columbus, OH: Merrill.

Doherty, W.J., McCabe, P., & Ryder, R.G. (1978). Marriage encounter: A critical appraisal. *Journal of Marriage and Family Counseling,* 4, 99-107.

Doherty, W.J. & Walker, B.J. (1982). Marriage encounter casualties. *American Journal of Family Therapy,* 10, 15-25.

Dreikurs, R. (1968). Determinants of changing attitudes. In S. Rosenbaum and I. Alger (Eds.). *The marriage relationship.* New York: Basic Books.

Elliott, S.S. & Saunders, B.E. (1982). The systems marriage enrichment program: An alternative model based on systems theory. *Family Relations,* 31, 53-60.

Ely, A.L., Guerney, B.G. Jr., & Stover, L. (1973). Efficacy of the training phase of conjugal therapy. *Psychotherapy: Theory, Research and Practice,* 10, 201-207.

Genovese, R.J. (1975). Marriage encounter. *Small Group Behavior,* 6, 31-44.

Graff, T.T. (1978). A structured communication program: The effects on female dyads in residence halls. (Doctoral dissertation, Brigham Young University). *Dissertation Abstracts International,* 39, 774A. (University Microfilm No. 78-13807).

Guerney, B.G., Jr. (Ed.) (1977). *Relationship enhancement.* San Francisco: Jossey-Bass.

Gurman, A.S. & Kniskern, D.P. (1977). Enriching research on marital enrichment programs. *Journal of Marriage and Family Counseling,* 3, 3-11.

Gurman, A.S. & Kniskern, D.P. (1978). Research on marital and family therapy: Progress, perspective, and prospect. In S. Garfield & S. Bergin (Eds.), *Handbook of psychotherapy and behavior change, second edition.* New York: Wiley.

Hawes, E.C. (1984). *Couples growing together.* Wooster, OH: Social Interest Press.

Hawley, R.W. (1980). The Marriage Encounter experience and its effect on self-perception, mate perception, and marital adjustment (Doctoral dissertation, University of Nebraska, 1980). *Dissertation Abstracts International,* 40, 5791A. (University Microfilms No. 8010866).

Hof, L. & Miller, W.R. (1981). *Marriage enrichment: Philosophy, process, and program.* Bowie, MD: Prentice-Hall.

Jessee, R.E. (1978). A comparison of Gestalt Relationship Awareness Facilitation and Conjugal Relationship Enhancement programs (Doctoral dissertation, Pennsylvania State University, 1978). *Dissertation Abstracts International,* 39, 649B. (University Microfilms No. 7812055).

Joanning, H., Brock, G.W., Avery, A.W., & Coufal, J.D. (1980). The educational approach to social skills training in marriage and family intervention. Analysis of social skill. *Nato Conference Series 3: Human factors, Vol. 11,* 175-191. Singleton, W.T., Spurgeon, P., Stammers, R.G. (Eds.). New York: Plenum.

Kefir, N. (1981). Impasse/priority therapy. In R.J. Corsini (Ed.), *Handbook of innovative psychotherapies.* New York: Wiley.

L'Abate, L. (1981). Skill training programs of couples and families. In A.S. Gurman and D.P. Kniskern (Eds.), *Handbook of family therapy.* New York: Brunner/Mazel.

Langenfeld, S. & Main, F. (1983). Personality priorities: A factor analytic study. *Individual Psychology,* 39(1), 40-51.

Lester, M.R. & Doherty, W.J. (1983). Couples' long-term evaluations of their Marriage Encounter experience. *Journal of Marital Family Therapy,* 9, 183-188.

Mace, D.R. & Mace, V. (1974). *We can have better marriages if we really want them.* Nashville, TN: Abingdon.

Mace, D.R. & Mace, V. (1975). Marriage enrichment—Wave of the future? *The Family Coordinator,* 24, 131-135.

Milholland, T.A. & Avery, A.W. (1982). Effects of marriage encounter on self-disclosure, trust, and marital satisfaction. *Journal of Marital and Family Therapy,* 8, 87*89.

Miller, S., Nunnally, E.W., & Wackman, D.B. (1976). *Alive and aware: Improving communication in relationships.* Minneapolis: Interpersonal Communication Programs.

Miller, S., Nunnally, E.W., & Wackman, D.B. (1979). *Couples communication I: Talking together.* Minneapolis: Interpersonal Communication Programs.

Miller, S., Wackman, D.B., Nunnally, E.W. & Saline, C. (1981). *Straight talk.* New York: Rawson Wade.

Monthly Vital Statistics Report: United States.

Neuhaus, R.H. (1976). A study of the effects of a marriage encounter experience on the interpersonal interaction of married couples. (Doctoral Dissertation, Columbia University Teacher's College, 1976). *Dissertation Abstracts International,* 37, 6793A. (University Microfilms No. 77*6720).

Nunnally, E.W., Miller, S., & Wackman, D.B. (1975). The Minnesota couples communication program. *Small Group Behavior,* 6, 57-71.

Pendagast, E.G. & Sherman, C.O. (1980). A guide to the genogram. *The Family,* 5(1), 101-112.

Peters, M.L. (1981). Short-range and long-range effects of marriage enrichment as an adult learning project using a marriage workbook (Doctoral dissertation, Auburn University, 1981). *Dissertation Abstracts International,* 42, 2442A. (University Microfilms No. 8127311).

Pew, W.L. & Pew, M.L. (1972). Adlerian marriage counseling. *Journal of Individual Psychology,* 28, 192-202.

Rappaport, A.F. (1976). Conjugal relationship enhancement program. In D.H. Olson, (Ed). *Treating relationships.* Lake Mills, IA: Graphic.

Reeves, J. (1983). Financial counseling—from a behavioral perspective. Paper presented at the Conference of the International Association for Financial Counseling. Provo, UT.

Regula, R.R. (1975). Marriage encounter: What makes it work? *Family Coordinator,* 24, 153-159.

Rogers, C.R. (1951). *Client-centered therapy.* Boston: Houghton Mifflin.

Stedman, J.W. (1982). Marriage Encounter: An "insider's" consideration of recent critiques. *Family Relations,* 31, 123-129.

Sutton, J.M. (1976). A validity study of Kefir's priorities: A theory of maladaptive behavior and psychotherapy. Doctoral dissertation, University of Maine at Orno.

Swicegood, T.V. (1975). A marriage enrichment group for the newly married: A supplement to pre-marital pastoral counseling with description and analysis (Doctoral dissertation, Princeton Theological Seminary, 1975). *Dissertation Abstracts International*, 36, 4569A. (University Microfilms No. 76 1282).

Taubman, L.C. (1981). The effects of the technique of the dialogue, as taught in a Marriage Encounter weekend, upon self-disclosure, communication, satisfaction, and awareness (Doctoral dissertation, University of South Carolina, 1980). *Dissertation Abstracts International*, 42, 433B. (University Microfilms No. 8114357).

Travis, R.P. & Travis, P.Y. (1975a). Marital health and marriage enrichment. *Alabama Journal of Medical Sciences*, 12, 172*176.

Travis, R.P. & Travis, P.Y. (1975b). The pairing enrichment program: Actualizing the marriage. *The Family Coordinator*, 2, 161-165.

Travis, R.P., & Travis, P.Y. (1976a). Self actualization in marital enrichment. *Journal of Marriage and Family Counseling*, 2, 73-80.

Travis R.P. & Travis, P.Y. (1976b). A note on changes in the caring relationship following a marriage enrichment program and some preliminary findings. *Journal of Marriage and Family Counseling*, 2, 81-83.

Wampler, K.S. (1982). The effectiveness of the Minnesota couple communication program: A review of the research. *Journal of Marriage and Family Therapy*, 3, 345-355.

Ward, D. (1979). Implications of personality priority assessment for the counseling process. *Individual Psychologist*, 16(2), 12-16.

Watzlawick, P., Beavin, J.H., & Jackson, D.D. (1967). *Pragmatics of human communication*. New York: W.W. Norton.

Wimbish, D. (1980). An exploratory study of the factorial validity of Allred's interaction analysis with college women. Unpublished manuscript, Brigham Young University, Department of Family Sciences, Provo, UT. to monitor the nature of their progress toward that end.

Part III:
Special Issues in Marital Therapy

Chapter 6
Sex Therapy: An Adlerian Approach
by
Carol Davis Evans and Robert R. Evans

Walking into our offices today are individuals, couples and families with sexual questions that are explicit, implied or hidden, yet fundamental to their visible troubles. Many books describe likely therapeutic solutions to these questions from many theoretical perspectives, yet the power of the Adlerian approach to sex therapy is not well known. The major goal of this chapter is to elaborate and apply this power. We assume that the reader is already familiar with Adlerian theory; we have included a bibliography that covers the now-standard sex therapy in sufficient detail to employ. We present here the application of an Adlerian approach to problems of sex therapy, in the form of a working model and illustrations of its use.

Many people already familiar with sex therapy techniques would improve their practice by learning Adlerian principles, and adept Adlerians should be able to apply their theory to the challenges of sex therapy by learning sex therapy principles. We are suggesting a way to create these two bridges.

To accomplish this, we note Adler's stance and present basic Adlerian assumptions that bear, in particular, on sex therapy. While it is impossible in one chapter to provide a comprehensive discussion of the subject, we provide a flowchart mapping a therapeutic sequence that, with examples, supports our theme and builds a substantial foundation.

How does the Adlerian approach, not devoted to sexual issues per se, provide such a good foundation? One may peruse virtually any journal on human sexuality and find evidence of the debate over whether a particular "dysfunction" is "caused by" or "based upon" more physiologically or psychologically defined factors. Adlerians know that sexual functioning cannot be divided into parts existing separately and independently of the rest of human living.

Adler's Stance on Sexuality

First, Adler himself noted the importance of sex. "Adler considered it one of the three great life tasks every human being must meet, the others being work and social relations," the Ansbachers wrote in the preface to their classic compilation of Adler's work, *Cooperation Between the Sexes* (Adler, 1978, p. viii). He recognized sex to be not mere physical activity or drive-regulated behavior, but a foundation of the whole family and thus society. Whereas Freud's emphasis was more on biological functioning, for Adler sex was a very sophisticated social behavior. Shulman agreed, stating:

> The amount of cooperation required in sex is probably greater than that required in most other human relationships. Indeed, in my opinion, the ability of husband and wife to cooperate in bed is a mirror of their ability to cooperate in other aspects of their relationship (Shulman 1967/73, pp. 84-85).

But like behavior in those other aspects, sexual behavior, according to Adler, can be learned and unlearned. It is therefore amenable to therapy and to change.

Second, sex therapy needs to be an option simply because of popular demand. The layman knows that something like sex therapy exists, and is likely to assume that marriage counselors know something about it. Clients today are quite willing to identify marital problems as sexual; they have expectations that their own or (more often!) their spouse's sexual behavior can change; and they are willing or even anxious to discuss sexual issues with the therapist in the context of dealing with other marital issues.

A peculiar fact may increase these expectations even more. What statistical evidence exists suggests that couples report relative sexual happiness. Tavris and Sadd (1975) wrote in the much-cited Redbook report, a large—100,000 respondents—though not representative study, that only about one in twelve wives reports or is believed by her husband not ever to reach orgasm. More importantly, Tavris and Sadd reported that a third of the respondents reported their sexual happiness as very good and an additional third said it was good. *One might expect people to be more interested in bringing their satisfaction up to nationally advertised expectations levels, rather than identifying their problems as a serious "dysfunction" requiring explicit "sex therapy."*

Third, many Adlerians believe that once the Lifestyle is known, the patterns in the client's life are understood and can be applied perhaps even more effectively (than ordinarily used) to the sexual area—so sex therapy per se is not needed. While this is true some of the time, specific sexual therapy techniques not only are expected by clients but also give the therapist additional openings for effective intervention.

Fourth, Adlerian Psychology (as the first social psychology) considers human behavior in the context of society. Today, sexual behaviors range across a broad spectrum, evolved over the past century from a time of Victorian denial (where physicians could not view a patient's nude body) to the much-argued permissiveness of the "sexual revolution." Overlaid on this situation and contributing to its flux is the "information boom," studded and laced with sexual data, opinions, options, implications and instruction. Sex is broadcast, however, relentlessly by the mass media via books, newspapers, magazines, movies, radio and television, and it is treated academically, popularly, pornographically and every other way.

Four Illustrative Cases. What might be done, for example, for the following couples?

> **Case One.** Adam and Ann were referred by Adam's urologist for sex therapy to solve his "impotency." They had not had intercourse for nearly six months, and Adam asked if something could be done. Ben's NPT (nocturnal penile tumescence) tests showed adequate erectility, suggesting a diagnosis of impotence with psychogenic origins. Ann was in full agreement, having been aware of Adams's degree of arousal some early mornings, yet angry at his rejection of her and fearful of losing him.

> **Case Two.** Bill and Beth came in as a couple because we insisted that we see them as a couple. Beth had originally called and didn't want her husband to know she was seeking help for "low sex drive" and

for the pain associated with intercourse. She reluctantly agreed to invite him on the basis that we prefer working with both spouses, believing therapy is more effective that way.

Case Three. Charlotte and Charlie came in for a "pair of sexual problems." Embarrassed, she reported not having had orgasms for years, and Charlie called his rapid ejaculation "having a hair trigger." They had argued following a passionate but brief intercourse after a friend's wedding reception. Charlotte had neared orgasm as Charlie climaxed, and her years of resentment tearfully exploded into his years of embarrassment. While she had been getting it over with quickly and he had been accommodating, now he wanted to "learn control" and she wanted to "feel more like a queen than a tramp."

Case Four. Domingo and Dolores fought over Domingo's lack not only of erections but also of sexual interest. They wanted to start a family, and their family wanted them to start a family, but Domingo, driven in his career, was only midway through professional school. Dolores was angry and ready to separate and he was embarrassed and desperate.

How to proceed with these typical cases depends, of course, upon the therapist's theoretical and practical model. Outlining the basic assumptions that particularly apply Adlerian sex therapy will demonstrate the potency of an Adlerian approach.

Basic Assumptions

The following assumptions come from several sources: Adlerian Psychology, the authors' training and clinical practice, and the field of sex therapy. The assumptions are consistent with each other and imply a foundation of some sources and solutions for sexual difficulties.

1. Behavior is interactional.

Behavior is formed in a social setting—the family of origin. There is no "I" without a "we." There is no psychology without sociology. Dreikurs (1955) wrote: "Every action is interaction" (p. 70). Sexual behavior is a social phenomenon. For the sexual relationship to be good, many other aspects of the relationship must also be good. A complicated set of social skills is necessary for good social functioning: How to cooperate, to listen, to talk, to ask, to notice, to savor and appreciate, to care, to focus, to empathize, to help, to lead and to follow, to overlook, to remember, to forget, to commit, to observe, to attend to, to be vulnerable, to represent oneself, and especially, to risk. Some implications of this position for sex therapy are as follows:

(a) Both people are seen together. Therapy is balanced so that neither partner can be blamed for the problem. One of Masters' and Johnson's most frequently cited observations is, "In a sexual problem, there is no such thing as an uninvolved partner" (1982, p. 383; 1976 notes; paraphase of 1970, p. 9-12).

(b) If only one partner is available for therapy, the work must be done in context and must be interaction-based.

(c) Each person is seen as maintaining the problem in some way, and will therefore need to be included in the process of change. There are no "good guys and bad guys."

2. Reality is unique to each individual.

The individual's subjective, phenomenological view of the world is the key to that individual's view of sexuality and thus one's own sexual functioning. A woman who has never had an orgasm because she places top priority on "pleasing" and is therefore less likely to stand her ground, ask for what she wants, and attend to her own body pleasure, requires a different kind of therapy than a woman who has never experienced an orgasm because she is uncomfortable being out of control and vulnerable.

In this chapter, we assume that the therapist knows how each client's private view of the world affects sexual individuals' phenomenological reality to stimulate better acceptance and therefore therapeutic effectiveness.

3. Behavior is internally and externally holistic.

Sex therapy draws from many fields: biology (physiology, medicine, endocrinology, pharmacology), psychology, sociology, anthropology, health and so on. Just as the presenting (and hidden) problems may be defined in these different vocabularies, so is the research and clinical work carried out and published in disparate settings. We assume the therapist is always alert to new opportunities to learn, find and integrate theory and data from these allied disciplines, which overlap more than is commonly assumed. The concept of holism unites this apparent diversity.

In this chapter we will treat sexuality in the form of a holistic model then, assuming that thoughts, feelings, chemistry, behavior, social interaction and so forth all function together, indivisibly. We will use the principle that sexual functioning cannot be separated from the rest of human functioning to delineate a particular therapeutic process and steps toward its accomplishment.

4. Human behavior is purposeful and follows a pattern.

To achieve significance within the family setting, the individual develops those traits considered by that individual to be the most useful. To that extent, given behaviors have no intrinsic value or measure, but must be interpreted according to their function; this is a "psychology of *use*." The person organizes cognitions, beliefs, feelings and behaviors into a pattern governed by rules derived by that person, and thus unique to that individual—the Lifestyle (See Chapter 3).

5. Every couple develops its own interactive style.

This development could be called "the couple Lifestyle," which is more than the sum of the two partners' separate Lifestyles; it is their dynamic *product*. This product depends, as Dreikurs put it, "on the interaction of their particular goals and purposes. Each somehow senses what he or she can expect from the other, and their agreement implies a certain acknowledgement of cooperation in pursuit of each one's goal" (Dreikurs 1955/1960, p. 72). Further, Adlerian theory holds that even though persons are not cognitively aware of their personal goals, they yet make demands and behave consistently with them and face other people's reactions to them.

6. Each therapy plan is unique.

Because of the above assumptions, the procedures for change suggested in this model will take into consideration and will vary according to: (a) the level of difficulty of the problem observed and interpreted (rather than the problem as presented), and (b) the uniqueness of the couple's and individuals' patterns.

Flow of the Model

The manner in which any therapy progresses can be modelled as a sequence of events from the time of first client-therapist contact through the termination of therapy. The approach proposed here is particularly fitting for Adlerians to use in conducting sex therapy, even at an elementary level. Referral to other specialists or redirecting one's focus of therapeutic content is feasible at any point. Phases of this process are, at the assessment level, intake, initial interview and then deciding what should be done first: medical treatment, marital therapy or family therapy, individual therapy or sex therapy. This last option, or direct therapy for the sexual problem using an Adlerian approach, will proceed through simple therapy, psychosexual and Lifestyle assessment and specific sex therapy. With the decisions linking these phases, we propose the flowchart in Figure 1. Let us first discuss the process and then elaborate the principles of the flowchart.

Because this chapter only addresses sex therapy, and sexual issues may be the presenting issue by clients or by referral, the main flow pursues the linked objectives of solving the sexual problems identified by clients and the interactive issues defined by the therapist(s). Since sexual issues also may emerge in the midst of counseling or therapy for other concerns, that point will be assumed for present purposes to be the entry point, at which the clients either are referred to us or arrive on their own volition. When clients raise a sexual issue they wish to resolve during ongoing therapy, the same model may be seen to fit with obvious adaptations.

Referral and Intake

When physicians are the referral source, clients have usually been examined for organic sexual dysfunction. To assume that all possible organic factors have been covered, however, may be erroneous. The therapist should directly ask, for example, how often and to what degree nocturnal erections are experienced by the man coming for "impotence," or what cultures has the gynecologist run for the woman complaining of painful intercourse. When these issues are presented by clients without prior medical workup, referral should be made to an appropriate physician, presumably one with whom the therapist is able to discuss the case. Clients can, following medical treatment, return for sex therapy if they still want it. This is the ethical and practical sequence, regardless. Furthermore, when referral is from another therapist, the same early assessment routine should be followed.

Intake forms vary widely, but usually require certain minimal data for clerical use. Carefully designing a form for the clients to write out typical family constellation data, role of prior therapy, educational and occupational situation, health status and reasons for seeking therapy provide more than just the beginnings of assessment. They focus nervous, angry, embarrassed or anxious people on data, thus calming them and providing safe areas for beginning the inquiries of the initial interview.

Initial Interview

The four primary goals of the initial interview are:

- To establish rapport indirectly
- To gather data for developing therapeutic hypotheses
- To intervene minimally and powerfully near the end of the session and
- To assign therapeutic homework.

Specifically, these goals may be approached by accomplishing or at least beginning six distinct tasks during this first session.

- **Create rapport while obtaining background information.** In marital and sexual therapy, the task of establishing trust and confidence is much more difficult than in individual therapy. The partners are often at war and polarized on how they see the problem; each one is hoping to gain the therapist as an ally. The success of therapy may well depend on the therapist's ability to establish a balance or neutrality that helps both partners feel they can be represented and understood.

- **Obtain a brief description of the problem from each person.** Implicitly there are separate perceptions, and each is validated.

- **Ask each spouse to list other major complaints.** Thus, all pertinent problems can be stated and put on record, then put aside pending later consideration at the therapist's discretion.

- **Obtain a brief history of the marriage.** Include information on who is living in the household, the courtship, cohabitation, reasons for marrying, pregnancies, miscarriages, abortions, children and their domicile, duration of marriage, previous marriages and their terminations (and nature of deciding on all of these).

- **Ask both partners some things they like most about the other, their selves and the relationship.** Partners' likes are indicators of the strengths of the relationship and of the respective individuals. This information is useful later for planning strategies and interventions.

- **Ask both partners what they want to achieve in therapy.** Since this leads directly to the therapeutic contract, specifics and accuracy are important. Demonstrable behavioral objectives are imperative; fuzzy abstractions typically lead to disagreement. (Occasionally, the difficulty one partner has with specifying what one wants evokes a realization of why the other cannot deliver it.)

Other things being equal, the model assumes that the therapist will respect the clients' request; if they come in asking for sex counseling, that is the place to start. With their attention and energy focused on sexual issues, the couple will probably be more motivated to move there. However, when conflict, resentment and bitterness in a relationship are so intense that one or both partners are unable to become aroused or are unable to cooperate in the sexually therapeutic homework, then marriage counseling must be done before the couple can work effectively on their sexual problems. Segal (1983) synopsized this difficulty with simplicity: "Doctor, make him an erection while I tell him what an ass he is."

Style of questions. The beginning session sets the stage for therapy. Even more than in other issues of couple counseling, it is important in sex therapy to balance attention paid the two persons. Spending equal time supporting each person and asking for their separate views on each issue identified demonstrates and helps establish the neutrality that assures both partners they will each be represented and understood. (In the first interview, confrontation is typically ill-advised but should also be balanced whenever used.) In discussing how one creates a comfortable climate with clients on what they often react to as delicate matters, at least with outsiders, Pomeroy (1976), learned many methods as part of the Kinsey team, has made these suggestions:

- Communicate a liking for the client; don't be neutral;
- help the client "save face";
- give reassurance continuously;
- do as little writing (note taking) as possible, or none at all, compiling notes after the interview;
- begin with questions about factual, nonsensitive subjects;
- avoid questions that can be answered with a "yes" or "no." We reiterate the advice to balance: Ask each client the same questions.

Content of questions. Certain styles of questions elicit the interactional nature of the difficulty, an aspect that very few couples can notice in the emotional midst of arguing, defending and feeling bad. The following general questions can illuminate the dynamics of the presenting problem. Although the therapist obviously requires this information, the very process of collecting it often proves illuminating for the client(s) as well.

- What is the problem as perceived by each partner?
- What is the history of the problem as perceived by each partner? Explore:
  —its development
  —its duration
  —how it has been intermittent, acute, chronic
- Why are they coming for therapy *now?*
- What have been the concurrent events?
  —births, deaths, affairs, illness, debts, accidents...
  —other crisis, in the minds of the clients
  —sudden or gradual shifts from original expectations for the relationship?
- What has each client done about it?
  —what helped
  —what didn't make any difference
  —what hindered
- What does each client think "caused" the problem?
- How did each client respond to what the other did to solve the problem?
- What does each partner expect of therapy?
- How would your life be different if you did not have this problem?

Routing to therapy tracks. During this first interview everything done should lead to the first hypotheses of therapy, and the strategy depicted in the flow chart (See Figure 1). The first hypothesis answers the implicitly multiple-choice question at this point on the flowchart: "Is sex therapy appropriate?" The answer would be affirmative if there are no apparent medical or other organically questionable conditions present, and if the clients demonstrate: (1) Their ability and willingness to do sexual homework (2) reasonable skills in problem-solving and (3) a stable life situation, free from crises such as illness, grief, dramatic career changes or family conflict.

Figure 1
Flowchart of Therapy Foci and Decisions

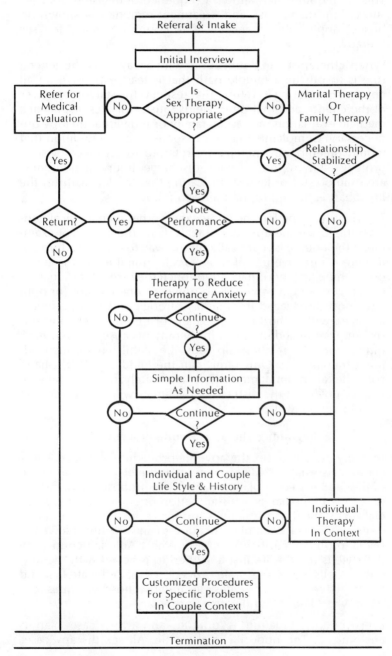

This simple flowchart shows a sequence of decision points—shown in diamonds—and treatment emphases—shown in boxes—applicable to most client couples coming for sex therapy.

When a therapist is in doubt about which way to go, the general rule is to pursue a middle path that is least expensive on all counts considering its return, that respects the stated objectives of the clients, and that often yields satisfactory results, making medical evaluation or marital, family or individual therapy unnecessary. Complaints that imply some organic condition that would preempt sex therapy are referred to a gynecologist or urologist: Any reports of pain, discharge, injury or numbness are examples of or factors indicating that the left path on the flowchart is the appropriate one to follow.

The right-hand path is the choice if for other than medical considerations, sex therapy cannot feasibly be the focus. For example, if the couple is practically on the way to divorce attorneys; if there is intrusive use of drugs or alcohol; if a child is acting out, compelling inordinate attention; if they are "stuck" in a cycle of who is right or who is in power; if one has not (or both have not) disengaged from family of origin; if either partner is involved with a third party, sexually or not; if either spouse is severely depressed; if one is in therapy because of the other's ultimatum—the relationship must be stabilized through adjunct therapy first. Only rarely can the middle and right-hand paths be taken simultaneously, or alternately, because the subversive power of the distracting dynamics will be greater than the unifying power of sexual risk.

Beginning Therapy: Simple Procedures

In many models of sex therapy, the procedure is to give a very elaborate sexual and life assessment at the beginning, and then to proceed with case planning. The style proposed here instead proceeds immediately with an action-oriented therapy, since elaborate initial assessment is expensive for the client and is often unnecessary. Simple procedures can sometimes solve the sexual problem. Further, whereas in most Adlerian counseling the style is to educate first and then to proceed with therapy, our model starts with simple procedures that educate first and then proceed with the Lifestyle and psychosexual questionnaire when and if that becomes necessary.

Every couple situation is unique, and every case plan is customized. The opposite is also true: All sex therapy cases have certain things in common and a few simple procedures will be useful with most cases. At the beginning of therapy, therefore, one basic determination is required: Is the couple stuck in a worry cycle (performance anxiety), are they in need of information, or both?

Performance Anxiety

Generally, if a couple defines the most intimate aspect of their lives together as unsatisfactory enough to seek help, their motivation includes anxiety. Combined with this anxiety is a typical pressure to perform—i.e., to have an erection, to control ejaculation, to stimulate the other pleasurably, to have an unmistakable orgasm, to participate with passion and spontaneity. Such pressures create an atmosphere in which the Performance Anxiety Cycle is set in motion: The cycle is usually imperceptible until well established. The paradox of the problem, as Satir (1975) was fond of saying, is that the problem itself is not the problem—the *solutions* are.

The Performance Anxiety Cycle may have no clear beginning. A simple incident such as consuming excessive alcohol, for example, or having a heavy cold may lead to loss of erection. Telling himself, or being then told by his spouse that he is a "failure" or has a "problem," the man is likely to worry and analyze and therefore generate fear. His fear prevents feelings of arousal when with his partner, whose rejection he probably fears more than that of anybody else. Consequently, he avoids her and/or responds less enthusiastically than either deems worthy, thus the cycle is under way.

The goals for working with performance anxiety are simple (see Fail-safe and Sensate Focus in Specific Procedures discussed later in this chapter): Create a situation where failure is impossible (put intercourse off-limits, with no breast or genital touching), and ask the couple to be close and sensual with each other ("Sensate Focus" exercise). This prohibition prevents possible failure and the sensate focus helps create a situation where people can feel aroused. Take for example Case One of Adam and Ann presented earlier, where the forgoing procedure was employed.

After Adam's initial and precipitous erectile loss, both he and Ann each murmured apologetic excuses, rolled over and pretended to go to sleep. At the next attempt at intercourse, Adam was only partially hard, and could not effect penetration. He became less affectionate, lest this affection lead to sex, and even

Figure 2
The Performance Anxiety Cycle

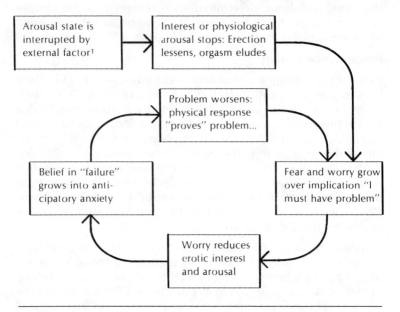

[1] This diversion may be initiated by virtually anything, but most commonly surprise, illness, alcohol, insult ("you are a failure"), guilt, fatigue, drugs (including alleged "aphrodisiacs").

began to avoid responding sexually when Ann seemed interested. She read his first detumescence and the subsequent increasing avoidance as a disinterest in sex, an embarrassing stage in his aging process, and a recognition of her own perceived loss of beauty and appeal. Her way of coping was to share her love for Adam in nonsexual ways and to place no sexual demands on him, thus saving both of them embarrassment.

When they came to our office, they had not had intercourse for six months. They had also not risked confiding in each other about their fears and good efforts. They seemed heartbroken about their affectional rift and somewhat helpless that Adam's *problem* was diagnosed as "in his head," but hopeful that sex therapy might offer some solution.

At the end of the first interview, our prescription for this couple was as follows: Intercourse was to be off-limits, and he was to make love to her "without his penis," (he could bring her to orgasms with manual or oral stimulation, but his penis was not to be involved).

Adam and Ann returned to our office for a second session encouraged by Adam's erection during the exercise. They waited for two weeks and finally broke the rule and had intercourse. We warned them not to be overly encouraged. When Adam had an erection, he was to "make it go down" in order to gain better control. He found this difficult. In five sessions they had broken the performance anxiety cycle. They were both greatly relieved. He was erecting well, and they were enjoying even more sensitive physical love on a par with their lifelong caring and commitment. It was unnecessary to offer much sexual information or to take further time for Lifestyle analysis, and they went happily into retirement.

Informational Impasse

Informational lack or distortion will frustrate the clients' efforts to have a rewarding sexual relationship. Accurate information is needed about oneself, one's partner and the interaction patterns that result from pursuing the goals that these people depend upon. Often people lack accurate information primarily because of precautions well drilled during childhood: Hands slapped while exploring genital feelings, threatening preachments and/or punishments for sexual interests. Family, religious and cultural myths lead not only to inaccuracy, but also to great voids. Such advice as: "Do what comes *naturally*," "Your husband will teach you all you need to know," or "All you need are the basics, you can learn with a prostitute," deter a person from seeking the best information about self or the other gender. Some clients can be educated easily with information from a book, a handout, anatomical diagrams, puppets, videotapes, therapists' writings or outside sources. Many a husband, for instance, has reacted with surprise and recognition, and subsequently reported improved lovemaking, after seeing a slide that clearly shows the similarity between the clitoris and penis, thus enabling him to realize how much his wife's clitoris rather than vagina is "where the action is."

One case without apparent performance anxiety, but requiring information therapy (the inner right-hand path in Figure 1) was that of Case Two, Beth and Bill. As usual, the presenting problem could not be either understood or addressed when in isolation from the couple's interaction.

Beth and Bill came to be treated for *dyspareunia*, or intercourse that was painful to Beth, and to find out how to increase her "sex drive." She hesitated to bring Bill, who had been hurt by her rejecting him. But he was relieved to know she had initiated the call for help and was impressed that she would open up to a stranger for him. When we put intercourse off limits and prescribed long periods of nongenital, nurturing holding and affection, Beth showed visible delight and Bill was relieved at being spared what he was beginning to believe was his failure as a lover. Since the therapists explicitly barred sex, neither spouse could blame the already typical lack of sex on anger, defense or lessening love, and both could instead focus on pleasure.

At the end of the first interview, we had Beth make an early appointment with her gynecologist to examine for possible low-grade vaginal infection which could be treated concurrently with therapy. One of several common bacterial strains was found and antibiotics were prescribed. Bill's urologist prescribed the same for him to counter possible alternating inflammations or of his being a host.

Anatomy lessons that were never learned by either were now provided via colored slides and standard genital exam homework. Bill had not known the location or even the importance of the clitoris, and Ann could not teach him since she didn't know either. Ann did not know the sensitivities of male genitals, and Bill was unaware of any more subtle gradient than erection and ejaculation. Homework carried out in private helped each learn their own pattern of arousal, which they then taught to each other. Bill had never learned the fundamentals of female sexual arousal and had assumed pain was typical but temporary; Beth had been deprived of learning her own sexual pleasures. Thus their combined sexual inexperience, focus on orgasm as goal, and stress over Beth's discomfort generated a pattern of confusion and decreased pleasure for him coupled with frustration, pain and lack of orgasmic release for her. Acquiring necessary sexual information encouraged them to develop physical skills, which led to greater confidence and therefore less avoidance, finally yielding the satisfaction they sought.

Homework for Beginning Therapy

Homework is assigned in the first interview for several purposes. Homework reinforces the couple's decision to try new solutions to their problems with outside guidance. It also helps the couple apply their insights from the therapy hour, particularly those affirming that both partners have been working to solve the problem all along, just in defensive and misdirected ways. With homework, new discoveries about each other, learned in the interview, can be examined further in "real life."

Homework is adapted from a set of "tools" or techniques from other approaches to sex therapy, according to the unique nature of the couple and their apparently viable therapeutic issues. Examples, discussed in more detail later are:

- **Fail-safe.** Clients are instructed that breasts and genitals are off-limits, but they are to touch each other affectionately more than usual.

- **Committed playtime.** Time to regain confidence in each other must be scheduled—literally—and protected from intrusion.

- **Sensate focus.** Masters and Johnson's (1982) exercises, starting with their less-known Stage 1, expressing, and continuing with Stage 2, learning, remains paradoxically powerful. (With the degree of erotic contact staged also, this is a major tool.)

- **Kegel exercises.** Muscle-toning exercises for the pelvic web not only tone and strengthen muscles but increase awareness of sensation. Good for men and women, these exercises need to be started early, since physical development requires time.

- **Alone together.** This unstructured date has strong requirements—it is purely and simply a time to recreate and generate new enjoyment of each other's company.
- **Caring behaviors.** The couple learns to negotiate (asking
  for and granting to the other) unmistakable tokens of caring and commitment.

Lifestyles of Individuals and Couples

If these simple procedures are not enough and the problem
continues to exist, it will become necessary to assess the
partners' individual Lifestyles, particularly as they pertain to
creating and maintaining the sexual problem.

Detailed help in making these individual and joint assessments
may be found in Chapter 3. Here, however, we will focus briefly
on the sexual issues in the Lifestyle: What additional information needs to be gathered during the Lifestyle assessment to
narrow the focus more within the sexual area, and how general
assumptions and basic mistakes about life, self and others
reflect on the presenting problems and can be emphasized to
motivate change as the interpretation is fed back to the clients
for re-orientation.

Additional information needed for sexual Lifestyle assessment.
For sex therapy, the Lifestyle assessment needs to include an individual and family sociosexual history to determine how and
what each individual learned about many specific concepts.
The Adlerian therapist must, of course, abstract from these data
the process, or "dance," between the partners that results in
their visible difficulty. This may be inferred by fitting each
client's answers under the rubric, "How did this person fit that
to one's own model of life?" The relevant topics for such an
assessment of patterns are:

- Information about sex and reproductive functions (what
  was learned about where babies come from, menstruation, nocturnal emissions, intercourse, petting);
- Attitudes about personal being and interactions (cleanli-
  ness, attractiveness, bodily beauty, bodily care, sensual
  awareness, color-taste-smell-feeling-looks, sharing oneself
  with others);
- Beliefs of how one loves and nurtures another person
  (trust, cooperation, willingness to work, kinds of support,
  expression of positive feelings, response to friends, kind-
  ness, nature of illness, sensitivity to others' plights, victo-
  ries and fortunes);

- Problem-solving and assertiveness (respecting others' boundaries and limits and maintaining one's own, saying "yes" and "no," communicating clearly and effectively);

- Gender roles, being male and female (expectations of males and of females, self and others; reaction or attitude toward these expectations, such as comfort, pride, or resentment).

- Values and morals, right and wrong (relative versus absolute rights or wrongs, degrees and changeability of integrity and loyalty, trust as earned and as assumed, cooperation and competitiveness and conflict, self-respect and respect for others).

These patterns may become most apparent by asking for specific sexual recollections while gathering early recollections with other Lifestyle data. Such specific questions might include: "When was the first time you noticed genital feelings? What happened the first time you felt aroused with another person? Same sex? Opposite sex? How did you learn to masturbate?" This list, rather than being a fixed interview schedule, urges inventive discretion of the individual therapist in posing questions that would reveal the patterns of this particular couple and of these individuals, and the nature of the presenting problems. Knowing these patterns and the beliefs and strengths of the couple, the therapist has most of the necessary information for planning a customized intervention for change.

Assumptions and sexuality. Lifestyle information such as beliefs learned from ordinal position, family and personal values, life experiences and so forth reflect on sexual satisfaction and patterns of sexual interaction. Some examples of how this feedback may be presented to clients follow:

- "From your place in the family as the youngest child, you've learned how to be creatively fun-loving and playful. Your Early Recollections show a great sensual appreciation of smell, sight, touch, taste and rhythms. These sensitivities will be helpful in teaching your more serious partner about this kind of joy, for even though you have not had her experience of having been married before, the delicious delight of learning and savoring can be catching."

- "Both of you learned in your families of origin how to be responsible and to work hard. Sex therapy, or any kind of therapy for that matter, is hard work and will require people to be responsible for themselves and for each other. Your early learning will serve you well in this task."

- "Your learning to be a good sexual partner requires that you be able to lead sometimes and follow other times. Your experiences as a middle child have already taught you how to do that."

- "Part of the problem with seeing life as a competitive arena is that you must also compete in sex. Since competition involves losing and you're afraid to lose, you avoid sex. When you begin to enjoy being with your spouse, your buddy, sexually and to really focus on your own body pleasure instead of on your performance, you'll find yourself more aroused."

Charlie and Charlotte, Case Three, who presented mutually reinforcing problems of rapid ejaculation and inability to orgasm, had been married for seven years and had a three-year-old daughter and an infant boy. As Charlie felt rejected sexually by Charlotte, he spent less time with her and the family, becoming more involved in his work. Charlotte, feeling abandoned with her children, began to believe that "he only wants my body, not my home, babies or company." She solved her problem by becoming overly involved with home and children and less with Charlie and his demanding work.

Charlotte, the youngest of five children, had three older brothers who made a princess of her. She had "center stage" Early Recollections, with men clamoring to please her, and she showed great dependence on these attentions. In his family, Charlie was the second boy, fifteen months behind the brother whom he eventually overtook, becoming the psychological first. For him, work was a competitive arena where he was determined to succeed and was constantly measuring himself and his progress. Though he was once enamored of his wife's "little girl" goodness and charm, he was now weary of her dependence and excessive demands to be noticed and treasured.

Strengths of their relationship were clear. Charlotte took seriously her feminine roles of being a good mother and the attractive—even showpiece— corporate wife. She started out as a playful sexual companion, but gradually discovered it more fun to attract attention than to enjoy it once found, and for her sex had become a bore.

Charlie provided the kind of Lifestyle that Charlotte loved—a beautiful house, expensive clothes, fancy parties, and admiring corporate peers. He also was a hard worker and could therefore be motivated in therapy to make some difficult changes if given the right kind of assignments. He was a problem-solver and a "can-do" person.

Such Lifestyle information offers an opportunity to change not only this couple's sexual functioning, but through this rewarding shift to change their relationship in other valuable ways as well.

Charlie's focus on competition had led to his paying little attention to his own sensual pleasure or to Charlotte's. His highs were derived from smashing finishes in racquetball; the subtleties of affectionate touching and foreplay were outside his awareness. He kept score, counting the number of times they had intercourse over a period of time. When Charlotte was not interested in sex, Charlie masturbated and brought himself quickly to relief.

As part of the therapy, we asked them to engage in prolonged, sensuous, mutual touching without going to orgasm. He was uncomfortable at first and felt silly, stopping before ejaculation. The second and third times were easier. Soon he was able to reach a perceptibly higher level of arousal without feeling the need to ejaculate. Eventually he learned that the process of reaching orgasm was more enjoyable than the orgasm itself. In his competitive stance toward life, Charlie had focused so much on "the score" that he had never learned to enjoy his body or Charlotte's. His new success in the sexual area facilitated his using his home more as a place of rest and recreation; he played more with his children and learned to spend relaxed time with his wife.

Therapy for Charlotte required helping her to take responsibility for her own orgasm and for her life generally. For seven years she had waited for Charlie to make sex good for her, and he never quite did. She had never told him how since she had never taken the initiative to learn for herself.

We prescribed long and sensuous genital touching, so that Charlotte could focus on her arousal without distraction. She learned to stimulate herself to orgasm and to teach that process to Charlie. In these weeks she taught herself to fantasize and developed her pelvic muscles to heighten her arousal. (See Kegel Exercises in Specific Procedures, discussed later in this chapter.) She also learned to ask Charlie for what she needed to reach orgasm. We suggested that she ask him, "Please don't go until I climax." By twelve weeks after they began therapy, Charlie stayed home happily and Charlotte enjoyed making him welcome.

Customized Sex Therapy

A therapeutic strategy can be refined once the therapist understands the individuals' and couple's Lifestyles, sociopsychosexual histories, homework performance patterns and nuances of numerous therapy sessions and can estimate the sexual consequences for this couple. The further down the flowchart (see Figure 1) therapy has proceeded, the richer the profusion of pattern data, but paradoxically, the greater the difficulty in selecting factors to formulate an intervention. By analogy, the grander the array of tools, the more important it is for the user to be a master craftsman.

Techniques are for the therapist what tools are for the craftsman. Techniques have evolved from wide and even disparate sources across time. The product they help fashion depends upon the skillful application of the best tool or technique for the particular raw material, objective and circumstance. While anyone can pick up a particular tool, the apprentice will not get the same result as the journeyman, and the master craftsman or professional may use fewer tools more deftly, adapting to momentary challenges and finish more quickly. Misuse of a power tool, applying a blade that is duller or sharper than expected or misjudging attributes of the raw material may do irreparable damage to product or user. Poor timing may waste time. Cutting corners may cut quality, which will show in the end. People are more concerned that the purpose is met.

The Adlerian concept of use applies to the therapist as well as to the client. Each technique has multiple uses, but operates best as designed, fitting with the usual sequence. And while dumb luck may occasionally be had, it is hardly a technique upon which to rely.

"Customizing" sex therapy is simply applying all available techniques to the emergent situation in accord with working principles. Using again the "tools" metaphor, off-the-shelf parts need careful integration to create a smooth, custom job. In customizing sex therapy, the critical concept is fitting the operating principles of standard techniques to the couple's unique interaction pattern (situation) and to therapeutic objectives. Phrased as a question, knowing this couple and their Lifestyle goals and our therapeutic goals, what procedures and techniques can be used to accomplish the most important of these? The fourth couple in the case examples introduced early in this chapter, Dolores and Domingo, Case Four, seemed during their first session to be appropriate candidates for sex therapy (central track of Figure 1). They were, indeed, both anxious about performance and needed sexual information. However, working on these was not enough. Their therapy illustrates a very customized procedure utilizing a manageably few additional "standard tools."

Although they had been married for two years at the time they began therapy, Domingo and Dolores had not yet had intercourse. On their wedding night, Domingo was impotent. Prior to their wedding, he had avoided sexual contact of any sort with Dolores, who wanted to be sexually active even before they were married. On their honeymoon trip, Domingo tried unsuccessfully to have intercourse; his tentative erection did not last long. After they returned home, he tried again a few times, again unsuccessfully, and thereafter avoided situations that might lead Dolores to expect sexual excitement.

We began our work with them by teaching such fundamentals as male and female anatomy, arousal and response cycles and by giving safe, sensual homework. We put breasts and genitals off-limits, but asked them to hold and touch affectionately in many other ways.

The emotional impact on both partners was intense. This beginning work was profound as they transcended unspoken fears together. Simultaneously they both experienced relief. She was relieved that they were coming for therapy and by the expectation of an ultimate resolution of their problem; he was relieved by her increased affection and reduced demands that he perform.

Time was an important element for this couple. They needed to do the safe, affectionate exercises many, many times. The atmosphere of safety evolved slowly during the weeks. They carried out their homework with great faith, which gave ample time for us to also take a comprehensive sexual history and general Lifestyle assessment. This process of talking, hearing, understanding and validating also contributed to their experience of safety. Their faith was increased during the second month as they noticed some first stirring of penile tumescence.

In the Lifestyle assessment, several noteworthy patterns became apparent. Dolores liked to judge. She watched and waited with implied rulership, as one who did everything right and who expected others to do everything right, too. Her early memories were full of such evidence. Domingo wanted to do everything right in order to achieve and to please. Their joint Hispanic cultural background further complicated the problem: They both perceived the role of the male as pursuer and the female as the one to parry his advances many times before surrendering. Each was angry with the other for being forced into a role that was inconsistent with "the way life should be."

From their sociosexual history, we found that Domingo had never learned to masturbate. His strong desires to please his parents plus their warning against genital touching had prevented such bodily pleasures from early childhood. Dolores described demanding romantic fantasies and dreams of being pursued by men of great wealth and sexual prowess. In her family of origin, she was the oldest of seven children and was placed in charge of their care, brightening the drudgery of her parental day with these sexual mirages, but lacking the skill to elicit such romance from a live human being. Dolores and Domingo met in college. He came from a well-to-do family, was good looking and was pursuing an exacting profession, which, understandably to her, kept him from being available for his unlearned and her imagined sexual exploits. Dolores, he expected, by virtue of her surrogate motherhood, would be competent as a homemaker and skilled as a mother so that he could leave the domestic part of their lives to her and get on with his pursuit of more important goals.

Domingo first began to have erections and feel aroused after their exercise sessions—in which the pressure was off by prescription. We told him to continue doing the affectionate, non-demand exercises, and planned our major intervention, which was to identify her as the problem bearer. We labeled her as having the "sexual dysfunction of virginal vaginismus," (an obvious reading of primary evidence) and asked him to begin preparing her for intercourse, nurturing her with tenderness and understanding. We asked him to begin to dilate her progressively with lubricated pinky, finger, two fingers and three, warning them this must proceed slowly over about three weeks, and that even should he be firmly erect he should not dare penetrate her until she was adequately prepared.

As any therapist should be anticipating, since it was no longer he, but she, with the problem, she could no longer judge him, but instead focused on herself, and he was now the pursuer, caretaker and helper. With no possibility of his having intercourse with her, he had already learned to become aroused and was erecting daily. Finally they gave up waiting for her slow dilation and had intercourse. She was delighted to be pursued and enjoyed the surrender.

General Principles from Standard Techniques

A few powerful procedures, previously mentioned as basic homework assignments, will be discussed as they apply to common symptoms with attention paid to the interaction patterns. It may be noted that only procedures 5 and 6 are homework assignments that an individual carries out alone. The others impose, stimulate and assume cooperation, and are organized in the therapy session and carried out at home. The procedures are: (1) Fail-safe, (2) Sensate Focus, (3) Committed Playtime, (4) Bibliotherapy, (5) Kegel Exercises and (6) Stop-start. More general working principles will follow.

Specific Procedures

- **Fail-safe. Prohibiting the feared sexual activity defines failure out of existence.** Unsatisfying intercourse is the most commonly addressed sexual problem. The means of failure is unimportant to the proscription; the process itself is powerful. As people develop sexual dysfunctions (e.g., erectile difficulties, untimely ejaculation, elusive orgasm, pain, difficult penetration), they tend to get into the Performance Anxiety Cycle. When the focus is on the organs that are not responding as demanded, whether one's own or the partner's, emotions such as rejection, anger, frustration, disappointment and jealousy grow. Both partners feel like failures—the one as the active lover and the other as the unsuccessful recipient. Prohibiting intercourse and other activity that may result in orgasm breaks this cycle of failure.

  Fail-safe is mandatory in performance anxiety cases and when the symptom-producing cycle is one of the demand/refuse. This technique is also recommended in many other instances thus understanding the principles leads the reader to the most plausible application. Assigning Fail-safe to a couple in the demand/refuse cycle can be tricky. It may be necessary to explain to the demanding partner that there are advantages to be gained by not making the other feel like a demandee. Excess theorizing or educating, however, can reduce the impact of this technique.

- **Sensate Focus.** With Fail-safe prescribed, the couple arranges the most comfortable private setting for expressing their cares nonverbally and through body touching, and they learn and teach what is comforting and erotic. Masters and Johnson's (1976) now classic exercises, starting with their less-known Stage 1, expressing[1], and continuing with Stage 2, learning, remains paradoxically powerful. With the degree of erotic contact staged also, this technique is a fundamental tool of sex therapy.

  Privacy is the first priority. Regardless of the couple's comfort with sexual intimacy, some malaise is to be expected. They should isolate themselves against distraction from telephone, work, family and friends for about two hours of prime time. First they should set up a quiet, relaxed atmosphere, in a room warm enough for nudity without covers and freshen themselves, bathing together if possible. One partner (the therapist may specify or help them establish which goes first) takes the active role, the other remains passive except for letting the active one know of any uncomfortable, painful or alarming intrusions.

  Stage 1 is expressive. The active mate touches and caresses the other (but does not massage or examine) to express love, caring and nurturing without words. "Talk with your hands and body" is an apt instruction. Any expressive kind of touch is permitted (e.g., kissing, squeezing, caressing), provided it is not sent or received as erotic, at least the first time. Partners should express their appreciation for the privilege of this intimacy, but nonverbally. The activity is for the enjoyment of the active partner (contrary, as noted, to the original Masters and Johnson description), not to please or arouse the passive one. After about a half hour, the partners switch places. Any comfortable positions may work.

  Stage 2 is for learning via feedback. The passive partner lets the active one know what is pleasurable, as nonverbally as possible. While sighs and movements do communicate, the "hand-riding" technique that Masters and Johnson

---

1 As described here, the exercises are not the same as originally published; Masters and Johnson altered them soon after publishing them (1976) as they described their revised procedures to trainees. The reader familiar with other versions should consider these differences. The essential difference is that Stage 1 is expressive, not manipulative, regardless of how lovingly done. See also Masters, Johnson and Kolodny, 1988.

recommend adds a direction-giving dimension: The passive partner's hand "rides" the back of the active one's hand to suggest preferred pressure, direction, stroke length and so on.[2] Stage 2 offers the often long-fantasized moment to create and explore while learning how the partner may be gratified. Again, after perhaps a half hour, the partners switch.

If the clients do not report this to have been a profound experience, it may be a sign that real blocks to intimacy exist, possibly implying the need for nonsexual therapy.

Stages 3 and 4 apply the same dynamics as Stages 1 and 2, but breasts and genitals are included, with intercourse usually still off-limits. This exercise becomes a most important means for the partners to provide each other with explicit sexual preferences, active and passive, in the trusting and emotionally moving structure that the term Sensate Focus implies. It is a healthy procedure for every couple to enjoy periodically, as they grow and change, and may be recommended with confidence.

Goals of the Sensate Focus exercises are safety from failure; development of broader, more varied, tender and erotic sensation; learning of more intimate and trusting communication; and new confidence and commitment in the couple's intimate future. Sensate Focus is most often indicated for treatment of performance anxiety, freeing the relationship by taking the stress off sexual outcome. This freedom provides an opportunity for each partner to learn to feel cared for without demand being placed on them. Sensate Focus two through four may be prescribed, in addition, for couples who need erotic information, skill in arousing the partner and enjoyment with being aroused (practice and permission), and renewal of intimate interest.

- **Committed Playtime.** Every couple, assuming they have a relationship based upon shared intimacy, emotional bonds and a lasting commitment such as marriage, requires "down time" to relax, recreate, reconstitute and reground those criteria. Some couples manage this nearly

---

2 For many clients a preferred method is to reverse "hand riding," with the passive partner riding and guiding the active one's hand in the preferred manner.

* This is the same as described in text, is not reversed.

daily in a comfortable mix of unstressed time together in the midst of other activity that is not of a bond-reinforcing nature. By far the majority, however, live not so much highly stressed lives as lives that simply prevent them from giving attention to this preventive maintenance. The Committed Playtime contract is not so much an exercise as a program designed by the couple to reconnect with each other.

With the help of the therapist, the couple begins to schedule protected time for themselves. A few hours weekly can suffice, provided that they firmly withdraw from routine or spontaneous distractions: friends, family, shopping, making repairs or adding errands ("while on that side of town") that cut into the committed time. The couple contracts for any leisure activity that is pleasurable to both, nonsexual or erotic, for the key principle is scheduling-and-doing. If the partners get together as often as they can in their spare time, after the honeymoon phase of this new experience, they will find less and less of it as obligation and more spontaneous activities will increase.

Couples with any marital strain can benefit from Committed Playtime. It is recommended particularly when either spouse complains of being ignored, "never coming first" or losing interest. Note that some couples will report "doing that already," but somehow keep up their guard against intimacy—most commonly by doing things with other couples, thus precluding intimacy. Even in marriages that are highly businesslike and reserved, Committed Playtime rejuvenates and extends the original contract. The bonds are clarified in intimate time, and reinforcing that true intimacy is a two-person phenomenon.

- **Bibliotherapy.** Some clients find the printed word more helpful than talk, and so like to receive or be directed to written materials such as books and pamphlets. Most people learn better through visual means, so charts, diagrams, slides and chalkboard information are helpful during therapy sessions. They can share what they buy at the bookstore with one another at home, at their own pace, order and selection. Many books are available in regular and used book stores. There are dozens of college human sexuality texts which can be lent for general information or found in libraries; some of the best are Masters, Johnson and Kolodry (1988); Rathus (1983), and Haas and Haas (1987). A rather encyclopedic text is Francoeur

(1982). The best manuals remain, for women, Barbach (1978) and for men, Zilbergeld (1978). Permission for erotic contact can be enhanced by suggesting study of Comfort's first volume (1972). (The above and other recommended books are listed in the Bibliography for Clients at the end of this chapter.) Assigned homework is outlined on handouts so that clients can read, reread and discuss them as they choose. Some word processor-stored materials can be customized to the specific Lifestyle and situational needs of specific clients.

- **Kegel Exercises.** Pelvic muscle exercises may be prescribed in many ways, but however done they should be introduced with several caveats. First, they are of benefit to the person performing them, male or female. Specifically prescribed to reduce urinary incontinence (by Arnold Kegel, a gynecologist), they simultaneously strengthen, tone and increase sensitivity of the vagina and web of muscles that support it and comprise the pelvic floor. In the male (these muscles tie to the penis base—the only large musculature involved in this organ—and Kegel Exercises enhance ejaculatory awareness and control.

Although all clients can benefit from practicing pelvic muscle exercises since they enhance pelvic arousal, these are prescribed primarily for developing orgasmic response in women and for attaining better erectile capacity and ejaculatory control in men. Specific assignments can be found in Barbach (1982), Heiman, LoPiccolo and Lo Piccolo (1976), McCarthy (1977) and Zilbergeld (1978).

- **Stop-start.** This exercise was designed for men who ejaculate too rapidly, a very common problem that is also very ill-defined. Still most often called "premature ejaculation," it is a highly relative problem, defined by both partner's feelings of disappointment. Stop-start works best if the man is ejaculating a few seconds after penetration of the vagina. If, however, the couple is upset that the man only lasts five or ten minutes with rhythmic movement, the more reasonable therapeutic focus is education for both partners about anatomy or intercourse and, foremost, increasing the partners' sensuality. "Much of the obsession with lasting longer is due to the exaggerated importance most of us have given to intercourse," argued Zilbergeld (1978, p. 258). But caution is wise; both clients' private logic should be learned to prevent resistance and loss of confidence in the therapist.

"Stop-start" is a variation of a design by Semans (1956) that has become a classic in this field. It is an exercise of three main stages, in each of which the penis is stimulated until before the point of "ejaculatory inevitability," as it was labelled by Masters and Johnson (1975, p. 102). (This is the point when prostatic contractions begin, the ejaculation reflex takes over, and the man is unable to prevent ejaculation from occurring in a few seconds.) Stimulation is not to resume until excitement declines, as may also the erection. This Stop-start process is repeated three times, with ejaculation the outcome, but considerably later than usual and implicitly under some control.

The process requires that the man *learn to tolerate increased levels and durations of pleasurable genital sensation*—not to "think about the football game instead." In Stage 1, the man stimulates himself. In Stage 2, his wife stimulates him, with the same objectives and rules. In Stage 3, the wife sits astride her husband's thighs as he lies on his back and moves his penis in her pubic hair and vulva, eventually rising and sitting to contain it in her vagina momentarily, then moving off. This "quiet vagina" phase is followed by movement, increasing each time the man signals the approach of inevitability, until the duration of intromission and the tolerance of vaginal stimulation is satisfactory.

Usually Stop-start is practiced concomitantly with both partners' Kegels Exercises and some regimen to increase orgasmic potential in the wife. The more she is involved with efforts of her own, the less is the pressure and self-consciousness for the husband.

Final remarks on exercises. These are but a few common procedures; others are to be found in sex therapy texts. The therapist should peruse these works and create many other fitting exercises.

Concluding Do's and Don'ts for Clients

Below is a final list of suggestions for clients with sexual concerns. They are so general that they can be used with most couples in most situations.

- Know the conditions for your own sexual arousal. What specifically do you need in order to have a satisfying sexual response? Pay attention to and write down specific situations that are exciting and arousing for you, and that are indicative of a good sexual experience.

• Learn to relax. Practice relaxation exercises until you are able at will to put your body into a calm state. Give yourself time to feel, to breathe and to enjoy.

• When you are not feeling aroused and your conditions for a good sexual experience are not being met, make love to your partner in ways other than through sexual activity. Expand your horizons. Know several alternative ways for getting close; intercourse isn't the only option.

• Tell your partner what you like. Learn to do this both in sincere verbal ways and nonverbally via touch.

• Keep yourself involved by focusing on your own sensitivity and arousal. Avoid becoming an observer of yourself, since this is counter to arousal.

• Increase touching in your relationship. Know that touching works. Trust and desire sometimes build slowly.

• Become an excellent lover without using your genitals. Be affectionate and loving without expecting intercourse.

• Don't get your identity from your partner's sexual response. Don't try to force a response from the other person.

• Let arousal be something that grows between you. Don't always approach with a goal.

• Make your partner the focus of your loving. "Who" is more important than "how."

• Especially after you've been together more than a few years, don't expect your partner to be aroused on every occasion. Expect to take turns seducing.

• Experiment. The more the above steps have been taken, the easier to try new approaches, positions and moods.

• Most important: Share your sexual "game plan" with your partner, don't require guessing. Anyone would feel complimented—and might even reciprocate.

Bibliography for Clients
Chapter 6

Barbach, L. (1982). *For each other: Sharing sexual intimacy.* Garden City, NY: Anchor/Doubleday.

Belliveau, F. & Richter, L. (1970). *Understanding human sexual inadequacy.* New York: Bantam.

Comfort, A. (1982). *Becoming a sexual person.* New York: Wiley & Sons.

Francoeur, R.T. (1982). *Becoming a sexual person.* New York: Wiley & Sons.

Haas, K. & Haas, A. (1987). *Understanding sexuality.* St. Louis: Times Mirror/Mosby.

Heiman, J., LoPiccolo, L., & LoPiccolo, J. (1978). *Becoming orgasmic: A sexual growth program for women.* Englewood Cliffs, NJ: Prentice-Hall.

Kelly, G.F. (1979). *Good sex: A healthy man's guide to sexual fulfillment.* New York: Harcourt Brace Jovanovich.

Lichtendorf, S.S. (1983). *Eve's journey: The physical experience of being female.* New York: Berkey.

Mahoney, E.R. (1982). *Human sexuality.* New York: McGraw-Hill.

Masters, W.H. & Johnson, V.E. (1975). *The pleasure bond.* Boston: Little, Brown.

Masters, W.H. & Johnson, V.E. (1976). Intensive Sex Therapy Seminar. St. Louis, MO: Reproductive Biology Research Foundation.

Masters, W.H., Johnson, V.E. & Kolodny, R.C. (1988). *Masters and Johnson on sex and human loving.* Boston: Little, Brown.

McCarthy, B. (1977). *What you (still) don't know about male sexuality.* New York: Thomas Y. Crowell.

McCary, J.L. (1971). *Sexual myths and fallacies.* New York: Van Nostrand.

Offir, C. W. (1982). *Human sexuality.* New York: Harcourt, Brace, Jovanovich.

Rathus, S.A. (1983). *Human sexuality.* New York: Holt, Rinehart & Winston.

Zilbergeld, B. (1978). *Male sexuality.* Boston-Toronto: Little, Brown.

Chapter 6 References

Adler, A. (1978). *Cooperation between the sexes* (H.L. & R.R. Ansbacher, Eds & Trans.). Garden City, NY: Anchor/Doubleday.

Dreikurs, R. (1955/1960). Adlerian analysis of interaction. In R. Dreikurs, *Group psychotherapy and group approaches.* Chicago: Alfred Adler Institute of Chicago. (Reprinted from *Group Psychotherapy, 8 (4)*, 298-307.

Dreikurs, R. (1981). "The three life tasks." In L.G. Baruth & D.G. Eckstein (Eds.), *Life style: Theory, practice, and research* (pp. 24-41). Dubuque, IA: Kendall/Hunt.

Hartman, William E., & Marilyn A. Fithian (1972). *Treatment of sexual dysfunction: A bio-psycho-social approach.* Long Beach, CA: Center for Marital and Sexual Studies.

Masters, W.H. & Johnson, V.E. (1970). *Human sexual inadequacy.* Boston: Little, Brown.

Masters, W.H. & Johnson, V.E. (1975). *The pleasure bond.* Boston: Little, Brown.

Masters, W.H. & Johnson, V.E. (1976). Intensive Sex Therapy Seminar. St. Louis, MO: Reproductive Biology Research Foundation.

Masters, W.H., Johnson, V.E. & Kolodry, R.C. (1982). *Human sexuality.* Boston: Little, Brown.

Masters, W.H., Johnson, V.E. & Kolodry, R.C. (1988). *Masters and Johnson on sex and human loving.* Boston: Little Brown.

Mosak, H.H. (1977). *On purpose: Collected papers.* Chicago: Alfred Adler Institute.

Mosak, H.H. & Shulman, B.H. (1961). *Introduction to individual psychology: A syllabus.* Chicago: Alfred Adler Institute.

Pomeroy, W. (1976). "How to Take a Sex History." (Xeroxed notes from Sexual Attitude Reassessment workshop, no further citation given.)

Satir, V. (1975, October). Personal notes from Satir Workshop ("Month-long"), Banff, Alberta, Canada, sponsored by Family Training Institute Ltd. Lacombe, Alberta, Canada: Family Training Institute.

Segal, L. (1983). Personal quotes from conversations and talks at Mental Research Institute, Palo Alto, California.

Semans, J.H. (1956). Premature ejaculation: A new approach. *Southern Medical Journal,* 49, 353-358.

Shulman, B. (1967/1973). The uses and abuses of sex. In B. Shulman, *Contributions to individual psychology* (pp. 81-90). Chicago: Alfred Adler Institute. (Reprinted from *Journal of Religion & Health. 6(4)*.

Tavris, C., & Sadd, S. (1975). *The Redbook report on female sexuality.* New York: Dell.

Wolfe, B. (1948). *Successful living.* London: Routledge & Kegan Paul.

Zilbergeld, B. (1978). *Male sexuality.* Boston-Toronto: Little Brown.

Chapter 7

Divorce Mediation

by

Brenda B. Even

Most of us would be surprised to learn that the number of divorces in this country has not yet reached record proportions and will not until 1990, when the largest contingent of the baby boom population moves into the 25 to 29 age range (those years when most divorces take place). A number of experts believe our present population contains the largest contingent with the potential of first marriage and, by the end of the decade, will boast the largest contingent with the greater risk of divorce. With the thought of an increasing divorce rate comes the concomitant thought of increasing problems related to divorce: The disintegration of families, conflicts over child custody, disputes over money and property, ongoing hostility and enmity. It is our contention that these problems need not occur, if the divorce mediation movement concurrently sweeping the country establishes itself firmly. In fact, Bahr (1984), reported the following advances of the mediation process:

- Two-thirds of mediated divorce disputes are resolved.

- Mediation reduces delinquency in alimony and child support payments.

- Mediation makes post-divorce adjustment easier, especially for children, since it reduces parental conflict.

At first glance, divorce mediation claims results that appear ex-aggerated or unrealistic. At its best, it must be over-rated; at its worst, it could be disastrous. It should be examined, at least, however, as a concept, a process and an alternative to the ad-versarial process. The purposes of this chapter, then, are (a) to present the concept of divorce mediation as a unique, but clearly defined intervention technique and (b) to examine the Adlerian connection to divorce mediation in terms of both basic assumption and specific approach. Consequently, the chapter focuses on the growth and development of the divorce mediation movement, the divorce mediation process itself, its connection to Adlerian Psychology and the future prospects of mediation.

Divorce Mediation:
Development and Growth of a Concept

The question has been raised numerous times: Is mediation an idea whose time has come? Professionals who work closely with couples who are engaged in marital conflict answer yes, because they believe mediation involves a process that today is breaking new ground, but that tomorrow will be the accepted way for solving one of society's most difficult dilemmas—dis-solution and restructuring of the family.

The editors of the periodic magazine *American Family* (Vroom, Fasset & Wakefield 1981) who in cooperation with the Family Mediation Association produced the essay "Mediation: The Wave of the Future," likewise concur. Their response addressed the major transition being experienced by our society's families at this time.

"The symptoms of transition," Vroom et al pointed out, "are well known:" The decline of the extended nuclear family, the high divorce rate, the growing number of single parent families, the increase in family violence, drug and alcohol abuse, teenage pregnancy and suicide and the growth of cults that replace the natural family. Paralleling these problems are the trends toward delayed marriage, dual career families, fewer children, single male or female headed households, group liv-ing and other experiments with new lifestyles.

And as if this were not enough, we now must deal with the devastating impact of AIDS on the family system.

In a similar article for *The Futurist*, Vroom, Fasset and Wakefield (1982) commented on the causes of this transition, which are becoming clearer. They cited these causes as:

Inflation and the high cost of housing; the baby boom and the "graying of America;" unemployment, underemployment and career uncertainties; television; affluence; the women's movement and sex role uncertainties; and the growth of the large government and service sector bureaucracies that are undermining the traditional mediating institutions of family, church, school and community (p. 29).

The emergence, then, of the mediation movement seems a timely development. It is hoped this movement can address some of the negotiation issues associated with the conflicts and uncertainties that batter and subsequently overwhelm the marital or family unit. Until very recently, the most likely course for a divorcing couple was for each to hire a lawyer and prepare for battle. Now there is the mediation alternative.

Mediation Defined. The following descriptions quoted from Vroom et al (1981), indicate the scope and possibilities of mediation:

- Mediation is not a thing. The mediator is not a separate party, but is rather a presence to be shaped by the parties and the issues for use in negotiating. Therefore a mediator must be resilient and flexible.

- Mediation is the process of power equalization because you cannot bargain, except between relative equals.

- Mediation is a process which posits a neutral third person who will guide the parties toward a resolution of their marital disputes, either preliminary to, or outside of, litigation.

- Mediation is a process that offers families a means of resolving disputes through a cooperative decision making process.

These are but a few of the many statements offered to define this process, which attempts to minimize the adversarial nature of mutual and/or family disputes. Most succinctly then, mediation is a process of restructuring the family by the parties most intimately involved. It is an opportunity for a couple, with the aid of a neutral third party, (a) to make decisions about future living conditions and arrangements; (b) to resolve such issues as spousal maintenance, custody, property division and visitation; and (c) to model a future relationship.

Although the idea and conceptualized process of mediation appears to offer a favorable alternative to the adversarial approach to divorce, the application of the process is relatively new. According to Pearson (*Marriage and Divorce Today Newsletter*, February 7, 1983), "Forty-five percent of sole practitioners began their mediation practice in 1981." What is more, few private sector programs have been operating for more than three years. Even in the public sector, mediation is a relatively new practice. The well-known Los Angeles Conciliation Court did not begin to offer mediation until 1973. Until recently, California was the only state to mandate mediation in contested custody cases. Under the mediation provision of the 1981 Family Law Act, court-appointed mediators had to meet the minimum qualifications of social service experience with families. At the present time a number of states have not only considered mandated mediation, but also have established legislation to enforce its implementation. In Canada, where similar prospects are probable, the outlook is similar.

Many believe "that mediated settlement is the only approach to divorce" (*Marriage and Divorce Today Newsletter*, May 7, 1984). In fact, John Haynes, a recent president of the Academy of Family Mediators, predicted that in the near future, half of the divorces in the country will be mediated, rather than litigated. Others, however, believe mediation as a viable entity may not survive because of the lack of highly trained mediators. Some believe that without a more highly systematized and regulated training program, the movement will evaporate (*Marriage and Divorce Today Newsletter*, May 28, 1984).

First, however, the specific tasks, steps and techniques of the process must be spelled out. Because of the newness and rapid growth of the field, experts say that the research has yet to catch up with emerging trends. Without a central clearing house of information, no one knows exactly how many people are practicing divorce mediation, how they are being trained, by what ethical standards they are determining charges, or what access the poor have to such services. The Denver Custody Mediation Project, a major federally funded study on divorce mediation, is attempting to coordinate some of the research efforts. To date, the project has reported on a variety of topics related to the mediation field, such as the successful traits of a mediator, weaknesses in the mediation field and differences between public and private mediators (*Marriage and Divorce Today Newsletters*, February 7, 1983; January 17, 1983; *Los Angeles Times*, July 6, 1983).

In May of 1984, the Symposium on Standards and Practices for Family and Divorce Mediation convened in Denver, Colorado. From that conclave emerged the final draft of the *Model Standards of Practice for Family and Divorce Mediation*. More effort, however, must be put toward developing and applying both research and ethical standards. Issues of training, supervision and certification of practicing mediators are still being addressed.

The Divorce Mediation Process

Divorce mediation is a cooperative process of restructuring the family by the parties most intimately involved. With the aid of a neutral third party, divorcing and separating partners reach a mutually satisfactory settlement regarding the division of marital property, child custody, visitation rights and spousal maintenance. According to Coogler (1978, p. 99), considered by many to be the "Father of Mediation," couples come to a mediation center for one of the following reasons:

- Something about their marriage is not working, and they are considering the possibility of either divorce or separation.

- The couple has not decided whether to seek a divorce, but has decided to live separately for some period of time, after which they might either resume their marital relationship or obtain a divorce.

- The couple has already separated or plans to do so in the near future, and either one or both parties have finally decided to seek a divorce.

- The couple is already divorced, and the provisions made in the divorce decree regarding support, visitation and custody are not working.

Mediation is not appropriate in the first instance, as such a couple more aptly needs information about what is involved should they decide to seek a divorce or separation. In the remaining instances, mediation is indeed appropriate as each situation calls for a mediation procedure to develop workable arrangements for parents and children at a difficult time in their lives. Thus, a therapist could feel comfortable in recommending such action.

A word of caution, though: Mediation is not for everyone. According to Horowitz (*Los Angeles Times*, July 6, 1983), "The pitfalls of mediation are most apparent when there is a lack of equal 'bargaining capacity' of the parties, creating a high risk of one or both not having full information regarding legal rights." Unquestionably, therapists must be able to discern whether dominance of one partner by the other and lack of information about legalities are factors when they recommend mediation.

Advantages of divorce mediation include that the process

• is clear, predictable and time limited,

• avoids lengthy and bitter court battles,

• is fiscally sound,

• fosters cooperation and self-determination in handling present and future life circumstances,

• promotes positive family reorganization,

• reduces the pain felt by children of divorcing parents, and is controlled by the divorcing parties.

Coogler (1978, p. 2) summarized the advantages of mediation as follows:

• The issues to be decided are clearly defined.

• The issues are limited to those whose resolution is needed for reaching settlement.

• Procedural methods are established for collecting and examining factual information.

• All options for settlement of each issue are systematically examined.

• Options are selected within socially acceptable guidelines.

• Uninterrupted time for working toward resolution is regularly allocated.

• Impasses are promptly resolved by arbitration.

In addition, Coogler (1978, pp. 1-9) stressed that the parties are not overwhelmed by the process because it teaches them how to be responsible for themselves. Consequently, they are better able to cope with their lives following the divorce. With divorce mediation, more time is devoted to working out a settlement than is typical in the adversarial legal process, and all of the involved parties are included in the planning. Cooperative, rather than the competitive, processes are encouraged during the course of the mediation. Through the use of mediation, Both parties have access to a setting in which they will have a full opportunity to be heard. Therefore, within a structured setting, and using clearly defined guidelines, a neutral mediator or a mediator who is knowledgeable in communication and negotiation skills, as well as in rudiments of divorce law, aids the parties in resolving the issues of their divorce.

Four recognized mediation models are in use around the country (Silberman, 1981): (1) The solo lawyer mediator; (2) the solo therapist; (3) the lawyer-therapist team; and (4) O.J. Coogler's variation, the "Structured Mediation System," which is the more known and developed form of mediation. It utilizes the interdisciplinary team approach, with carefully delineated roles for therapist and lawyer. Involved in one of these models, the couple then proceeds through a series of steps, most succinctly outlined as follows by the Family Mediation Association (1982):

Mediation Step-by-Step

Initial Contact

A. Phone contact
B. Brief explanation of process
C. Mailing material that details process
D. Appointment arranged

Orientation Session

A. Review of expectations of the couple
B. Brief history of the couple
C. Discussion of taping and confidentiality
D. Overview of mediation

    1. No comparison with adversarial process
    2. Couple makes choices
    3. Determination of equitable division of property
    4. Emphasis on cooperative conflict resolution
    5. Recognition of need for reduction in Lifestyle
    6. Realization that each spouse has a right to the contribution of the other

E. Overview of rules

1. Spousal maintenance
2. Child support
3. Custody
4. Property division
5. Impasse/arbitration
6. Taxation

F. Contracts
G. Recognition that there is no right solution
H. Distribution of mediation rules and financial forms

First Mediation Session

A. Additional questions answered
B. Temporary maintenance agreement if appropriate

1. Time-limited
2. Not precedent-setting
3. Definition of
   a) Support-child
   b) Support-spouse
   c) Housing
   d) Custody/visitation
   e) Use of bank/charge accounts
   f) Handling of debts
   g) Conduct of individual personal lives

C. Agenda

1. Custody
2. Division of property
3. Finances/budget
4. Need for resource experts

Subsequent Sessions—Agenda

A. Custody
B. Division of property
C. Finances/budget
D. Support

Memorandum of Agreement

A. Record of spirit and detail of agreement by parties
B. Checklist

1. For mediators
2. For attorneys

C. Need for return to mediation?

Advisory Attorney

   A. Meets with mediator and couple together
   B. Explains legal rights and ramifications in an informational way.
   C. Reviews with them in memorandum prepared by the mediator and the divorcing parties
   D. Drafts Settlement Agreement in legal terminology
   E. Review Settlement Agreement with couple
   F. Files agreement for the couple

In order to understand in detail the ramifications of the step-by-step process of mediation, it is strongly recommended that one seeks formal training in the mediation process, which includes a rudimentary knowledge of state or provincial laws. Guidelines for successful implementation of the mediation process emphasize the following elements:

1. It is a non-adversarial approach

2. It requires joint decision making

3. It stresses cooperation, not competition

4. It equalizes power—one controls the decisions that affect one's life

5. It stresses a win/win approach, instead of no/win or win/lose

6. It necessitates the demonstration of mutual respect

7. It teaches the parties how to be responsible for themselves during the process, so that they are better prepared to cope later

8. It emphasizes seeking the decision that will serve the best interests of the divorcing parties, as well as the offspring they may have

9. It includes encouragement as a necessary ingredient

In addition, not only should the clinician receive training in the mediation process, but it is our contention that the therapist must be grounded in some fundamental understanding of human behavior and theory. Therefore the following section will attempt to provide the reader with the compatibility of Adlerian theory and the mediation process.

The Adlerian Connection

A number of terms included in the previous commentary on guidelines to successful mediation bring to mind Adlerian theory. The terms "choice," "cooperation," "power," equality," "respect," "responsibility," "best interest" and "encouragement" are basic to Alfred Adler's Individual Psychology. Although there are no documented ties between Adlerian Psychology and divorce mediation, Coogler did, in fact, possess both a law and a counseling degree from Georgia State University. He, in addition, attended parent education programs offered by an Adlerian therapist. This may in some way account for some similarities. The uncanny similarities are as follows: Both the psychology and the process of mediation deal with social context, and the social embeddedness of people, each likewise recognizes the purposiveness of behavior, although their reasons for doing so differ, and both share the central philosophical attitudes of mutual respect and social equality.

Other parallels that are stressed include the importance of a democratic atmosphere, individuals taking responsibility for their own actions, the importance of choice and the need for the mediator to be an encourager for the couple. Perhaps, however, the single most important element of both is the belief in social interest, that striving toward the improvement of one another's lot in life. In essence then, when reviewing Adler's principles outlined in the first chapter, one could well be reviewing guidelines designed for mediators.

Similarly, a recap of the common techniques employed by Adlerian therapists, (Manaster & Corsini, 1982) and these outlined in earlier chapters of this book, reveals another set of commonalities. Anecdotes, clarification, confrontation, conflict resolution, emotional support, homework, humor, interpretations, reasoning, shock techniques, suggestions and silence are all techniques employed at some juncture by the divorce mediator, although often not with the same purpose as that of the therapist. Initially, examination of the following chart can assist practitioners in delineating the differences between the role of the mediator and the role of the therapist.

A summary of the role of the Adlerian therapist may add to one's understanding of how the approach can enhance the mediator's work with couples and families. The following review from Dewey (1978, pp. 37 & 38) identified the role of the Adlerian therapist:

1. Acts as an educator....

2. Becomes a helping friend, not an "anonymous therapist." Shows warmth and genuine interest, expresses feelings and opinions, is a fellow human being, who makes mistakes, as all humans do, but who demonstrates (the) courage to be imperfect.

3. Positions (self) as an equal....

4. Demonstrates Social Interest and self-acceptance, practices mutual respect; stresses cooperation rather than power.

5. Rarely uses psychoanalytic labels or classifications. Sees all maladjustments as manifestations of discouragement....

6. Plays an active role. Guides the conversation. Does not use free association.

7. Emphasizes use, not possession. Shows how one uses one's feelings to fortify one's ideas. One uses one's emotions to move toward one's goals....

8. Emphasizes purpose, not cause. A man says he hates his wife. Rather than looking for the cause of the hate, the therapist attempts to determine what purpose the hate serves for him (to get even with her, to punish her, to excuse himself and so forth.)

9. Emphasizes movement, not description.... Encourages clients to become aware of (their) actions, not just the actions of others. (Note how a victim arranges to always get the short end of the stick.)

10. Tries to understand the client's Lifestyle and 'private logic'. How (the client) views (self) and his (or her) world,...Uses Family Constellation,...Early Recollections and Dream Interpretation....

11. Works for motivation modification, not just behavior modification....

12. Teaches client to compensate for shortcomings in constructive ways....

Undoubtedly, the mediator likewise assumes many of these traditionally therapeutic roles. At times the mediator serves as a helping friend; at other times one exhibits the courage to be imperfect. The mediator also positions self as an equal, demonstrates social interest and self-acceptance, and must not label or classify. Similarly, the mediator plays an active role, taking responsibility for keeping the couple on task and emphasizing usefulness, purpose and movement toward agreement. The mediator teaches the client to compensate for shortcomings in constructive ways. However, the mediator does not try to understand the client's Lifestyle and private logic. Nor does the mediator work for behavior or motivation modification.

Although the principles and values underscoring the beliefs of mediator and therapist, the techniques used and the roles assumed are in many ways alike, the basic task of the mediator differs from that of the Adlerian therapist. Whereas the task of the Adlerian therapist is to understand and change behavior, that of the mediator is to complete a settlement agreement. Still, the likenesses are intriguing; in fact, they may possibly encourage numerous Adlerian therapists to consider the possibility of adding to their repertoire of skills the role of mediator.

Future Directions

Already a number of mediators are expanding their view of divorce mediation. They are moving from the use of mediation in the divorce situation only to a more broadly based approach, which applies the process to other family difficulties such as teenage rebellion, elderly parents and domestic violence, to name a few. Other areas in which mediation could be an appropriate tool include school-related issues, pastoral concerns and corporate difficulties. From the Adlerian point of view, mediation in this broader sense would indeed fit Adler's view of *gemeinschaftsgefuhl*—that willingness "to see with the eyes of another, to hear with the ears of another, to feel with the heart of another..." (Dewey, 1978, p. 42). No doubt, Adler would have encouraged, if not led, such a broad-based attempt to assist individuals in their tasks of love, work and community.

Chapter 7 References

Bahr, S.J. (1984). The divorce mediators. *Health*, p. 58.

Coogler, O.J. (1978). *Structured mediation in divorce settlement.* Lexington, MA: D.C. Health.

Dewey, E. (1978). *Basic application of Adlerian psychology.* Coral Springs, FL: C.M.T.I. Press.

Family Mediation Association (1982). Training Handout.

Horowitz, J. (1983, July 6). Divorce: Few rules to govern the new breed of mediators. *The Los Angeles Times.*

Manaster, G.J. & Corsini, R.J. (1982). *Individual psychology.* Itasca, IL: F.E. Peacock.

Silberman, L.J. (1981). Professional responsibility problems of divorce mediation. (Monograph No. 1) *The Family Law Reporter, 7,* 4001-4012. staff, (1983, January 17, February 7, July 6; 1984, May 7, May 28, August 29) Marriage and Divorce Today.

Vroom, P., Fassett, D, & Wakefield, R.A. (1981). Mediation: The wave of the future. *American Family. (4)*, 8-13.

Vroom, P., Fassett, D, & Wakefield, R.A. (1982). Winning through mediation: Divorce without losers. *The Futurist,* 16, 28-34.

Chapter 8
Working with Remarried Couples
by
Lynn K. O'Hern and Frank R. Williams

A marriage between two persons who have been married before includes all the joys and delights of any new marriage, as well as the difficulties and conflicts. In addition, however, because remarriage is so complex, the difficulties may seem to far outweigh the joys in the initial stages of the marriage.

Even though many people in second marriages come to therapy because of issues identified with the children or ex-spouses, the focus of therapy will eventually turn to the couple and on how they work together on the presenting problem. John and Emily Visher (1979) pointed out the following:

> If the relationship between the spouses is strong and withstands attempts by the children to split or weaken the alliance, the family unit is able to cope successfully. In stepfamilies there are more strains than in most intact families, and as a result the alliance or coalition between the couple seems particularly important and also more difficult to achieve and maintain (p. 122).

Because of the importance of the couple, this chapter has been included to point out both the similarities and differences between counseling couples in a first marriage and in subsequent marriages.

Although such factors as techniques, counseling styles and theories may be similar for all marital counseling, the therapist must understand the complexities and unique issues of the remarried couple. For example, while an issue in the first marriage may be the inability to separate from parental involvement, in a subsequent marriage a similar issue may instead involve separation from a former spouse.

In therapy, it is the couple who eventually must do the work, with the therapist serving as facilitator, educator and model. As the number of remarried couples increases as a result of the high divorce rate, the majority of clients seen in marital counseling in the future will have some, if not all, of the concerns outlined in this chapter.

Part I: Preparing for Remarriage

As in first marriages, couples who remarry rarely do the recommended work before they remarry. Part I is presented for therapists who may be working with about-to-be remarried couples or already remarried couples who are struggling. Ideally, the remarried couples can go back and complete the tasks presented below in order to make this marriage as complete and successful as possible.

Elizabeth Einstein and Linda Albert, in their four-part series on *Stepfamily Living* (1983), provided a solid guide for "Preparing for Remarriage." Einstein and Albert defined the four parts of this process as: resolving, rebuilding, relinking and remarriage. Each is important in the eventual process of remarriage, and each can be worked on even after marriage occurs if it has not successfully been completed prior to the marriage.

Resolving

Resolving includes the grieving necessary for healing. It includes clarifying feelings through expressing anger, hurt, depression and sadness. It means taking time to redefine oneself and surrender to the reality of aloneness and loneliness in this new phase of life. It means acceptance that the old is no longer a part of one's life and the new is yet to be defined. It also means beginning to reshape one's life and map out new directions for the future. Many who write about the grieving transition call this the "ending"—the process of ending something that was and that never again will be.

Rebuilding

The second step, *Rebuilding*, is a lonely time. Many of the old behaviors and patterns still exist—the children must be cared for, the job goes on and the homemaking must be accomplished. At the same time, the world looks different. The reality of being alone, of not being a part of a couple, and of redefining oneself as a single or as a single parent becomes a major task. Attempting to take this new definition out into the world by dating, meeting new people and entering into the world as a single creates new stresses and new conflicts and demands new skills. This is also the time of reshaping what one wants out of life, setting goals for the future, and risking new relationships and additional commitments.

It is during the rebuilding time that many people attempt new behaviors and involvement with someone for an extended period of time. If this new involvement is hurried into another marriage, additional problems could be created. If one enjoys and learns from the new involvement, it can be a beneficial part of the process. This rebuilding period can also be a time of reflection on the previous marriage. As Dreikurs (1946) stated, "A proper evaluation of one's previous marital experience might easily smooth the way in a new marriage" (p. 196).

Relinking

A new sense of direction characterizes the *Relinking* stage. Some of the practical aspects of living may become more satisfying and less burdensome. Beginning to trust oneself suggests hope for the future. One awakens to the possibility of another long-term commitment. Most people have improved interpersonal skills and most people have learned a lot about themselves in this long process. This stage, then, is a time of relinking with another partner, beginning again to dream of the future and sharing oneself and one's family.

If this new relationship leads to marriage, people often assume the relationship can fulfill all that the first marriage did not. In addition, out of fear of a second failure, little of substance generally is discussed in order to avoid conflict. Obviously, such avoidance can later produce significant difficulties. During this courtship, expectations should be clarified, relationships with other people such as ex-spouses and former in-laws should be understood, future plans for children must be discussed, and financial and other practical issues must be negotiated. Although these issues are usually left until after the "honeymoon" stage of the remarriage, the process is much easier when completed prior to any long-term commitment.

Remarriage

The *Remarriage* state involves the attempt to create a new couple or a new family in the most healthy and productive manner. As with any new couple, the following can be said:

> A married couple is seen in the light of Adlerian Psychology as two separate individuals, both operating according to the guidelines of their basic convictions, intentions and expectations, each striving to achieve one's own place in life, but at the same time, each also working to build a life with the other, and in the process using more or less courage, more or less selflessness, more or less positive cooperations (Belove, 1980, p. 194).

The trend for most remarrying couples is to include the children in the actual marriage ceremony. Many of these ceremonies begin with promises of peace, love and never-ending happiness that may in reality feel uncomfortable and unreal to the children if they have not been a part of the planning. The ceremonies of remarriage can be creative, exciting and much more mature and realistic than many first weddings. The children and significant others should be in on the planning and the process. The ceremony is to some extent as much theirs as it is the couple's. Not addressing the children's concerns and needs in the planning can create resentments and hurts with long-lasting negative consequences. One boy, having gone to the second and third marriage of his father and the second marriage of his mother, said proudly one morning, "Gee, I've been to three of my parents' four marriages."

Einstein and Albert (1983) ended their book by suggesting that the work done between the end of a marriage and the beginning of a new marriage can be the most important investment ever made.

> When you have successfully resolved your relationship with your former spouse, you are free to begin a new commitment without emotional baggage interfering. When you have spent time exploring who you are, learned to meet your needs and are functioning

as an independent person, your strong sense of identity will provide you with the strength to survive some testy times with your stepchildren. When you and your new mate work hard at important courtship tasks that are unique to stepfamilies, you will have a headstart on a challenging situation. And, when you hold a creative celebration to herald the new beginning to your family, friends and community, your happiness and joy will provide a wonderful start for reaping all the potential that lies ahead for you with stepfamily living (p. 23).

Part II: Tasks of the Couple

The preceding section outlined the ideal processes for a couple to experience before remarriage. Even though most couples will not have accomplished these processes prior to remarriage, they are presented here to highlight the necessary work to be done. For most couples, the work that should have been accomplished before remarriage will have to be done during the initial phase of therapy. If not completed, growth is unlikely within this second marriage. The tasks of recoupling as well as working on the personal aspects and the public aspects or remarriage are defined and addressed here along with many of the typical concerns of each task.

Recoupling

Recoupling is the first and perhaps most all-encompassing task. When people have been a part of a couple that has divided, either by death or divorce, the task of coupling does not come as easily as perhaps it did the first time. Recoupling is an ongoing task throughout the marriage, and certainly cannot be accomplished in a short period of time. Furthermore, recoupling will be affected by the successful implementation of the other two tasks: personal and public issues.

Recoupling comprises the time and effort two individuals take to create the necessary boundaries and limits around themselves as a couple. Of the many unique ways of doing this, the ones chosen will be personalities of the individuals and the couple as an entity. If the individuals remain separate, both functionally and emotionally, the couple boundaries remain too loose. If, however, the individuals mesh themselves together so that they lose their individuality, their autonomy and the family will suffer. Neither extreme is productive. The ability to balance the two extremes becomes the goal of therapy.

Individuals remarrying tend to wish to maintain too much autonomy in hopes of avoiding the painful process of endings that was experienced in their first relationships. If this emotional separateness continues, it contributes to the gradual erosion of the relationship when the couple is faced with the new challenges of marriage. Of all the many subsystems within the stepfamily or remarriage system, the couple is the most fragile and many times the only dyad that will or can disintegrate.

Couples in the process of recoupling should take time and, of course, focus on the age-old need for open communication, as discussed in the previous chapters. The problem, however, is time alone with each other. For those remarriages where children are involved, there is literally no substantial period of time for coupling without also parenting. Times seems even harder to find than in first marriages with children because in the remarriage there are often two families of children to accommodate, as well as the typical daily routines of work and homelife. Take for example the following hypothetical situation.

Jane and Bob have Jane's daughter from Sunday to Friday and Bob's son from Friday to Sunday. This schedule, which was determined at the time for each divorce and was undoubtedly practical at that time, means the couple rarely have any time alone. They feel obligated to spend the weekend time with Bob's son, since it is their only opportunity to be with him, and obliged to have some special time during the week with Jane's daughter, since most of their time together involves work and school. In a first marriage, with children at home all the time, there is generally little difficulty in leaving the children alone or with a sitter on a regular basis to spend time together as a couple.

Time, then, sometimes must be consciously structured—with specific agreed-upon hours taken solely for the couple. This time should be structured with those activities necessary for the bonding usually done in first marriages prior to children. Such activities include having fun, talking openly, sharing personal stories, creating dreams for future and solving together the ongoing concerns of the family. These structured times should not be for routine television watching, attending the kids' soccer matches or participating in regular events with the rest of the family.

Not only is time as issue, but remarried couples also bring with them myths and distorted beliefs about remarriage and step-family living. These myths (Coleman & Janon, 1985) include:

- "Things must work out." While this myth may also be present in first marriages, it is much more pronounced and destructive in second or subsequent marriages. Often couples go to any length to avoid facing problems. "Love will conquer all, this time" is the attitude. The initial phase in remarriages is often a fantasy that everything is okay and will always be okay in the remarriage/stepfamily. The couple, then, will attempt to avoid problems in order to make sure the marriage works. This myth is the basis for several others.

- "Keep criticism to oneself and focus on the positive." Couples may believe that if only this had been done in the first marriage, then perhaps the marriage would not have failed. This myth fosters avoidance of conflict, ambivalence and a tendency to deny reality. Couples "walk on eggs" as the result of this attitude.

- Another myth, related to the first, is, "If things are not going well, focus on the past and make sure it doesn't happen again." The past marriage(s) are criticized while any immediate problem is avoided, if possible. Blaming the previous marriage for what is currently happening causes major problems. Pretending is often the second phase in remarriages. Even though one or both persons know there are problems, they go about their relationship "pretending" all the negatives from the past will eventually work out in this relationship.

- The desire to "see oneself as a part of a couple first and as an individual second" is another attempt to avoid personal issues and to "make this one work" at all costs— usually creating undue personal stress.

- "What is mine is mine and yours is yours" is a prevalent remarriage myth and impedes an "our" orientation. This separateness is especially common in the financial and parenting arrangements of remarriage. Two types of prevalent financial organizations are a "common pot" or a "two-pot." With "common pot," all income is put into one pot and then decisions are made about how it is spent. "Two-pot" is usually "three-pot" where there is a household account and each also maintains a separate account. This arrangement works as long as both partners are contributing to the financial common account. Where there is disparity, problems are often created.

- Another marriage myth also present in remarriages is that "marriage makes people significantly happier." Many remarried couples will pretend they are happy because they not only cannot be unhappy, but they also have to be happier this time around. This myth relates to the common misbelief that one must be part of a couple to be okay.

- Finally, "What feels good for us might be harmful for the children." Many remarried couples ignore their own relationship for the sake of the children as a way of making things up to the children. This tendency often results from guilt over the first divorce and a belief that the children have suffered unduly.

Personal aspects

Working with personal aspects is the second task for remarried couples. There are many aspects of a relationship, some not very obvious, that must be discovered, lived with and negotiated. One aspect is a difference in patterns of living. Visher and Visher (1979) stated "...certain styles of adult behavior have been developed, and distinct living styles have emerged. Successfully joining two very different systems requires considerable tolerance and flexibility on the part of the individuals involved" (p. 129).

Everything from language and patterns of sharing affection to who takes out the garbage can create constant tension. It is important to help couples understand there is no right or wrong way. "The fact that patterns have solidified over a number of years and have suddenly become questioned may lead to daily conflict, contributing immeasurable to the degree of anxiety and tension experienced by the couple" (Visher & Visher, 1979, p. 130).

The second area of personal tension relates to the history of each spouse, including relationships prior to the marriage, ex-spouses and, of course, the children—whether they live at home, with the other parent or are adults when this marriage occurs. The extent to which these prior relationships continue to intrude on the necessary bonding of the new couple will slow the process and place undue tension on the couple. Most of these former relationships—particularly with ex-spouses and children—will have to be maintained at some level. It is only with careful exploration of feelings and clear negotiation of the boundaries that these relationships can be maintained at a level that is comfortable for the new couple. "When the emotions from a past marriage have not been laid to rest, they can continue to affect a person's future adjustment during the period of divorce and after remarriage" (Messinger, 1984).

The boundaries of old relationships will, of course, change with time, as new events occur and as children's needs change with age. For example, the out-of-town parent may be constantly visible and present during the soccer season, but mostly absent the rest of the year. The most difficult of these relationships is usually the ongoing relationship with the ex-spouse. This relationship must be redefined from lover, friend, confidant and spouse to co-parent and eventually may be even friend of the new couple. "A parenting arrangement between ex-spouses that worked during the separate parenting period may not work when a new partner is introduced" (Messinger, 1984). If the ex-spouse remains too actively involved in the new relationship, the new couple cannot create their unique living patterns. This in no way means that the ex-spouses cannot be friends or that one must accept the myth that ex-spouses have to hate each other.

As Ahrons and Perlmutter (1982) pointed out, "The general mistrust of a continuing relationship after divorce is reflected in the prevailing stereotype that former spouses must, of necessity, be antagonists; otherwise, why would they divorce?" (p. 36). They go on to explain that this myth is reinforced by clinicians who usually only see the difficult former spouse relationship in therapy. However, all remarriages require some juggling when determining appropriate ways to handle new situations. While confusing, these new patterns can be challenging if seen as another step in building the new couple's relationship. The following example is a common complaint by remarried couples.

Betty was faced one morning with news of the unexpected death of an old friend. Overcome with grief, she picked up the phone and called her ex-husband for comfort. Understandable when John, her new husband, found that she had called her "ex" instead of him, he felt rejected. Over time, Betty will understand that spontaneous reactions may not always be the best for the new relationship. Had she taken a moment to think it through, she would have realized she could have gotten support from her new spouse and not endangered their new relationship. Such occurrences in the first few months, and sometimes first few years, create tension because assumptions made are not always grounded in reality.

John understood, after talking it through, that Betty's behavior was an old reaction based both on how the former couple handled similar situations and the fact that this person had been a mutual friend of Betty and her ex-husband. John's understanding that it meant nothing about how Betty felt about him or his role as her spouse helped him to stop interpreting her behavior in erroneous, and usually hurtful, ways. This kind of open communication is the most productive way of managing the personal tasks of remarriage.

Misinterpretation of facts or behavior in communicating about an ex-spouse is the most difficult issue for remarried couples. A simple statement of concern made to an "ex" can be interpreted by the new spouse as left-over feelings for the former spouse. An act of appreciation could be interpreted as a hidden wish that the former couple were still together. These are the small things that, left unresolved, will continue to build as resentments and unfinished hostilities between the new couple.

Another issue for newly married couples, but more emotionally laden when faced by remarried couples, is that of finances. A first marriage usually begins with few financial resources, or if any exist, they are fairly unencumbered. A second marriage begins with money, property and insurance, which is usually all tied to previous relationships with either the ex-spouse or children. The actual amount of money is undoubtedly greater at this time in their lives, particularly if both partners are working, but there are also greater expenses, involving the former relationships. Financial issues must be handled with ongoing understanding, communicating and negotiating without misinterpreting the facts. In outlining tips for remarried couples, Jean Lown stated that "couples who fear they'll appear too concerned with financial gain, may hesitate to discuss finances. However, what seems to be a very unromantic notion is a sound idea which can save you and your spouse a lot of heartache and legal fees in the long run" (1985, p. 26).

Perhaps more difficult than finances for the new couple is the issue of children—including problems with grieving children, ex-spouses concerns, disciplining, divided-loyalty issues, money for raising children and whether the couple should have children together. The relationship with the children consistently creates the most tension, undoubtedly because all the other issues also relate to the children. This is where the Adlerian child rearing principles can be of most assistance for the couple. For though there may not be a right or a wrong way to rear children in the blended family, couples need to be together on how they are going to handle children. The couple's task is to remain open and flexible while understanding, negotiating and communicating about the children, but must also have a proven body of child rearing principles from which to guide their decision. One thing for certain, "more chaos is not needed."

Public Aspects

The third task for remarried couples is to work on public aspects of the relationship, or the external influences that are part of all social relationships. These external influences, which affect all marriages, are compounded by their complexities for remarried couples.

The largest influence is the community in general. Do new couples continue to relate to former friends, choose new friends, relate to her friends or his friends? Do they continue in the same church, the same neighborhood social group, the same athletic club? Do they continue relating if it means being in association with an ex-spouse and possible an ex-spouse and that person's new partner? Do they continue to relate to the former in-laws? And how do they relate to each other's parents, who might be blaming the new spouse for the breakup of the old marriage? Are the new in-laws (stepgrandparents) expected to treat the new children as they do their biological grandchildren?

There are no right answers. Each area must be discussed, feelings shared and a mutually agreeable avenue in each situation decided. It is possible for couples to find new social groups— e.g., a new church or a new set of couples for friends. For the couple to survive, each partner must be willing to negotiate, understand and make changes. It comes down to clear, open communications, to not misinterpreting the intentions or the facts. For example, a phone call from an ex-mother-in-law does not mean that she is unaccepting of this new marriage or the new spouse; a stepgrandparent forgetting the birthday of a new stepgrandchild may not mean they are uninterested and want no part in this child's life.

A second public issue is that of choosing where to reside. when one partner moves into the home of the other, which happens to have been the home of the former marriage, there are some complicating details. Even though practically and financially this arrangement may be the best alternative, changes should be made as soon as possible to make this house the home of the new couple. In practical terms, this transformation may require buying new furniture and rearranging the old, changing pictures on the wall, adding on a new room, redecorating or whatever it takes to make it feel like "our" house rather than "your" house. If financial limitations prohibit extensive remodeling or refurnishing, it is helpful to do some brainstorming about what can be done that would cost little money and still make the house seem new and different and "ours."

The home is one of many elements that can threaten a new spouse. Old pictures, vacation spots, cars, gifts and so forth can have the same effect. "In the blended family, struggles for dominance can and do take place over just about everything having to do with possessions" (Berman, 1982, p. 4). At the same time, therapists must understand that "a new house may help somewhat, but it is not a panacea" (Berman, 1982, p. 4).

The last aspect of this third task involves those rituals that bring the extended family into the public, such as graduations, marriages, holidays, school functions and funerals. Who goes where? What is the role of each member? How does each person feel about the situation? All these are important considerations. Each new situation demands additional preplanning, creative thinking and negotiating, more consideration for others, and a greater degree of tolerance by all members of the family. None of these negotiations is easy, but they do not have to be heartbreaking either. One ten-year-old said he was always excited when he could say that all four of his parents came to family night at school; and he is also pleased to know that even when everyone is so busy, at least one of the four will attend each of his soccer games and music recitals.

Part III. Counseling a Remarried Couple

It is imperative for any person helping a remarried couple to understand the dynamics of this new relationship. The previous information is given to help therapists understand that this marriage will deal with quite different forces than the first. The more information and comfort the therapist has with the issues, the better that person can assist the remarried couple.

The role of the therapist is as "educator, a model and a facilitator" (Mosak, 1979). Few remarried couples need long-term, indepth therapy. Most need practical permission, information and options.

Counseling Process

The process of counseling a remarried family includes all the basic elements described by Dreikurs (1967), including establishing a relationship, understanding the couple, providing insights and reorientation and education. We have defined that process as follows:

A	= intake	D	= family work
B	= family evaluation	E	= couple work
C	= couple evaluation	F	= reorientation
		G	= termination

Figure 1

                B   D

        A   F   F

                C   E

1. During the intake process information about the history of the couple and family and the presenting issue is taken (A).

2. Then either a more thorough family assessment is done (B) or a more extensive evaluation of the couple (C), depending on the information gathered in (A). Often a movement is made to immediately reduce the family chaos (D) before proceeding.

3. If it is determined during step A that the issue is primarily the couple relationship, the next step will be to focus on the couple (E).

4. Following the couple work (E), the whole family is seen at least once to reorient the family to the changes made by the couple (F) before termination (G). "Reorientation is a process that occurs during all stages of therapy, but has special importance after insight has been attained" (Dinkmeyer & Dinkmeyer, 1982, p. 119).

5. If it is determined that the family system needs more extensive work (C), the family will be seen a number of times (D), which may lead to work with the couple (E), and on to reorientation (F) and termination (G).

In the first session, basic information about the family and couple is gathered. Much of this and subsequent information may be similar to that gathered in the initial interview chapter, but with added emphasis on:

- The length of the current relationship, including time lived together and length of marriage, as well as length of previous relationships.

- The length of time since separation and divorce of each person and significant relationships since divorce.

- The children (if applicable) of each person, their ages, where they live, and/or visitation practices and the ages of the couples' children together.

- Expectations of each person about: Each other, remarriage, finance, sexual relationships, relations with other people of same and opposite sex, and the extended family.

Also discussed during this first session will be the counseling process, the expectations of the couple, and the therapist's commitment to the couple and the couple's commitment to the counseling process. A contract can be established including the number of sessions expected and common goals. The therapist will also share a diagnostic hypothesis with the couple before the conclusion of the first session.

> Because remarried couples often begin therapy in the midst of crisis, there is usually a need to do some "quieting of the chaos" and education about step-families and remarriage. As homework, the therapist may request the couple write a history of their relationship, in their own words, giving the high and low points and clearly stating what they want from therapy and what they want from one another in order for the marriage relationship to be what they would like it to be. This often reveals hidden agendas, as well as mistaken beliefs and myths that they have been unwilling to discuss or unable to understand.

An actual case study, as experienced by the authors of the chapter, may provide the reader with a sense of the aforementioned dydactic commentary.

A Case Study: John and Barbara

Barbara and John set an appointment initially as a couple. During the telephone call John explained that his son, Josh, was 13 and living at present with his mother in another city. Barbara's daughter, Michelle, 8, had adjusted well to being in the stepfamily and was getting along well with John. The couple had a son of their own, who was two years of age. They had been married four years.

The present problem centered around how Josh was affecting John and Barbara's relationship. Because they identified themselves as having the problem, the decision was made to see the couple rather than the total family.

Initial Session

John and Barbara came for the first appointment and after initial introductions, John began:

John:
I didn't want to come. I don't think there is any real problem, but since Barbara thought we ought to come, I was willing.

Therapist:
John, what do you think is Barbara's reason for wanting you to come?

John:
Well, she feels we're growing further apart and that if we don't do something we'll end up like our first marriages.

Therapist:
What do you think?

John:
I think everything has been blown out of proportion. I know that we have some problems, especially about Josh. We could work those out if Barb would talk about it.

Therapist:
What is it that Barbara won't talk about?

John:
Ask her. She's the one that's upset about Josh. He's an ordinary boy. He has his problems and gets in trouble once in a while, but no more that I did when I was a kid. Barb made him move out. It was either he

goes or we go and I didn't want to leave, so we made arrangements for Josh to live with his grandmother.

Barbara:
It's not true that Josh is an ordinary boy. He's trouble and I wasn't going to have him around Eric. John always protects him and doesn't see any problems. He wants him to come back. In fact, he had demanded he come back or the marriage isn't going to continue. That's why we're here. I don't think we can work it out by ourselves.

John:
The most important thing is our family—the whole family. That includes Josh. It's not his fault he is the way he is. If it hadn't been for his mother and the way she treated him and our marriage, which was disastrous, everything would be fine. He's had his problems, but he's overcoming these now. The important thing in all of this is the kids and the family.

Therapist:
Barbara, you are saying you didn't want Josh back in the family and John you are saying that the future of the marriage depends on it. It sound as if you are at an impasse. Before we talk some more about this, let's get some background about you and your marriage.

We found out that John and Barbara had been together for five years and married for four. Each had been married before. John had been separated for three months when he met Barbara and moved in with her two months later. Barbara had been divorced for two years at the time they began living together.

Barbara's daughter Michelle had been with them from the beginning. Josh came to live with them six months after the marriage, sent by his mother, Rona, who said she couldn't handle him and that he needed to be with his father. There had been no warning or discussion about Josh joining the family. This unexpected change in their family was the beginning of their conflict. Previously, Josh had visited irregularly and indicated each time that he didn't want to be there. John and Barbara initially had stated that they did not want more children, but were excited when Barbara became pregnant and Eric was born. Both John and Barbara were employed outside the home and had good jobs. They felt they had only minor financial problems, but they had not been resolved. They were living in a home that Barbara had purchased after her divorce.

During the initial interview, we also found out what the couple knew about stepfamilies. Most couples have little understanding about stepfamilies and remarriage and are seeking information in addition to working through problems. This educational task is a very important part of the process in remarriage/stepfamily counseling.

Therapist:
Barbara, what had happened in your relationship that brought you here?

Barbara:
I don't think John loves me any more. He only cares about whether Josh is with us or not. He doesn't pay attention to me or my feelings.

John:
That's not true! You ignore me! We don't make love any more, you gripe about money, you complain that I don't spend time with Eric. I love you, but Josh is important to me. He's my son.

Barbara:
I tried to be a mother to him, but he wouldn't let me. He was nasty to me and Michelle and would go around hitting her and you wouldn't do anything about it.

John:
Michelle was always antagonizing him. She deserved getting hit at times. But he was only ten then. He's grown up a lot.

Barbara:
He got worse. When Eric was born he pouted and was angry all the time and when he hit him, that was it!

John:
You also wouldn't speak to him. You expected me to love and be close to Michelle and I did, but you wouldn't do the same with Josh.

Therapist:
It sound as if Josh and his unexpected entrance into your family was the beginning of a lot of problems and that over the last couple of years the two of you have gotten into some patterns of living that have created a distance between you.

John:
I guess so, but I think we can work it out.

Barbara:
Well, I want to, but I don't know if I can handle Josh coming back.

Further discussion indicated that there were other problems in the relationship. John had moved out for a time shortly after Josh had left and tried to keep Josh with him. During this time he had entered into another relationship but gave it up and returned to the marriage to try to work things out. It was at that time that Josh was sent to his grandmother's. John's continual denial of any real problems, his blaming of the first marriage, and his focus on the children and family were indications of how he was believing several of the remarriage myths.

During this first session we spent part of the time sharing some of the basic complexities and problems of stepfamilies, including a discussion of the remarriage myths. John and Barbara agreed that they believed many of these myths. We also illustrated our hypothesis with a diagram.

Figure 2

Josh

E

L

B

Barbara   **John**

E

L

The relationship between John and Josh is biological (B), legal (L) and emotional (E). The relationship of Barbara and John is emotional and legal. The question remained, "What is the relationship of Barbara and Josh?" At best, it could be emotional. When the couple was in a shaky place, Josh would then be able to use the lack of any tie to Barbara and the problems between Barbara and John to further create problems, always with the purpose of keeping his father attached to him and not to Barbara. Barbara and John were able to see that when there are problems between Josh and Barbara, the key to resolution would be to strengthen the couple relationship.

John:
I'm beginning to see that only if Barbara and I have a good relationship and talk about the problem can we deal with Josh.

Barbara:
That's what I've been saying. You just don't listen to me! If we can get along and we can decide together how to handle Josh, then maybe he can come home, but not until then.

Therapist:
I agree with that assessment and want to suggest that we look further at the couple relationship and then come back to talk about Josh's entrance into the family.

John and Barbara agreed to follow this process. The importance of working with the couple's relationship first was discussed and a contract for additional sessions was made. They were given a homework assignment to independently list what they wanted from their relationship.

There were still things about the couple relationship, about relationships with ex-spouses and other basic stepfamily issues that we needed to discuss. After this first session, it was determined to move to Step C (See Figure 1) rather than B, because the major immediate issues belonged to the couple. In addition, Josh was not a daily problem because he was not in the house, so the daily living tasks were being handled adequately.

Second Session

During the next session more information was obtained. Before discussing the homework, we wanted to learn more regarding the relationship with the ex-spouses; about the roles that each was playing in this marriage e.g., wife, husband, mother, father and how they differed from the first marriage; the use and abuse of power; how much space and time alone was needed by each; their process of decision-making; the expression of affection and need for nurturing; their values and interests; and what kind of a support system they had as a couple and as individuals.

We learned that John did not get along with his ex-spouse, Rona, and that from time to time this caused problems for the new relationship, especially when money was involved. Barbara and her ex-spouse, Tom, had a good relationship.

Most of the every-day decisions in the family were made by Barbara, with John simply complying with such decisions as disciplining of the children, housework, paying bills and social activities. John said he didn't care what happened in those areas as long as he could go out once in a while with his friends. This was not a problem with Barbara, who also had a small group of women with whom she was socially active. They had very few couples as friends and did little together socially.

When it came to issues of power and control, things were not so harmonious. John felt he had enough power and did not think he abused what he did have. Barbara disagreed.

Barbara:
You pushed your power all over the place when it came to Josh, and when you didn't get your way, you left.

John:
If you had been nice once in awhile and didn't have to always have your way, we wouldn't be in the predicament we are in now. Every time we turned around you were saying either Josh goes or the marriage is over—and then you withdrew sexually. So who had the power and who uses it!

Both John and Barbara felt that neither had enough space from the other, but also expressed frustration about not having enough time together, especially to do things alone. When family activities, such as soccer, picnics and other outings were scheduled by Barbara, John was willing to participate.

After opening up many areas of concern and conflict, then making a list for future work, their homework listing their desires for their relationship was discussed. Many of the areas that had been discussed earlier were on the lists on one or both:

John:
I want Josh to be able to come back to our family. I want to spend more time together as a family when Josh comes to be with us. I want more sex in our relationship. I want Barbara to come with me when I play softball. I want her to not bug me right after I get home at night about what needs to be done around the house.

Barbara:
I want to spend some time as a couple without kids. I want some help with Eric, especially at dinner time. I want you to spend time with Michelle. I want us to find friends we can spend time with. I want you to be affectionate with me at other times besides when we are in bed.

After discussing the lists at some length, the session was concluded. Homework for the next session was a request for the couple to discuss their lists more fully and to bring to the session those items which caused conflicts and/or those they wanted to work on immediately.

Subsequent Sessions

John and Barbara were not unlike many couples we have seen in first marriages, but they had additional concerns that are specific to remarriage. Unique to their remarriage system were the relationships with the children, ex-spouses, finances, housing, support relationships and power. In subsequent sessions (Step E of Figure 1) the couple worked on communicating more effectively and on conflict resolution, using the issues they had raised from their want lists. As in all marital therapy, homework was given to help them work on communications and negotiations.

Sessions were spent working through the issues, including:

Housing:
They decided to buy a new house that would feel more like "their" home.

Discipline and Child Care:
John began spending more time with Michelle and even began coaching her soccer team. He also became more involved with Eric at home. Barbara spent individual time with Josh when he visited.

Finances:
They went to a three-account system: His, Hers, Ours. This seems to work well with remarried couples.

Friends and Support:
They joined the local chapter of the Stepfamily Association, which provided a new support system. With less tension at home, they were willing to invite friends from their respective social groups to their home.

Couple Time:
John and Barbara began setting aside time to be together without children. In order to do the homework, they had to spend at least an hour each week alone. They decided they would continue this, but with fun activities as well as working through problems.

Communications:
They began to share on a much deeper level some of their own fears, without feeling threatened that the other would misinterpret feelings.

Termination

We spent several months working with Barbara and John. Some time was spent with each individually. Ultimately, some sessions were spent with the family together (Step F in Figure 1). One session was spent with Michelle and Josh both together and separately. They gave new insights into the family and their desire to work together, which was shared in a particular tearful family session. One session was also spent with Rona and John. At first Rona was reluctant to come in, but was convinced that it would be beneficial for Josh. At that time only Josh was discussed and new more compatible guidelines for the ex-spouses were established. There seemed to be unresolved issues remaining between Rona and John that required attention. They subsequently spent several hours together clearing up many of these issues. Since that time, both have expressed how freeing the experience was. Barbara felt it was a positive experience for their marriage as well.

In order for the remarried couple to establish the necessary bonding, it is critical that they spend time together in recreation and in discussion. While this is true in first marriages, the fact that children are present often becomes an excuse for not confronting the problems. With Barbara and John, counseling provided the guidance and the impetus needed for them to proceed. Although the counseling was terminated (Step 6, Figure 1) before Josh re-entered the family, much of the ground work had been laid for his successful return.

Summary

Dinkmeyer and Dinkmeyer (1982) defined marriage counseling as "a collaboration between the couple and the therapist" (p. 122). The purpose is to assess the beliefs and behaviors while educating the couple to reach new goals. The definition and purpose is the same for remarried couples as for first-marrieds. "The partners who come to counseling are basically... the same two who once loved each other and got married" (Belove, 1980, p. 193). The process of counseling involves weeding out the confusion and complexities that have dampened and/or reduced these feelings as a result of changes in their life situation. These changes are for most remarried couples immediate and overwhelming.

Chapter 8 References

Ahrons, R., and Perlmutter, Morton S. (1982). The relationship between former spouses: A fundamental subsystem in the remarriage family. In Messinger, L. and Hansen, J.C. (Ed.) *Therapy with remarriage families*. Rockville, MD: Aspen System.

Belove, L. (1980). First encounter of the close kind. *Journal of Individual Psychology, 36(2).*

Berman, C. (1982). Your place or mine? *Stepfamily Bulletin, 2(3/4).*

Coleman, M. & Janon, L. (1985). Remarriage myths: Implications for the helping professions. *Journal of Counseling and Development, 64* 116-120.

Dinkmeyer, D. & Dinkmeyer, J. (1982). Adlerian marriage therapy. *Individual Psychology, 38(2).* 115-122.

Dreikurs, R. (1946). *The challenge of marriage.* New York: Hawthorn.

Dreikurs, R. (1967). *Psychodynamics, psycho-therapy and counseling.* Chicago: Alfred Adler Institute.

Einstein, E. (1982). *The Stepfamily: Living, loving, and learning.* New York: Macmillan.

Einstein, E. & Alberts, L. (1983). *Stepfamily living series.* New York: E. Einstein.

Flach, F.F. Jr. (1984). What to do when at odds with former spouse. *Remarriage, 1(2).*

Lown, J. (1985). Money matters and remarriage. *Remarriage, 2(7).*

Mayleas, D (1977). *Rewedded bliss.* New York: Basic Books.

Messinger, L. (1984). *Remarriage: A family affair.* New York: Plenum.

Mosak, H. (1979). Adlerian psychotherapy. In R.J. Corsini (Ed.), *Current psychotherapies* (pp. 44-94). Itasca, IL: F.E. Peacock.

Powers, R.L. & Hahn, J.M. (1979). Couple counseling: A traditional marriage in transition. *Journal of Individual Psychology, 35(1),* 26-44.

Roosevelt, R. & Lofas, J. (1976). *Living in step.* New York: Stein and Day.

Sager, C.J., Brown, H.S., Crohn, H., Engel, T., Rodstein, W. & Walker, L. (1982). *Treating the remarried family.* New York: Brummer/Mazel.

Visher, E.B. & Visher, J.S. (1979). *Stepfamilies: A guide to working with stepparents and stepchildren.* New York: Brunner/Mazel.

Visher, E.B. & Visher, J.S. (1982). *How to win as a stepfamily.* New York: Dembner.

Wald, E. (1982). *The remarried family: Challenge and promise.* New York: Family Service Association of America.

Westoff, L. A. (1978). *The second time around: Remarriage in America.* New York: Penguin.

Index

Remarried couple 198
Reorientation 19, 23-24, 209
Resistance 51
Resolving 198
Review of First Impressions of the Relationship 101
Riedler, K. 104
Rogers, H. 50, 138
Ross, D. & Ross, S.A. 59
Routing to therapy tracks 158
Rules of Audience Participation 122-123
Ryder, R.G. 140
Sadd, S. 150-151
Sager, C.J. 97
Saline, C. 139
Satir, V. 78-79, 161
Saunders, B.E. 142-143
Schaefer. M.T. 50
Second Session 215
Seeking to understand 127-130
Segal, L. 157
Selecting Volunteers 120
Self 67-70, 73-74
Self-acceptance 192-193
Self-worth 41-42, 47
Semans, J.H. 178
Sensate focus 161, 165, 173-175
Sexual Relationship 64-65
Sharpley, C. 50
Shepard, C.F. 107, 110
Showing mutual respect 95
Shulman, B.H. 10, 150
Sibling relationships 68
Silberman, L.J. 189
Sluzki, C.E. 5
Snyder, D.K. 50
Social Interest 15, 192-193
Social relationship 41-42, 44
Soliciting attention 131-132
Spanier, G.B. 49
Sperry, L. 119
Spitting in the client's soup 22
Spouse Observation Checklist 49
Stedman, J.W. 140
Steinglass, P. 78-79
STEP 51
Stepchildren 201
Stepfamilies 197, 201, 203, 210, 213
Stepfamily Living 198
Stop-Start 173, 177-178
Stover, L. 138
Structured Mediation System 189